THE POWER OF
REAL
OPTIMISM

THE POWER OF
REAL
OPTIMISM

A Practical, Science-Based Guide to
Staying Resilient, Curious, and Open
Even When Life Is Hard

DR. DEEPIKA CHOPRA

SIMON ELEMENT

New York Amsterdam/Antwerp London
Toronto Sydney/Melbourne New Delhi

SIMON
ELEMENT

An Imprint of Simon & Schuster, LLC
1230 Avenue of the Americas
New York, NY 10020

Some names and identifying characteristics have been changed. Some dialogue has been re-created.

For more than 100 years, Simon & Schuster has championed authors and the stories they create. By respecting the copyright of an author's intellectual property, you enable Simon & Schuster and the author to continue publishing exceptional books for years to come. We thank you for supporting the author's copyright by purchasing an authorized edition of this book.

No amount of this book may be reproduced or stored in any format, nor may it be uploaded to any website, database, language-learning model, or other repository, retrieval, or artificial intelligence system without express permission. All rights reserved. Inquiries may be directed to Simon & Schuster, 1230 Avenue of the Americas, New York, NY 10020 or permissions@simonandschuster.com.

Copyright © 2026 by Things Are Looking Up LLC

All rights reserved, including the right to reproduce this book or portions thereof in any form whatsoever. For information, address Simon Element Subsidiary Rights Department, 1230 Avenue of the Americas, New York, NY 10020.

First Simon Element hardcover edition March 2026

SIMON ELEMENT is a registered trademark of Simon & Schuster, LLC

Simon & Schuster strongly believes in freedom of expression and stands against censorship in all its forms. For more information, visit BooksBelong.com.

For information about special discounts for bulk purchases, please contact Simon & Schuster Special Sales at 1-866-506-1949 or business@simonandschuster.com.

The Simon & Schuster Speakers Bureau can bring authors to your live event. For more information or to book an event, contact the Simon & Schuster Speakers Bureau at 1-866-248-3049 or visit our website at www.simonspeakers.com.

Interior design by Janet Evans-Scanlon

Manufactured in the United States of America

10 9 8 7 6 5 4 3 2 1

Library of Congress Control Number: 2025945808

ISBN 978-1-6680-8112-9
ISBN 978-1-6682-2549-3 (Int Exp)
ISBN 978-1-6680-8114-3 (ebook)

 Let's stay in touch! Scan here to get book recommendations, exclusive offers, and more delivered to your inbox.

*For my parents—
who taught me that real optimism
doesn't deny the dark,
but helps us see within it.
But mostly for my Jag, Dio, and Jia:
this is truly for you,
and the world I know you'll help create—
one shaped by your courage, your kindness,
and your wonder.
Mama is just so damn proud of you.*

There is a light that never goes out.

—The Smiths

Contents

Prologue xi

Introduction 1

Chapter 1 "Stay Positive!":
What We Get Wrong About Optimism and Why It Matters 11

Chapter 2 "It's All in Your Head":
The Seven Truths of the Brain and Its Power to Foster an Optimistic Mindset 33

Chapter 3 "Good Vibes Only":
What the Cult of Positivity Ignores About Human Emotions 53

Chapter 4 "Therapy Fixes Everything!":
Taking Mental Health Beyond the Couch 81

Chapter 5 "You Can Have It All!":
How the Impossible Ideal of "Balance" Hampers Optimism 104

Chapter 6 "Just Ask the Universe!"
A Science-Based Guide to Manifesting Your Dream Life 123

Chapter 7 "Believe in Yourself!":
A Scientific Approach to Creating Affirmations That Actually Work **146**

Chapter 8 "Trust Your Gut":
Reconnect with Your Intuition to Improve Decision-Making **168**

Chapter 9 "We Never Fight!":
How Optimists Embrace Conflict to Cultivate Strong Relationships **187**

Chapter 10 Optimism Is an Inside Job:
The Science of Self-Care **210**

Chapter 11 The 33-Day Optimism Challenge **234**

Acknowledgments 253
Notes 255
Index 273

Prologue

In light of everything, cracked open, not unscathed, but still here and carrying the flicker

In the summer of 2023—at the same time I was writing the proposal for this book—my two-year-old son, Dio, was diagnosed with an extremely rare illness. I will spare you the details (they are not necessary, I want to respect his privacy, and frankly, I can still barely talk about them without getting upset), but let's just say it was an extremely dark time in my and my family's life.

The worst part by far was the uncertainty; the condition was so rare—literally only two children in a million are diagnosed with it each year—that the doctors weren't able to give my husband and me any definitive answers about our son's prognosis or the chance of recurrence after treatment. Dio had surgery, and the doctors recommended an intense course of treatment for a year. But given how little they knew about the disease, they still couldn't promise the treatment would be effective. We had to make a terrible choice based on unreliable information. My husband and I hated the prospect of putting our sweet boy through anything this severe, but doing nothing seemed like a worse option. I could not let my child stay at risk.

We agreed to move ahead with the doctor's recommendations, and within a few days Dio was undergoing a second surgery, this time to implant a port in his chest where he would receive his treatments over the next year. *How is this happening?* I kept thinking. Just a few days earlier my son had been a happy toddler, wrestling with his older brother and playing with his favorite toy trucks in our living room. Now he was unconscious on an operating table, and we were all facing an uncertain future. Sitting outside the operating room, my husband and I watched, helpless, as we waited for the "surgery in progress" light to turn off. *With every agonizing minute, my thoughts raced. Why is it taking so long? Is something wrong? How has it been only thirty minutes? Haven't I been here for hours?* I kept telling myself not to cry, but the tears came anyway, silently and uncontrollably creating a pool behind my glasses. I was holding on to Dio's lovey so tightly against my cheek that it ended up becoming soaking wet from my tears. Just as he usually used it every night for comfort, I was now using it to do the same.

The surgery went well, but the worst was yet to come. For the next year, in addition to watching Dio endure his treatments at the hospital, my husband and I had to give him a daily dose of steroids. Pediatric steroids are usually administered orally, and the standard version most hospitals prescribe have a flavor and consistency that can only charitably be described as chalklike. Almost every child on an immune-suppressing treatment requires steroids, and yet, even well into the twenty-first century, scientists haven't bothered to come up with a formula that is even a little bit palatable? C'mon, people, can we get a new formula going already?!

Dio was far too small to swallow pills, so the pharmacist recommended crushing the medicine and mixing it with his food. "Just don't mix it with something he likes," they told us. "Because he'll never want to eat it again." It didn't matter what we tried—yogurt, ice cream, peanut butter, even that sugary flavored syrup you use for snow cones—Dio was not fooled. He wouldn't eat any of it. The first time we tried nearly broke me. Alex, my husband, had to physically restrain him in his high chair as I held his mouth open to force the spoonful of medicine-laced mush in. Of course he immediately spat it out—strawberry yogurt mixed with his potentially lifesaving medicine splattering all of our faces, his tray, our clothes. I couldn't blame him. I had tried a little bit of the mixture out of a sense of solidarity, just to try and understand what he was going through. I gagged to the point where I almost vomited. How on earth was this going to work? How was I going to do this every day? It seemed impossible—and awful. My mind flashed to accounts I'd read of prison guards force-feeding inmates or political protesters. It is an inherently violent and violating act—and here I was being forced to do it to my beloved son. His own mother and father—potentially traumatizing him in order to keep him safe. I wanted someone to make it make sense. Well, it didn't. It still doesn't.

As he continued to scream and cry, something inside me shattered. I left Dio with Alex and retreated to my office to hide. I felt like a frightened child as I literally crawled under my desk to get as far away from everything as possible. I let myself fall to pieces. "I can't do this," I wailed into the floor. "I can't do this. Why do I have to do this?"

The next few months were an absolute blur. It wasn't lost on me that, through what was perhaps the most pessimistic period of my life, I was writing a book about optimism tools and positioning myself as an expert on mental health and positive thinking (which I am!). As I write this now, I'm about a year out from the initial diagnosis and can say that, at the very least, the experience was a lesson in humility. Because even I, the Optimism Doctor, didn't take my own advice . . . well, not at first.

Every moment of that year was filled with some urgent task: rushing back and forth to the hospital, researching therapies and statistics, writing this book, and of course, taking care of Dio, my older son, Jag, and my unborn daughter. Oh, right, did I mention we were about to welcome a third child during this entire ordeal? Well, we were, and I could barely savor the excitement and joy I felt at the prospect of having my first baby girl because I *had* to focus on everything else that was going on instead. Not only that, but I couldn't help but think that, as the universe was about to bring us a new, by all accounts perfectly healthy baby, it might be about to take my baby boy away from me. I was in the darkest place I had ever been mentally or emotionally, and I spent a lot of time there, deep within those thoughts.

All my friends told me I was brave and strong and seemed to have it all together. But I didn't feel like I had it all together. I didn't feel brave. I felt like I had no other choice. If you're sitting there thinking you don't know how you would get through something like this, trust me, you would. You would be amazed at what you would soldier through if you had to.

When I wasn't in full-on soldier mode, I resorted to a bunch of old coping techniques—the things I did before I understood how the brain works and just wanted to gain a sense of control over my life. I sought out old spiritual teachers—people I had met in high school—to help guide me through my grief. During the few weeks we waited on pathology reports, I journaled and recited affirmations, hoping I could will them into reality: *Dio is healthy. The tests will come back negative. Dio is healthy. My family is healthy.* I visited psychics, believing that if I knew what the future held, I could somehow intervene. I banished—or at least tried to banish—every negative scenario from my mind. I had to stay positive— for myself, for Dio, for my family, for my sanity. The doctors had told us the mass they had removed was likely one of three things: it could be benign; it could be a rare disease that was potentially treatable but for which there wasn't a whole lot of information or data suggesting outcome measures; or it could be a third disease, one that was equally rare and pretty much immediately fatal. I would not let myself believe anything but the best-case scenario. I told myself, time and time again, that it had to be benign.

Of course, dark thoughts still crept in. *What if this is the start of goodbye? What if this is the first of many lasts?* All the small, mundane, routine moments became so big and automatically sent tears streaming down my face: our nightly ritual of reading a page in our big book of animals; rocking on our favorite chair; the full-belly laughs when we told our inside jokes; the after-dinner dance parties. Despite my desperate attempt to stay positive, I felt such despair during that time that it changed me forever. I wouldn't wish three minutes of these thoughts on any parent, let alone three weeks.

Even though I had tried all these things—in vain—before, the need to regain some sense of control over the situation led me down a rabbit hole of magical thinking, denial, and—I'll admit it—delusion. I preferred the illusion of control to the reality of uncertainty. I was searching for answers where none existed.

One evening as I was rocking Dio to sleep in the darkness of his bedroom (a nightly ritual we had carried out since he was a baby), he looked up at me with his big brown eyes and said, "Mama, you are doing a good job." This was my sweet, tender, sensitive little boy, sensing my sadness at his pain and taking care of me the way I was taking care of him. It crushed me. I looked down at him, tears welling up in my eyes, and said, "Dio, *you* are doing such a good job." And then he said, "We are doing it together, Mama."

The pathology reports finally came back, and while the mass wasn't benign like I'd hoped, it also wasn't the immediately fatal scenario, either. While the treatment wasn't guaranteed to work forever, there was at least a treatment. And treatment meant hope. I asked the doctors if they knew what might have caused this, but they couldn't give me an answer; the disease was so poorly understood that they had no scientific explanation. "As far as we know," they told me, "it's just bad luck." I couldn't accept that, though. The scientist in me believed there had to be a reason.

As the months went on, we settled into more of a routine. I dreaded Tuesdays, when Dio had treatment, but I made it through by reminding myself that this course had an end date. On the day of his first treatment, I started a countdown, and each Tuesday, after we left the hospital, was one Tuesday closer to this particular part of the ordeal finally being over.

Unfortunately, I had no idea if this would actually *ever* be over. Even as Dio neared the end of his treatment, whatever optimism I felt about his prognosis gave rise to new worries. As of this writing, Dio is still a very small child, and his disease remains a complete mystery to the smartest scientists and doctors alive. "It could still come back," I told myself. "This might not be over. What if the next time is even more serious? What if doctors never find a cure? Will he need to worry about this for the rest of his life?" At a time I had assumed would be full of relief and optimism about the future, I was filled with a new sense of dread and fear.

In some ways, this period was even more emotionally difficult for me than the immediate aftermath of Dio's diagnosis. At least then there was something I could do to potentially fix the situation. There were decisions to be made, appointments to be scheduled, prescriptions to fill and administer, healthy meals to prepare, doctor's notes to obtain. I hated the treatment days, but at least I could tell myself we were doing something actionable. Now the only thing I could do was wait. All of a sudden, I faced the prospect of a literal lifetime of uncertainty and a fate I could do nothing to control.

I didn't want to project my anxiety onto my kids (the youngest of whom, Jia, joined our family a few months into Dio's treatment). I especially didn't want to upset Dio, who would have enough to worry about without managing the anxiety of his mother. I spent a lot of time crying in my car. Every trip to the market, every run to my PO box, every drive home from dinner with friends was a chance to let all my emotions out. I sobbed until my eyes were red and my nose started running. I screamed. I wailed. I heaved. I pounded my fists on the steering wheel and searched every corner of my psyche for a reason why this was happening and a way to heal the pain. I asked "Why me? Why our family? Why my baby?" Until I had to remind myself: "Why not me?" My life has been blessed in many ways, but I am not special. Bad luck can strike anyone.

As I have so often discovered in life, relief came in the most unexpected form. One night, just before Dio went in for his final treatment, I decided to unwind by watching the movie *A Family Affair* on Netflix. (I know, I know. You probably were not expecting me to reference this random movie at this point in my story, but I promise there's a point, so just go with it!) In the movie, Zac Efron plays Chris, the boss of Nicole Kidman's daughter, and he and Kidman's character, Brooke, start dating, even though he is much younger than she is. Is it a good movie? No. I can't really recommend it, but one scene from late in the movie has stuck with me. In the scene, Brooke is fretting over her relationship with Chris to her late husband's mother, played by the indomitable Kathy Bates, because she's worried the relationship is doomed to fail. As she's stressing, Bates's character stops her and says, "The end is none of your business." (I actually remember the line as "Kid, the future is none of your fucking business," but Google is telling me I added that color on my own.)

As I'm writing this, it's been several months since I watched this film (which a top critic on Rotten Tomatoes literally described as "fine"), and I cannot stress enough how much this scene resonated with me. The end *is* none of our business. We cannot predict the future, so why do we spend so much time trying? Why, as the aphorism goes, should we borrow trouble from tomorrow when all we can really worry about is right now? This otherwise forgettable line in a perfectly okay movie helped me realize I didn't need to control what happened in the future—I couldn't. It didn't matter if the universe had a plan for me or if everything in life was chalked up to bad luck; there were certain things I could control and certain things I couldn't. All I could do was focus on what I could control and be open and curious about the rest of it. All the research I had done and the expertise I had could take me only so far; I had to live life in order to really learn from it. I had already spent this long in darkness, and my family and I have gotten through this horrible, unimaginable period together. So why should I spend the time I have now—the time where my son is not in treatment, is able to start school, and can travel again (even though we still have to be very careful when we do)—paralyzed with worry and anxiety? Why would I choose darkness when there is so much light?

I want to use this time to live, to celebrate. During the year Dio was in treatment, I had forgone a lot of big celebrations because I didn't feel like celebrating anything. I didn't celebrate my fortieth birthday. I didn't throw a party for the birth of our baby girl. I didn't even celebrate selling this book to a major publishing house. But now, right now, I want to celebrate everything. For example, I just booked a trip for the five of us to go to Napa, which is where we went when Dio was first diagnosed and we were waiting for the pathology report. Even though the place holds such shitty memories from the last time we were there, I want to return to it so we can rewrite the memory during this new phase of our life. I want to do it all again, as a family. I want to recapture the magic we briefly lost. I don't want to be afraid anymore.

I decided to share this story at the beginning of the book for a few reasons. First, it seemed dishonest not to. How could I write about optimism without acknowledging how difficult it can be for even an optimism expert to practice it when life gets stressful? How could I offer advice without admitting that sometimes, I'm the last to take it? I also shared it in the hopes that any readers who are going through something particularly difficult will draw some strength and hope from it. Bad things can happen to anyone, and while your situation is likely not the same as mine, it's important to know that you are not alone. We all struggle at times—no matter how confident or put together or strong we may appear. I hope you can take some solace in that.

Of course I also wanted to share my story, in part, to help me process what the hell had just happened to me and my family. Writing, as you'll see throughout this book, is one of the most powerful ways to process emotions and cultivate optimism. Connecting with others is another powerful tool. Sometimes simply expressing an emotion or sharing the most painful parts of ourselves alleviates some of the burden we feel and helps us gain a sense of perspective.

But most of all, I see this story as a clear example of what real optimism is and isn't. Optimism is not about believing that everything will turn out the way you want it; that everything will go according to plan, or that positive thinking about the future can stave off disaster. It's about accepting that life is hard—sometimes *really* hard—but it always has something to teach us. If we can stay open to those lessons, we will survive. What other choice do we have?

As I write this, I don't know what the future holds for Dio or for our family. Right now he is happy and healthy, but I am aware that that could change. Or something else could happen that rocks our world in a way we couldn't expect. I feel this anxiety a lot. In my free time or the quiet moments of the day, I can feel it sneaking up on me. But I try to remind myself that *the future is none of our business*. Because I don't need to know what will happen tomorrow to know that I will survive it. I will survive it because I have before. This is the essence of real optimism.

Introduction

*You can overcome a lot of things,
but you cannot overcome being human.*

In the fall of 2016, I got pregnant with my first son. When the doctor gave me and my husband the news, I was equal parts thrilled and terrified. I had always wanted to become a mother, and pregnancy seemed like such a wonderful adventure. At the same time, I had always harbored intense anxiety about carrying and delivering a baby. I'm a bit of a hypochondriac (okay, okay, definitely more than *a bit*), and as far back as I could remember, I dreaded the experience of childbirth. Still, I tried to push any panic-inducing thoughts out of my mind and focus on my impending status as a new mom. I tried to picture a positive, healthy pregnancy. I imagined caressing my ever-expanding belly, singing sweet lullabies to the life growing inside of me, nourishing my body and my baby with an all-organic diet and regular prenatal massages. Maybe I'd take up yoga—even though I haven't made it through a full yoga class in decades. Maybe I'd put on a flowy white dress, head to the nearest beach, and have someone shoot soft-focused photos of me and my bump at twilight like so many women on my Instagram feed! No matter how nervous I was, I strove to take pride and joy in the experience.

That is not what happened.

In my second trimester, I was diagnosed with hyperemesis gravidarum, an extremely serious, rare-but-not-rare-enough condition that causes some pregnant people to vomit, well, *a lot*. This is not morning sickness. This is morning, afternoon, evening, middle of the night, while you're driving, while you're sleeping, while you're talking to your mom on the phone or watching TV or doing anything that usually brings you joy, any time of the day or night sickness. I threw up over thirty times a day, every day, during the entire duration of my pregnancy. I threw up on every major roadway in Los Angeles. I threw up on the beautifully manicured sidewalks of Beverly Hills. Once I even threw up in the middle of a client's visualization session while asking her to imagine her ideal safe space. To this day, I cringe at the thought that I might have ruined whatever that place was for her.

I was so sick I had to stop seeing clients because I didn't have the strength to work—and, to be honest, because I felt like a fraud. I am known as "The Optimism Doctor," but during those ten months, I lost every thread of optimism within me. I was so miserable that I couldn't stand for anyone—not even my husband—to touch me. This was a big deal because under normal circumstances, I crave physical human contact so much that my body starts to feel depleted if I go without it for too long. (Yes, my love language is physical touch.) Before I got pregnant, I'd maintained an extremely strict diet—no gluten, no dairy, no refined sugar, no nightshades—to manage an autoimmune disorder. After the nausea set in, the only thing I could stand to eat were Egg McMuffins. No, not some SoCal, sprouted-grain, organic, Erewhon version of an Egg McMuffin: the OG McDonald's, fully processed, registered trademark, Egg McMuffin.* The only thing that made me feel the tiniest bit better was scratching the peel of a fresh lemon or orange and sniffing it. I craved the milliseconds of relief this brought me so much that I carried a piece of citrus fruit around with me all day and pulled it out at regular intervals to smell it. (I ruined several leather purses this way.)

These days, it's easy to look back on this period of my life with a sense of humor, but at the time, all of this compounded to make me feel really, *really* bad. Most days I struggled to get out of bed. And when I did get out of bed, I was so exhausted and sick that even simple tasks, like drinking a glass of water, making a cup of tea, or showering, felt impossible. I tried everything to feel better, but nothing worked. I am a clinically trained

---

* Ironically, those Egg McMuffins are probably the only thing that kept me out of the hospital, because despite the constant vomiting and the fact that I needed daily IV drips to stay hydrated, I still managed to gain thirty-two pounds.

behavioral scientist with a doctorate in clinical health psychology. I had spent my days working with clients to help them manage all manner of mental health issues—from anxiety, stress, and low self-esteem to crippling disorders like OCD and clinical depression. I am also a student of holistic wellness practices and have tried basically every tip or trick recommended by a wellness expert or self-help book over the past two decades. (Some have worked, some have not, but as a professional who has had a deep and complex relationship with my own emotional and physical health, I feel it's my job to try anything at least once.) The point is, I, more than most people, have the tools and training necessary to pull myself out of a funk and optimize my mental health. And yet the second I got pregnant, none of the tools in my toolbox worked. I meditated. I recited affirmations in the mirror. (*I am healthy. I feel wonderful, joyful, and at ease.*) I journaled and wrote down things I was grateful for. I prayed, even though I don't believe in any particular god. I attempted to take walks in nature. Before bed each night, I imagined waking up with a calm stomach, hoping I could manifest this dream into a reality the next morning. I visualized myself in a room full of white roses, which signify protection and healing. In my prepregnancy life, most of these practices helped ease my mind and calm my nerves. During this period, not a single thing brought me a moment of relief, let alone joy.

Then one night, seven months into my pregnancy and counting down the minutes until my due date, I resolved to do something—*anything*—to try to boost my mood. Earlier that day I had (somehow) thrown my best friend a bridal shower and now found myself staring at a bag of large rose petals, which I had left over from a decoration. I knew from my work that engaging one's senses is usually a great way to calm your mind. (I am, at heart, a vibe girl—totally into setting the perfect mood for the moment.) So I ran myself a warm (but not too warm) bath, threw in a few petals, dimmed the lights, put on my favorite Mazzy Star album (because this is what happens when you mix a vibe girl with a nineties indie rock/grunge girl), and tried to will myself to get into the tub. I knew the moment my body touched the water I would probably throw up, so I just sat there, staring intently at the petals floating softly across the surface while trying to ignore my roiling insides and the jabs of my son's feet against my rib cage.

And then, like a rainbow cutting through the clouds after a storm, I had a thought. "This sucks right now, Deepika, but it will not last forever," I told myself. "You *can* get through this. You *will* get through this." For a brief, shining moment, I felt lighter. I felt at ease. I even felt a little bit joyful. In short, for the first time during my pregnancy, I felt optimistic.

The moment didn't last long. Roughly ten seconds later, any mental and physical relief I felt was replaced with the sudden need to vomit, and my thoughts once again turned to how awful I felt. I continued to feel awful every day until my son was born. I continued to feel bitter and sad over the fact that I didn't get to enjoy my pregnancy. And I continued to lack the energy to do anything that had once brought me pleasure or satisfaction. But something significant had changed. Whenever I started to despair, I brought myself back to that moment beside the bathtub. I reminded myself that I would feel good again. That one day the vomiting would stop and I would once again be able to enjoy all the things I usually did. That this truly awful experience would make me stronger—and perhaps already had. It was this slight but profound mental shift—not the bath, not the affirmations, not the journaling—that helped me endure the rest of my pregnancy.

I like sharing this story because it reveals so much about what we get wrong about mental health. In our positivity-obsessed culture, we have come to believe that the goal of mental health is to eliminate stress and conflict and to try to be happy all the time. "Good vibes only," "find your bliss," "always look on the bright side"—these may seem like harmless slogans on a T-shirt or Instagram post, but their prevalence points to a deep desire in our culture to feel as good as possible as often as possible. This is understandable. Who wouldn't prefer to feel happy, energetic, and at ease in the world, as opposed to depressed, angry, or anxious? But equating good vibes with psychological wellness is not just inaccurate; it sets us up for failure. This is what I experienced firsthand during my pregnancy: When we try to fight the things we have no control over or bury our feelings under fake smiles and hollow affirmations, we fail—and often feel worse for the effort. The goal of mental health is not to be happy all the time. It's to learn how to face whatever comes our way with curiosity, compassion, and resilience. It is to elevate our emotional state in such a way as to allow us to live a life aligned with our deepest hopes, desires, and values. This is the promise of what I call *real optimism*.

What do I mean by real optimism? We tend to think of optimists as perpetually positive Pollyannas—always peering through their rose-colored lenses in search of silver linings and half-full glasses. To be optimistic, we believe, is to be generally unbothered by the actual state of things. But this is an oversimplification. Optimism is not about ignoring reality or being cheerful all the time. Real optimists are keenly aware that sometimes life sucks. The caveat is they see these setbacks and challenges as temporary, something they have the ability to learn from and overcome. Optimists do not quash negative emotions, but they also don't give themselves completely over to them. Instead they acknowledge that stress, anger, fear, and sadness are natural parts of the human experience and use those feelings to identify their needs and desires. Optimists know they can't control everything that happens to them in life, but they can control—or at least attempt to control—their response to it.

Why should we strive to become more optimistic? Because, simply put, optimism improves our mental and physical health and makes us more able to face whatever life has in store while staying committed to our goals and values. Science has shown that people with a greater sense of optimism experience more life satisfaction and improved mental health, marked by a decrease in depression and anxiety. Optimism increases personal resilience and improves one's ability to cope with stress and setbacks. Optimism also promotes and improves relationships (a key indicator of happiness), since optimistic people are considered to be more friendly, likable, and socially attractive. Optimism enhances one's physical health in many ways. One study found that individuals who scored high in optimism lived, on average, 11 to 15 percent longer than those who scored lower and were significantly more likely than pessimists to live to be eighty or older. Optimistic people have better cardiovascular health and bounce back from common respiratory illnesses much more quickly than those who are more pessimistic. Optimism has also been shown to promote creativity, innovation, productivity, and problem-solving, as well as to lead to better decision-making and increased self-esteem, confidence, and self-mastery. And because of all these associations, optimists are more likely to report longer, more satisfying relationships than pessimists.

I developed my approach to mental health and optimism after becoming disillusioned with so many of the popular approaches out there. To be clear, I am *not* the most optimistic person I know. In fact, I'm pretty sure I'm not even the most optimistic person in my immediate family. For the first few decades of my life, it never occurred to me to pursue psychology as a career because I assumed I wasn't cut out for it. Growing up, I was an extremely sensitive child. So sensitive that my parents had to shield me from sad movies or news stories because anything the least bit upsetting could put me out of commission. I could watch extremely violent crime movies like *Scarface* or *The Godfather* on repeat; those things didn't faze me. But anything about injustice or the inexplicable grief of human love and loss? Forget it. True story: When I was fourteen years old, I had to stay home from school for a week after I saw *Titanic* for the first time. I was so traumatized by Jack's death that I couldn't get out of bed. You read that right: The death of a fictional character and the end of a completely unrealistic (and extremely short-lived) romance laid me out *for a whole week*.

But then, a few years after I graduated from college and got my first job, a boss and mentor of mine suggested that a degree in psychology might allow me to channel my natural empathy and curiosity about people into an actual job. I decided I had nothing to lose. I got accepted to the clinical health psychology program of my dreams, earned my master's, and put in thousands of clinical hours before earning my doctorate and then completing a double postdoctoral fellowship at UCLA and Cedars-Sinai. Along every step of this very long and difficult process, I fell in love with the work more and more. I loved helping people overcome challenges, both circumstantial and psychological, so they could live the lives they dreamed of. I loved giving people the tools and self-knowledge they needed to improve their mental health. I loved seeing the progress they made as they learned to replace the fears, anxieties, and negative thoughts holding them back with internal narratives that helped them achieve their goals and embrace the future optimistically.

At the same time, I also became disillusioned with many of the methods I was being taught. While traditional talk therapy worked well for helping patients identify and process trauma or unhelpful belief systems, the approach forced us to spend most of our time focused on their past. Neuroscience shows us that the brain is an anticipatory organ; it is always looking ahead, not behind. While we all benefit from developing self-awareness and understanding how past events have impacted our mental state, awareness alone can't help us change our behaviors. That requires a different set of tools.

I started to observe how many of my patients, in search of these tools, looked to popular self-help culture for answers. In some cases, the strategies they found worked well. I have clients who swear by their meditation, yoga, breath work, journaling, or other practices, and that is great! In fact, research shows that such practices can have a profound positive impact on your mental health when used in a way that complements your natural brain chemistry and stress response. Routines and practices that are authentic to the way your mind works are great additions to your mental toolbox.

Unfortunately, not all trendy self-help practices fit this bill. Practices such as reciting affirmations, creating vision boards, or manifesting to the universe don't always require you to take action or shift your thinking and therefore often fall short of the promises they make. If you don't *believe* you're beautiful, you won't convince yourself simply by staring in a mirror and saying it three times out loud. If you don't *believe* you're worthy of love, you won't find a healthy relationship just by verbalizing it. And if you don't back up your dreams with action, you will never reach your goals because, trust me, the universe has plenty of other stuff to worry about other than whether you're living, laughing, and loving as much as you should be. Shifting your thoughts is difficult, but it's a lot easier to do when you understand how to work with your brain instead of against it.

As part of my work, I studied the brain and became totally obsessed with what I was learning. For example, did you know that the brain is terrible at distinguishing between fact and fiction? If you imagine something is happening, your brain responds as if it is *actually* happening. Once we know this, it's easy to see how our thoughts—even outlandish or incorrect ones—can affect the way we feel. The brain also seeks patterns in order to help it make better predictions and tries to confirm information it already knows so it can become even more efficient. This is great for detecting signs of danger, but it often leads the brain to spot threats where none exist.

All this knowledge allows us to understand why our thoughts and emotions can be so difficult to temper. The good news is, the brain is highly adaptive and malleable. It is always learning, which means we can teach it more of what we want. When we apply the right tactics for doing this, we can shift our thoughts gradually but dramatically, so they help instead of hinder us.

In 2013, I started my own practice and have continued to develop a unique approach to working with my clients that combines the most powerful aspects of traditional therapy—such as cognitive behavioral therapy—with science-based tools and holistic methods that help people redefine their expectations and increase resilience; identify and alter false narratives; and navigate difficult emotions and experiences with curiosity instead of fear. I also started finding ways to measure my clients' capacity for optimism in different aspects of their lives and then work toward increasing that capacity wherever necessary. Because the mainstream therapy community did not really have the right vocabulary for many of the methods I use, I stopped referring to what I do as therapy in the traditional sense and started to refer to it as self-worth work. One day after I had described my approach to a client, he told me, "So, basically, you're like my optimism doctor." I had never put it that succinctly before, but I realized he was exactly right and have embraced the moniker ever since.

The more I studied my clients, the more I noticed that the way everyone experiences life depends not just on what families they're born into or how their past has shaped them, but on how they choose to view the world and their place within it. The difference between an optimist and a pessimist cannot be explained by circumstance alone. Optimists do not live lives free from worry or stress. In fact, many of them have overcome enormous challenges that have shaped their characters and outlooks. The difference is that those who choose to look at life optimistically view these challenges as temporary and as opportunities for growth, rather than as catastrophes.

After reading this book, I hope you will have a deeper appreciation for not only *why* optimism is worth pursuing but *how* to do so—effectively and diligently. I hope it will help you let go of the need to be perfect and understand that mental health is not some ideal state of being; it is an ongoing lifelong process that requires self-compassion, softness, and acceptance. *You can overcome a lot of things, but you cannot overcome being human.* You are wired to experience the full range of human emotion—not just happiness—and life is definitely going to throw crap your way at times (maybe even a *lot* of the time). When you learn to face that crap optimistically, you learn how to move through life with greater ease and satisfaction, leaving you energy to focus on what truly brings your life meaning and joy.

In the pages that follow, I will share groundbreaking research into how the brain works and how that directly impacts the way we think, act, and feel in order to show how cultivating a real optimism practice can—gradually but significantly—improve your life. I will start by making the case for what *real* optimism is and why it matters. I will then explain how the brain processes information and how we can use its efficiency, neuroplasticity, and future-oriented nature to nurture a more positive outlook that will set us up for success in achieving our most important goals. I will explain how the cult of positivity skews the goal of mental health and how sitting within discomfort—not ignoring it—is the key to resiliency and growth. I will explain the origins of popular practices like affirmations, manifestation, and self-care and explain why, unless they're practiced in a way that honors the way our brains work, they can end up feeling ineffectual (and in some cases counterproductive). I'll explain why I think the concept of balance is bullshit and why it's better to focus on having a purpose and making empowered choices than to try to have it all. I'll explain why some aspects of traditional therapy—while helpful for becoming more self-aware and processing traumas—can often leave you feeling stuck; how even micro-moments of joy can drastically boost your mood; and why, if you want to create fulfilling long-term relationships, your argument style matters *way* more than how you show affection.

Throughout the book, I will draw on my more than fifteen years of experience working with clients and patients, providing workshops, studying the latest research, and developing strategies anyone can use to practice more optimism, combat anxiety, and achieve a healthier outlook on life. I will share stories from my life as well as the lives of my clients to show how optimism works in the real world and how it can help you no matter what you're struggling with. I will offer practical step-by-step strategies, practices, and techniques that work *with* our brain's natural programming instead of against it. And I will refer to interviews I have conducted with dozens of experts—including performance coaches, professional athletes, psychotherapists, and neuroscientists—to offer additional perspectives on how optimism can be applied in all facets of life.

While I don't believe this book is a substitute for quality professional care, I do believe that real optimism is one of the most powerful tools we have to increase joy, resilience, and hope in our lives. I believe that the more optimism exists in the world, the more loving, compassionate, and collaborative our world could be. I believe that optimism is the antidote to the fear and anxiety so many of us feel on a daily basis and that *only* by embracing an optimistic outlook can we ever hope to solve the most pressing challenges we face—on both a personal and global level. It may sound ridiculous, but I truly believe that optimism can change the world, but it won't happen all at once. Optimism is literally contagious; the more each one of us cultivates it within ourselves, the more it will radiate toward others. Call me an optimist but I believe that with the tools in this book, you can make your life and the lives of those around you a little bit brighter—and that is something even the most cynical person can agree is worthwhile. Let's get started.

CHAPTER 1

"Stay Positive!"

What We Get Wrong About Optimism and Why It Matters

Optimism doesn't erase struggle; it survives it.

Look, you seem cool and all, but I gotta be honest. I don't know why I'm here. Everyone keeps telling me I should just try and stay positive or whatever, but what's the point? It's not like it's going to change anything."

Nick was in his early twenties and had spent the last few months undergoing treatment for cancer. I was a twenty-five-year-old doctoral student working my first internship in UCLA's psycho-oncology department. My job was to provide therapeutic support to cancer patients and their loved ones to help them cope with their diagnoses and treatments. Nick was my first patient—and one of the toughest cases I've had in my career to date.

He was a stereotypical tough guy. From the moment we met, he exuded machismo and made it clear that he thought therapy was a waste of time. He'd been raised to believe that emotional vulnerability was a sign of weakness and feelings were best kept to oneself. As a result he was, let's just say, *struggling* to come to terms with his circumstances. As part of his treatment, he had undergone surgery, which had gotten rid of the cancer but struck a blow to his confidence and sense of virility. When I started seeing him, he had just completed his prescribed course of treatment but had to return to the hospital every few months in order to check if the cancer had returned. A pattern quickly emerged. In the weeks leading up to each appointment, Nick would begin to act out his stress in increasingly dangerous ways. At one of our earliest sessions, he showed up with bloodied knuckles left over from a fight he'd gotten into at a party the night before. A few weeks later, he wrecked his car after speeding through the winding streets of the Hollywood Hills and careening off an embankment. He somehow walked away from the scene without any serious injuries, but it was clear to me that he was risking his life on purpose, coping with his fear by trying to cheat death rather than talk about it.

Therapy is both art and science. While there are specific methods and tools you can use based on tested principles, every patient is different, and not everyone will respond to the same types of treatment. In order to truly connect with each patient, you need to get creative. And that starts by getting to know the person and meeting them where they are at. I knew right away that if I was going to help Nick, the first thing I needed to do was gain his trust. Everyone around him—his family, his friends, his fellow cancer patients, and even some of his doctors—kept telling him to keep his chin up, to not dwell on his diagnosis, to try to be optimistic. And he wasn't buying it.

It became clear that I wasn't going to have much success by trying to coax Nick to talk about his feelings or to list off all the ways a more positive outlook could benefit him. He had had a good life, a positive attitude, and a healthy social life; and he felt like cancer had stolen that from him. I needed to help him see that he still had a lot of life to live.

"Do you have any games coming up?" I asked Nick during one session shortly after his accident.

I knew Nick was an avid hockey player. He'd played since he was a kid and was extremely competitive. During the more intense parts of his treatment, he hadn't been well enough to play, but as soon as his health started improving, he rejoined his league and played every Sunday at a rink near his home. A few people had suggested that maybe he should take it easy while his body fully healed, but he wouldn't give it up. I'd noticed that, at many of our sessions, the only time he seemed to feel joy was when he was talking about hockey or anticipating an upcoming game.

Something told me that if I kept asking him about this subject, it would help me understand him more.

"I have one this weekend, yeah," he said, visibly relieved that I hadn't asked him about his treatments, his recent accident, or how he was feeling.

"Oh, cool," I said. "You're excited?"

"Yeah, pretty excited," he said. "It's going to be a tough match—the opposing team has a solid defense—but we've been practicing a lot this week, so we feel good about it."

"Nice. So you think you're going to win?"

"Well, there's no way to know for sure, of course, but yeah, I feel pretty confident that we can win."

To an outsider, this conversation may have seemed like nothing more than banter—a therapist trying to relax her client before she started on the "real work" of therapy. But I knew I had just found the key to Nick's case. Despite his (perfectly normal and understandable) negative attitude surrounding his health, Nick had not lost all sense of optimism. He was still optimistic about hockey—and this was the key to helping him understand just how powerful that could be.

"So you don't *know* if you're going to win, but you think you will?" I asked.

"Yeah," Nick responded, clearly a little skeptical at what must have seemed like a dumb question.

"But, if you're being realistic, you have just as much chance of losing as you do of winning, don't you?"

"Yeah, of course we could lose," he said, a little incredulous. "But what would be the point of trying if I thought we were going to lose? I always play like I'm going to win."

"So if you don't know you're going to win, why do you expect it?"

"Because it puts me in the right frame of mind. When I expect to win, I focus on what I need to do to win. If I expected to lose, I'd get too in my head. I play better when I expect to win. I have more of a purpose."

I smiled. "So basically you're telling me that when it comes to hockey, you're pretty optimistic."

He chuckled, finally catching on to what I was doing. "Yeah, I guess so."

"One more question, then: What if you went into each screening session with the same mindset you have when you play hockey. How might that change the way you feel in the months leading up to it?"

"Ummmm." I could tell Nick was still not entirely convinced, but I'd gotten him to think about his situation just a little differently. "I don't know."

I smiled. It was all I needed. "How about we find out?"

For the next several months, Nick and I worked together to help him consciously practice optimism. By drawing the connection between the way he thought about hockey and the way he could learn to think about his health, I showed him that not only could he benefit from a real optimism practice but that he already had the capacity to sustain one. Almost immediately, I started noticing changes in his demeanor. He became more open and vulnerable in our sessions. He stopped behaving recklessly in the weeks leading up to each screening. He made more time to do the things he loved and spend time with the people he cared about.

The more he noticed these positive changes, the easier it became for him to cope with his situation. He started taking better care of his health knowing that if the cancer didn't return, those habits would set him up for a healthy future, and if it did, his body might respond better to the next round of treatment if it was strong going into it. He began sharing his feelings and fears with his closest friends and relatives, which helped him appreciate the support network he had—and would have if he got sick again. He started thinking about the future—what he might want to do for a career, if he might like to move away after his treatment ended, what he wanted his life to look like once he was fully cancer-free.

By the end of our year of working together, Nick's outlook had totally transformed. By the time our therapeutic relationship ended, his cancer had not returned, but I didn't hear anything else about his life until several years later, when I received an email from him from out of the blue. He had come across an interview I'd done for a local website and looked me up online. He wanted me to know that he had remained cancer-free and that he was now a father and husband. More important, he said, he had maintained the sense of optimism he had cultivated back in that office at UCLA and was still benefiting from the practice. "You may not remember me," he wrote, "but I just wanted to say thank you."

Let me be clear, I am not suggesting that Nick's renewed sense of optimism prevented his cancer from coming back. Biology and good medicine did that. While several studies have demonstrated a link between an optimistic outlook and improved physical health, there is no evidence to suggest that a sunny disposition can cure cancer—or any other disease.

You're also probably wondering how something as simple as a hockey metaphor could change someone's life that profoundly. Well, here's the thing: When it comes to improving your mental health and changing your behaviors, the big transformations *always* start with little things—often things you may not fully appreciate when they happen. Nick's life didn't change because of one conversation; it changed because that conversation shifted his thinking in a way that allowed him to start making different choices about how he lived his life and interacted with the people around him. All he needed was proof that the effort to develop more optimism would pay off. Once he had that, he was able to realize how working to shift his attitude about his diagnosis could help him cope in the present.

Critically, the conversation he and I had did not require him to be positive or certain about anything, just as he was never certain he would win a hockey game. By shifting his perspective, Nick was able to reckon with his reality instead of trying to run from it. In doing so, he was able to process his very real anger, fear, and grief about what he was going through in healthy and constructive ways, instead of trying to bury his feelings or act out on them. Optimism did not require him to ignore the reality that his cancer might indeed come back or that—worst-case scenario—it could come back, spread, and kill him. It simply but profoundly changed the way he faced this possibility. It didn't suddenly grant him the ability to change the outcome of his next appointment. But it did give him the ability to experience more joy in the three months leading up to that appointment. By expecting to beat cancer, Nick had a reason to invest energy into his life. Optimism did not change Nick's future; it allowed him to live more fully and purposefully in the present, which set him on a different, more productive trajectory.

When we understand what *real* optimism is, we can begin to appreciate how our outlook on life affects our experience of life, and we can, with some effort, learn to shift that perspective to one that helps us live the life we want. While we can't always change our circumstances, when we choose to look at those circumstances optimistically, we immediately become more able to move through the world with purpose, perspective, and an open heart. To do this, we must do what Nick did: We must reconsider how we think about optimism and, in turn, examine how we view our own lives.

What Is Optimism?

Whenever I speak to a large group of people, I like to ask them to shout out the first word that comes to mind when they think of optimism. Inevitably the room immediately fills with echoes of "POSITIVITY!"

This is not surprising. Most people tend to use the terms *optimism* and *positivity* or *positive thinking* interchangeably. Even some psychologists and therapists do this. I, however, see them as cousins, not twins—similar but fundamentally different. While an optimistic outlook often promotes positive emotions and feeling positive can help us think optimistically about the future, it's important to draw a distinction if you want to harness the true power of real optimism without succumbing to problematic thinking.

Our society's obsession with positivity and positive thinking emphasizes a belief that the goal of life is to feel good as much as possible. Conventional wisdom maintains that we do this by focusing on the upside of any given situation while ignoring—or at least downplaying—the downside. Positive thinking holds that emotions like joy, contentment, and excitement are superior to those like anger, sadness, disappointment, or jealousy because we feel better when we experience them.

There is nothing wrong with wanting to feel good. In fact, the whole point of this book is to show how a real optimism practice can improve your overall mental health and foster positive thoughts, feelings, and events throughout your life. However, making positivity a goal often leads us to ignore the lessons that challenging experiences and feelings can teach us. Positive thinking also focuses on how we feel in the present moment, encouraging us to replace uncomfortable thoughts and feelings with ones that elevate our mood. Again, this is a natural, understandable impulse. Who wants to feel shitty if it's possible to feel good? The problem is, we cannot live authentically if we pretend that life isn't occasionally shitty. When we disregard or dismiss unpleasantness for the sake of placating ourselves in the present moment, we are basically trying to gaslight ourselves into believing we're okay when we're not.

Optimism, by contrast, invites you to look toward the future no matter what your present circumstances. It is a way of thinking that assumes that on the whole, future events will be positive rather than negative; good outcomes will outnumber bad ones, and even the bad ones are temporary. Optimism invites you—in fact, I would argue it *requires* you—to experience the full range of human emotion, because only by doing so can you process the reality of your circumstances and make informed authentic decisions about how to move forward.

I'm an extremely visual person, so when I think about optimism, I like to visualize myself sitting alone in a dark room. The room is completely empty and silent, and there's no light coming from anywhere. But as I sit there—with nothing else to do but take stock of where I am and what I'm feeling—my eyes start to acclimate and I notice something take shape in the darkness. It's a door. I don't know what's on the other side of that door, but the fact that I know there's a way out—that I won't be stuck in this room forever—allows me to stop focusing on the darkness and start focusing on the door. And the more I focus on the door, the more I start to notice it changing. The door is unlocked. Then it's ajar. Then I notice a faint light peeking out from behind it. I'm still in the darkness, and I still don't know what's waiting for me on the other side of the door, but I decide I want to find out. I become curious about whatever is in store for me, so I begin to walk toward it.

Curiosity is an extremely important component of optimism—and one that gets lost when we focus too much on trying to manipulate our emotions or snap out of whatever funk we're in. When we allow ourselves to be curious about both what we're experiencing in the present and what the future holds for us, we naturally become less preoccupied with trying to assign value to events or emotions. Instead, we open ourselves up to whatever our experiences have to teach us about ourselves, our world, and our humanity. When we walk through the door at the far end of the dark room, we can hope that something wonderful is waiting for us on the other side, but because we have already been through the darkness, we are prepared for whatever lies ahead. Curiosity breeds knowledge, and knowledge breeds resilience. When we seek out information and understanding, we become wiser and more capable. Real optimism opens us up to our potential while encouraging us to embrace the uncertain. We learn to discern between what we can and can't control and seek opportunities to learn and grow without holding on too tightly to specific expectations or outcomes.

Optimism Is a Spectrum

We tend to think that our inclination toward optimism or pessimism is inherent. You're either an optimist or a pessimist. You see the glass as half full *or* half empty. In reality, our outlook tends to shift depending on our circumstances.

For instance, on the whole, individuals tend to be more optimistic about their own lives or the lives of those in their immediate social circles but relatively pessimistic when asked to predict the future of larger groups, including society as a whole. For example, one study found that individuals were optimistic about their job prospects and salaries in the future even if they were pessimistic about their nation's economy. Similarly, people tend to be relatively optimistic about the future of their local neighborhoods and communities even while pessimistic about the prospects of their nation or the rest of the world.

Your levels of optimism can also vary wildly *within* your own personal life. Maybe you feel optimistic about your career and financial prospects, but when you think about your love life, you've decided that romance doesn't exist outside of fairy tales and you're simply not destined for happily ever after. Perhaps when your boss asks you to head a major project for corporate, you rise to the task without a doubt you'll excel. But when they ask you to *present* that project at next year's shareholder meeting, your palms start sweating and you start wondering if your boss will buy it if you suddenly come down with an inexplicable case of laryngitis the night before the meeting. You're optimistic about your ability to succeed in one area but not another.

Or maybe you're like me. As I explained in the last chapter, I am not the most naturally optimistic person. As I've gotten older and started learning more about the benefits of optimism and ways to practice it, I've become much more optimistic about most areas of my life except one. Whenever something threatens my physical health (or at least I think it *might* threaten my physical health), I immediately panic. Seriously, the second I get a sore throat, I convince myself I've contracted a life-threatening incurable condition. Some rare, unidentified virus that will no doubt rob me of my ability to speak, perhaps? Once I threw out a brand-new pair of prescription eyeglasses because they fell into an airplane toilet. Could I have sanitized them? Maybe . . . and trust me, I *tried*. But how would I know it killed everything?! I tried talking myself into keeping them, but I couldn't stop imagining what deadly microscopic organisms might be lurking in the crevices. In the end, I realized I was better off just getting rid of them. Why not save my mental energy for more pressing matters and practice overcoming my hypochondria some other day? (Luckily, I was in New York City, where driving is not necessary, because I definitely couldn't see clearly for a full thirty-six hours.)

The point is, even if you don't consider yourself an optimistic person, chances are there are at least some areas of your life where you engage in optimistic thinking, even if you don't appreciate or realize it. And as we'll learn throughout the rest of this book, with the right tools and attention, you can learn to apply that perspective to other areas of your life. Optimism is not an inherent, unmalleable state of being. It's a practice you subconsciously or consciously cultivate over time, and it lies on a spectrum.

Optimists Are Made, Not Born

While we all have tendencies toward optimism or pessimism depending on our situation, these tendencies are not as immutable as you might think. Research shows that only about 25 percent of the traits associated with optimism are genetic. The rest are determined by environmental factors like how we were raised, what experiences we've had, what lessons we've learned, and how we've taught ourselves to interpret the events that happen around and to us. So what determines whether someone is an optimist or a pessimist?

Several researchers have studied how optimism shows up in our lives and what factors determine whether someone is more prone to optimism or pessimism. One of the most prominent of these scientists is Martin Seligman, who began studying optimism in the 1960s after becoming curious about what made some people more positive and functional than others. Seligman gained fame after discovering a phenomenon he dubbed *learned helplessness*. For those of you who don't have a stack of psychology and self-help books piled on your nightstand like I do, learned helplessness describes what happens when people (or animals) become so accustomed to repeated pain or suffering that they can't control that they eventually stop trying to avoid it, even when an opportunity to escape their situation presents itself. Seligman discovered this after experimenting with dogs in a lab to see how they would respond to a series of random electrical shocks. Over time, the dogs that received the shocks without being offered a way to avoid them stopped trying to escape altogether—even when presented with an opportunity to leave the cages in which they were being held. They simply gave up, believing there was no way out even when there was.

What popular literature often omits from discussions of these experiments is another observation Seligman made while working with these animals: Learned helplessness is not inevitable. Of the animals subjected to the same conditions as the dogs who succumbed to their plight, roughly a third of them walked right out of their cage as soon as they realized they could. Seligman decided to find out why. Eventually he came to identify three ways in which pessimists and optimists view the world differently. When confronted with negative events, information, or feedback, pessimists tend to interpret the causes of those events as permanent, pervasive, and personal. Bad things happen all the time and are inevitable, and any personal setbacks or failures are usually a result of one's own inherent inadequacy—not a consequence of outside forces or other people. Optimists, meanwhile, when presented with the same information, will interpret the causes as temporary, situational, and within their control. Things can get better, they likely will, and they can (at least somewhat) manipulate that destiny.

Let's say you're stood up by a date. If you think of your romantic life pessimistically, you might spiral into a flurry of negative thoughts: "Rejected yet again! This always happens. I'm never going to find love. That's it! I'm never dating again!" [Immediately deletes all dating apps and declares a vow of celibacy on social media.] Meanwhile, if you believe that the situation is isolated and bears no reflection on your worth as a potential partner, you'll likely interpret it more optimistically: "Oh well. Maybe something came up or they just found someone else they vibed with better. Dating is hard, but clearly that person wasn't right for me. I'll try again later, but for now, since I'm at this nice restaurant, I'll treat myself to a glass of wine and call my best friend. That will make me feel better."

In other words, our sense of optimism depends primarily on the things we tell ourselves, the stories we create to help us make sense of the world around us and determine how best to respond. We originally wrote these stories based on feedback we received, observations we made, and lessons we learned in the past, especially early in life, when we were first trying to figure out what the world was and our place in it. Those stories may have been based on fact or fiction. They may have served us or hindered us. But the point is, we invented them. And if we invented them, then we can reinvent them. When we start to reexamine those stories through fresh eyes, through the lens of additional experiences we've had and lessons we've learned since we first wrote them, we start to appreciate how they've shaped our outlook. When we change these stories, we change our outlook. And when we change our outlook, we can change our lives.

Optimism Is Adaptive

It's easy to look at the history of life on planet Earth as a testament to the importance and power of pessimism. According to Darwinian theory, the survival of a species comes down to its ability to spot, avoid, and defend against threats.* What better way to defend oneself than to assume danger is lurking around every corner and prepare for the worst?

Pessimism is certainly important—to a point. Sometimes assuming bad outcomes can help protect us from serious harm, especially if we don't have all the facts about a situation. When we teach small children to distrust strangers, for example, we're essentially instilling them with a pessimistic attitude in order to keep them safe while they learn to better judge their surroundings and develop their instincts. But even in non-life-threatening situations, a healthy dose of pessimism can help keep our mental health in check. In fact, scientists have found that, under certain circumstances, setting low expectations can help us cope with risk and manage our anxiety so that it doesn't get the better of us. This strategy, known as *defensive pessimism,* can actually improve our performance within those risky situations.

But think about how exhausting it would be if we assumed *only* the worst-case scenario all the time. If we saw every living creature as a potential threat and spent all our time preparing for possible catastrophes? Left unchecked, our innate pessimism could quickly become paranoia, an extremely maladaptive state of being defined by irrational and pervasive fears.

In order to counterbalance our inherent pessimism, some scientists theorize that humans evolved a sense of optimism so they could detect and defend against potential dangers while still planning for and working toward a positive future. One of the things that distinguishes human beings from most other animals is the prefrontal cortex, a section of the brain concerned with learning, reasoning, and problem-solving (among

---

* And, of course, to procreate.

other things). Unlike most other species, humans are able to learn from the past in order to plan for the future. We can imagine future scenarios—both desirable and not—and use our power of deductive reasoning to determine how likely each scenario is and whether it's worth pursuing based on its potential upsides and downsides. This unique neurobiology is what allowed us to learn to cook, farm, build permanent homes, organize into societies, and generally shape the world around us instead of waiting for evolution to adapt us to the world. Without optimism, some evolutionary biologists argue, this incredible ability would have largely gone to waste, hijacked by a persistent belief that the future was less important than whatever was lurking behind the bushes, ready to pounce, right now.

Regardless of *why* we developed our generally sunny attitudes, optimism is clearly a central part of the human condition. In fact we as a species are so relentlessly optimistic that sometimes we do things that don't seem to make a lot of sense. For instance, several studies of global speech patterns have found an overwhelming and universal preference toward the use of positive language over negative language. This positivity bias—also known as the Pollyanna principle after the classic children's book character who was known for her relentlessly optimistic attitude—was first identified in the late 1960s, but the findings of that original study have been replicated multiple times. In one 2015 study, for instance, researchers evaluated the use of 100,000 words across ten widely spoken and very different languages. In every sample, they found a clear preference for positive words.

In one famous study, researchers asked soon-to-be-married couples how likely it was that they would eventually get divorced. Even though the rate of divorce in the Western world is roughly 50 percent, each of these couples reported that the chance of their getting divorced was basically zero. This tendency to overestimate the likelihood of future positive scenarios is known as the *optimism bias* and is often pointed to as a flaw of human psychology. If we were smart, wouldn't we look at the data and interpret our chances of success based on cold hard facts, even if they were at odds with our feelings and desires?

To that I say *no!* What good does it do any couple to assume their relationship will end? What good does it do someone to believe their dreams are unrealistic—even if they are unlikely? What good does it do to always assume the odds are against you instead of dreaming you might defy them? In other words, what *harm* does it actually do to be optimistic?

As I write this, my seven-year-old son, Jag, is obsessed with basketball. He is a half-Caucasian, half-Indian kid from Santa Monica who is destined to be no taller than five-eleven. Yet he is convinced he is going to play for the NBA. Given that the odds of a high school basketball player in the United States making an NBA team are roughly two thousand to one (and Jag is still well off from high school), I'm going to go ahead and confess that I have very little faith in this dream of his. But am I going to tell him that? Am I going to tell my sweet-faced, overenthusiastic first grader that his hoop dreams are more like pipe dreams? Of course not. And I don't know a single parent who would advise me to do so. Jag's dreams, like any elementary school kid's ambitions, are likely to change as he gets older. And if they don't, then the worst thing that will likely happen is that he keeps playing and enjoying basketball, eventually realizes the odds of going pro are stacked against him, and either gives up playing basketball or continues to play it for fun and exercise. And who knows? Maybe he'll defy the odds, get a scholarship to a Division I school, lead his team to win the NCAA Championship his freshman year, and become a first-round draft pick for the Lakers! Stranger things have happened, so again I ask, what's the harm?

Optimism makes life worth living. It motivates us to have a go at things we might not otherwise try and to accomplish things others never thought possible. Think of every great human achievement: democracy, space travel, the eradication of smallpox, and on and on. How could humanity have ever accomplished any of these without a little wishful thinking? On a more personal level, what would be the point of falling in love, starting a business, or going on an audition if we didn't think we could succeed?

Optimism Is Not Magic; It's a Muscle

When I first started working with Nick, he was skeptical that optimism could help him. In his mind, the idea that simply believing in a positive future could improve his circumstances was, frankly, bullshit. People who believed you could direct the future with your thoughts were at best wrong and at worst deluded.

The thing is, he wasn't wrong.

Optimism on its own can't influence the future. The reason it's so beneficial is because it promotes behaviors that help us create the futures we want. Or at least the ones we expect. When you believe that the future holds promise, your goals are achievable, and setbacks are temporary and surmountable, you are more likely to approach your life proactively and productively.

At the beginning of this book, I mentioned a bunch of research that shows a link between optimism and a number of desirable life outcomes. Optimism can help you live longer, cope with stress, be more productive and creative, and develop and sustain stronger relationships—all factors associated with well-being. The reason optimists thrive in these ways is not because they have some special in with the universe. They simply put more effort into doing the things that will help them prosper because they believe those efforts will pay off, even if they're not sure exactly how. They nurture their most important relationships, pay attention to their health, seek solutions to problems, reach out for support when they're struggling, and generally just take charge of their lives instead of leaving things to chance.

Optimism is like a muscle: The more you work to develop it, the stronger it becomes. As you start to see the results of your efforts—and the optimism practice that inspired those efforts—the easier it becomes for you to be optimistic in the future. A positive outcome reinforces the belief that positive outcomes are possible, even likely, in the future. In this way the optimism muscle gets stronger. It's a virtuous cycle, a feedback loop. Optimism begets more optimism.

Optimism Is for Realists

There's a great line at the beginning of the movie *Home Alone* (hi, yes, nineties girl again!), where Uncle Frank is freaking out that the family is going to miss their flight to Paris. At one point, Kevin McCallister/Macaulay Culkin's dad turns to Frank and says, "Think positive, Frank!" and Frank retorts, "You be positive. I'll be realistic."

This false dichotomy (which we all know exists just as much in the real world as it does in beloved Christmas movies) between positivity and realism posits that optimistic people are at least somewhat deluded. Just look around. Can't you see how many things are wrong with the world and how often terrible things happen? You have to be kidding yourself if you think everything is just going to work itself out in the long run!

But the truth is, optimists value a realistic view of the world just as much as pessimists do, if not more so. In fact, research shows that an optimistic mindset can actually make someone more equipped to face reality than a pessimistic one.

In one study, cancer patients who ranked high on an optimism scale asked more questions about their diagnosis and prognosis than those who ranked as more pessimistic. Rather than throw up their hands in defeat, they sought information that could help them strategize potential solutions to the problem in front of them. What's more, when they determined that they had done all they could to improve their chances of beating their disease, they turned their attention to processing how they felt about the situation, being honest with themselves about their emotions and struggles, and applying consistent effort to coping with the stress of their situation rather than letting it get the better of them. They didn't put on rose-colored glasses or bury their heads in the sand to avoid difficult feelings or negative energy. Rather, they embraced the reality of their situation and took charge of the aspects they could control. And when they determined they had done the best they could, they stopped putting effort into controlling the uncontrollable and instead focused on bolstering their own mental health and making the most of the present moment.

Other research reveals that optimists are more strategic than pessimists about where they devote their time and effort, gathering information in order to determine whether it's worth spending time on a task or abandoning it in favor of something with a bigger potential payoff. In one study, participants were given a certain amount of time to solve a series of anagrams, some of which were solvable and some of which were not. Those who scored high in optimism tended to give up on the unsolvable problems much more quickly than those who scored low in optimism, choosing instead to devote their limited time and energy toward the problems that could be solved. We tend to think of giving up as a negative quality—celebrating people who tough it out even when things seem impossible. While grit and determination are necessary for accomplishing big goals, they can quickly turn into folly when the challenge is at worst, impossible, or at best, not worth additional effort. An optimist's ability to make decisions based on all the information available to them—even if it's tough to hear—can therefore be an asset when trying to make good decisions and get things done.

That said, it's important to distinguish between real optimism and blind optimism. As its name suggests, real optimism requires strong, consistent engagement with reality. Blind optimism is expecting your desired outcome without considering the factors that would influence that outcome—such as chance, in the case of something like gambling, or the expectation that you will make the varsity basketball team without practicing your lay-up. When people criticize optimists or dismiss the usefulness of an optimism practice, they're often confusing these two types of optimism, which is why it's essential to distinguish them. If you want to realize the benefits of optimism, you must make sure your beliefs are backed up by facts and effort.

Optimism Breeds Resilience

Before we move on to discuss *how* to cultivate more optimism in your life, I want to take a moment to emphasize a critical point. While real optimism encourages us to think positively about the future, it can't exist without struggle because, put simply, life does not exist without struggle. We become more optimistic when we experience hard things and get through them. The more we do this, the more confidence we build in ourselves. The more resilient we become. The braver we are.

Like a muscle, optimism requires resistance in order to grow. If you've ever lifted weights, you'll know that if you want to gain strength and build muscle, you need to gradually challenge yourself, adding more weight or reps each time you practice. If you simply do the same routine over and over again, you'll never get stronger.

As Martin Seligman showed through his work, how we handle setbacks and resistance is one of the hallmarks of how optimistic we are. In one study, Seligman and his colleagues timed competitive swimmers in a race. They then told each of the swimmers that their time was two seconds longer than it actually was. In a subsequent race, the swimmers who ranked high on an optimism assessment actually swam faster than they originally had. Those who ranked low on optimism swam slower. All the swimmers had been disappointed by their original fabricated times. But while the optimists used this information as motivation to swim better, the pessimists internalized the results and thus performed worse.

The more we allow ourselves to grow and learn from the challenges we face, the more resilient we become. The act of doing this is inherently optimistic because it allows us to move through difficult times with a sense of curiosity and meaning. When we succumb to pessimism, despair, or self-pity, we lose an opportunity for growing, becoming more self-aware, connecting with ourselves and others, and meeting our full potential.

If you want to become more optimistic, you're going to need to challenge yourself, to embrace the hard stuff and the struggles and the resistance that will inevitably get in your way. This requires you to see setbacks that arise beyond your control as opportunities for learning and growth. It also requires you to take risks and seek out opportunities to help you reach your goals and achieve the life you want. This not only requires optimism, but it also helps us build our optimism muscle because, regardless of whether we realize the outcome we want, we gain information about the world and ourselves that we can use in the future. Every time we choose optimism, we choose ourselves.

Quiz: How Optimistic Are You?

For each of the following situations, pick the answer that best describes how you would respond or feel.*

1. You forgot your best friend's birthday.
    a. I've been so busy that it slipped my mind.
    b. I'm terrible at remembering important dates.

2. You didn't get sick all year.
    a. I paid more attention to my health than I have in the past.
    b. I wasn't exposed to a lot of sick people.

3. You and your partner make up after a huge fight.
    a. I am committed to the relationship and willing to try and make it work.
    b. I realized it wasn't that big of a deal, so I forgave them.

4. A friend expresses gratitude for helping them get through a tough time.
    a. I enjoy being there for others.
    b. I enjoy helping my friend.

5. Your friend hasn't responded to your last few text messages.
    a. They must be busy.
    b. Did I do something to offend them?

---

* This assessment was inspired by the forty-eight-item optimism questionnaire that was originally created by Dr. Martin Seligman. Unlike Seligman's original, this version is not meant to be used as a diagnostic tool, but rather a general measure of optimism. If you're interested in a more comprehensive optimism score, you can sign up to download Dr. Selingman's full assessment here: https://www.authentichappiness.sas.upenn.edu/questionnaires/optimism-test.

6. You meant to return an item that you bought and don't need, but you missed the window.
    a. I didn't get around to it because I had other things going on.
    b. I am lazy.

7. You knit your mom a scarf but she never wears it.
    a. I picked a color she doesn't like.
    b. She never likes what I get her.

8. Your doctor tells you that you have high cholesterol.
    a. High cholesterol is usually genetic.
    b. I have a poor diet.

9. You've been feeling exceptionally tired lately.
    a. I haven't been sleeping as much as I should.
    b. I'm getting older. I shouldn't be surprised.

10. Your boss praises your team for pulling off a successful project at work.
    a. I managed my team well and kept everyone on task.
    b. My team is extremely competent.

11. Your boss asks you for advice on a problem.
    a. I give honest and reasonable opinions, so even my superiors know they can trust me.
    b. I knew a lot about the issue they needed help with.

12. You failed a test.
    a. I didn't study hard enough.
    b. I don't do well under pressure.

13. You throw a surprise party for a friend and pull it off without a hitch.
    a. I'm good at planning parties.
    b. Everything fell into place!

14. You run for your local school board and lose.
    a. The person who won is more established in the community.
    b. I'm not great at promoting myself.

15. The person you're dating suggests you take a break.
    a. I've been a little sensitive lately.
    b. I'm too much.

16. You lead your team to a victory at trivia night.
    a. I'm really good at trivia.
    b. I knew a lot about the categories that night.

17. You go ice skating with friends and keep falling.
    a. Ice skating is difficult.
    b. I'm not very coordinated.

18. You overdraft your checking account.
    a. I forgot about a scheduled withdrawal.
    b. I need to be better organized about my finances.

19. You witness someone being harassed on the street and intervene.
    a. I pay attention to my surroundings.
    b. I assessed the situation and decided to say something.

20. At a party, you tell a joke that makes everyone laugh.
    a. I am good in a crowd.
    b. Everyone was having a good time.

21. You work up the courage to ask your crush out on a date. They say no.
    a. I was nervous and didn't play it cool.
    b. They could probably tell I was a mess.

22. A stranger flirts with you while you're out with friends.
    a. I am an attractive person.
    b. That person finds me attractive.

For every A you selected, give yourself 1 point. For every B, give yourself 0. If you scored:

0–5: You are naturally pessimistic. You tend to interpret negative events as personal, permanent, and pervasive.

6–11: You are optimistic in certain circumstances but tend toward pessimism most of the time.

12–17: You are naturally quite optimistic but still take a pessimistic view of the world some of the time.

18–22: You are naturally very optimistic. You tend to see negative events as temporary and isolated and don't take them as reflections of who you are as a person.

Don't worry if your score surprises or disappoints you! Look back at the questions and see how each one indicates opposing mindsets, not innate qualities. Are you more optimistic about certain parts of your life than others? Do you notice any patterns about how you explain the world? As you practice the exercises throughout this book, notice how your mindset starts to shift. Where would you like to be more optimistic in your life? How might a new mindset help?

CHAPTER 2

"It's All in Your Head"

The Seven Truths of the Brain and Its Power to Foster an Optimistic Mindset

Optimism is a choice we make about how to live our lives every day.

Nine times out of ten, whenever I meet someone new and they discover what I do for a living, they ask me some version of the same question. "Oh! So you must know all the happiness secrets!" they begin, leaning forward with excitement and hope glittering in their eyes. "Tell me: What is the *one* thing I can do to be more optimistic *right now*? What is the magic pill? I could really use one!" Um, yeah, I could use one, too!

Can I be honest? I hate this question. Okay, *hate* is definitely too strong a word, but I don't *love* this question. Not because I don't understand it—I absolutely do. It makes complete sense to me that someone, upon finding out they were talking to an optimism expert, would want to see if I could offer them some kernel of wisdom that would instantaneously help them increase their optimism. We are all stressed and pressed for time. We all want to improve our lives as much as possible, as soon as possible. We all have too much information to process and too many choices to make each day. So, no, I don't blame people for asking me this question. I just hate that, well, I never feel like I can give them the answer they want to hear—and I am not a fan of disappointing them.*

Our self-help-obsessed culture would have us believe that change can be easy if you just engage in the right activities. *Try this diet or mindfulness practice! Repeat after me: "I choose happiness! I am strong. I am confident. I am love!" Read this book. Take this course. Follow this guru. Download this app. Buy this supplement. Go outside. Get more rest. Practice self-love and self-care.* And so on and so forth. We are bombarded with so many "simple" solutions and quick fixes that we are constantly overwhelmed. We can't possibly do it all, but where should we even begin? And why does it feel so difficult all the time? Is change even possible? If so, then why does it feel so hard? What are we doing wrong?

Trust me, you're not doing anything wrong. The reason change feels so hard is because it *is* hard. In fact, even though change is one of the most constant realities of our existence, active, purposeful change is—from a neurological and psychological standpoint—one of the most difficult states for humans to be in. Our brains have evolved to resist change. They are wired to value the familiar, to revert to what they've always done and always known in order to make the most efficient decisions possible. If we weren't wired this way, it would be impossible to get anything done because we'd constantly have to process and learn from the same information over and over again. This is why we develop habits—automatic, almost unconscious, ways of thinking and behaving that allow us to conserve our mental and physical energy so we can dedicate it to other, more challenging pursuits.

We form our earliest habits automatically. When we're young and trying to make sense of the world, things just sort of happen to us. We acquire language, learn how to cross a busy street, and figure out how to eat based on the cues we pick up from our families, communities, and cul-

---

* If I had to give one answer, I'd say sleep. Getting consistent high-quality sleep is one of the most efficient ways to boost your mood, get more energy, and increase your mental clarity. But it's still up to you to direct that energy toward worthwhile pursuits and to apply consistent effort toward reaching your goals. Far from a magic bullet, but certainly good advice.

tures. We also learn what behaviors are safe (or not safe), form beliefs about other people and the way the world works, and develop a sense of self based on the same set of cues. If, when we're older, we decide to challenge these lessons, we must actively work to unlearn them. And that is extremely difficult to do.

When we want to change, we have to actively work to reprogram our brains so that their natural biological efficiency promotes the habits, beliefs, and thoughts we want to adopt, instead of defaulting to the old patterns we're trying to shed. The more we try to change at the same time, the more difficult the entire process becomes. Even a seemingly isolated change—like altering your diet—requires myriad smaller changes in order to work: changing how you cook, where you shop for groceries, and what you buy; changing your eating habits; learning new recipes, etc. If we want to succeed, we need to retrain our brains to accept that each one of these new behaviors is normal; if we don't, we will struggle until we eventually give up.

Change *is* possible. But it requires understanding how the brain works so we can work *with* our natural biology instead of against it. One of the biggest problems with so much self-help advice is not that it's bad. In fact, there is ample evidence that a lot (though definitely not all) of our most widely accepted ideas about how to promote well-being are scientifically valid. The problem is that much of it is presented in a way that fails to honor the brain's inherent complexity, efficiency, and evolutionary history. It sounds great to say that meditating or employing affirmations or goal-setting or seeing a therapist or fostering social connections can make us happier—and they *can*. But if we don't understand *why* and under what circumstances these strategies work—and if we don't actually *do* the work—we can't fully appreciate the methods, effort, and time required to see results and make them last. And when we don't have realistic expectations for what change will look like, then we'll be setting ourselves up for frustration and disappointment.

Because here's the real answer to that question I get asked all the time: There is no shortcut to lasting change. There is no magic pill or one-size-fits-all tactic or even just one thing you need to do to improve your well-being. And here's the real kicker: Even if you do everything right, sticking to your goals and doing your best and working really hard to change, you will never be perfect. You will never stop changing or wanting to change. You won't one day wake up to realize you've solved all life's problems. You won't change your way out of stress or challenges or failure or mistakes or bad days or crappy emotions or moods. Change is a constant process—and that is okay. In fact, it's exactly how things are meant to be. The goal of real optimism is not to somehow transcend the messy reality of being human; it's to lean into the full experience of it so we can better understand ourselves and the world around us. Real optimism is not some Zen-like, fully realized state of being. It's a choice we make about how to live our lives every day.

The Seven Truths of the Brain

Any sort of change that happens within us has to start in the brain. When we find ourselves struggling to change, it's usually because our brains are stuck in their default patterns and whatever interventions we're using are not sufficient to unstick them. We may have no real idea *why* we want to change or what we'd truly gain if we did so, so we give up before we really get started, lacking the motivation or true self-awareness required to see us through. That's why, before I dive into specific advice about how to cultivate more optimism in your life, it's important to understand how the brain works and why. We don't yet know everything there is to know about the brain, but we know a lot—and that knowledge can prove invaluable when setting out to build new habits.

Truth #1: The Brain Is Wired for Optimism

As we discussed in the last chapter, even though the human brain adapted to be able to perceive threats, scientists theorize that we developed a sense of optimism in order to mediate the stress that constantly anticipating danger would have on our brains. Recent discoveries in neuroscience support this theory by revealing the neurological underpinnings for optimism and networks in the brain associated with an optimistic outlook.

For example, studies show that the mechanisms for both optimism and pessimism lie in opposite parts of the brain, with the right hemisphere primarily driving pessimism and the left primarily driving optimism. In keeping with the evolutionary theory we discussed in the last chapter, scientists believe this is essentially a neurological yin and yang: with half of our brain concerned with anticipating and protecting us from danger and the other responsible for making sure we can cope with that danger in a way that allows us to thrive, mentally and physically. More specifically, a meta-analysis of several studies into how the brains of optimistic people function identified two particular areas of activity: the anterior cingulate cortex, which helps us imagine the future and process information regarding the self, and the inferior frontal gyrus, which is associated with interpreting cues and inhibiting our responses to them.

Neuroscience as a discipline is still relatively new, and we still have a long way to go before we fully understand how the brain works, let alone how it specifically determines whether our outlooks skew more optimistic or more pessimistic. And sure, you probably don't need to understand the difference between the anterior cingulate cortex and the posterior cingulate cortex in order to benefit from a deeper and more pervasive sense of optimism in your life. But I'm sharing this information for a few reasons. First, I just think the science is really cool. Even though my degree is in psychology, I've always been fascinated by the physical brain—how it learns and processes information; how it communicates with the body; how it shapes who we are. And the more scientists understand these processes, the more likely those in the medical field can come up with treatments and interventions for a whole host of neurological and psychological conditions.

In the meantime, though, if we want to improve our sense of optimism, we have to do it with the tools we already have. And that's the main reason I like understanding this science. These advances in neuroscience show that without doubt, our brains have the capacity for optimism. Even if you think you've lost it, the wiring is there; you just might need to reignite it.

Truth #2: The Brain Is Future-Oriented

The human brain is constantly trying to predict what will happen next so that we can prepare for it. From an evolutionary standpoint, this makes sense, because the ability to detect signs of danger in the surrounding environment helps our species survive and evolve. But scientists are constantly finding new and surprising ways that this shows up in our lives. For instance, did you know that the body produces insulin at the mere sight or smell of food? Known as the cephalic phase insulin response, this is a well-documented process designed through evolution to help us digest food more efficiently. Ever felt your stomach start to growl the second you enter a restaurant and catch a glimpse of the dishes other guests are being served? Or salivate when you smell your favorite dessert baking in the oven? That's your brain preparing your body for what it assumes you're about to eat.*

Our brain's fortune-telling prowess also helps us in social situations. When conversing with people, we detect patterns in their speech that help us anticipate when they're about to end their sentence so we know when it will be our turn to speak. We do the same thing when listening to music. One study showed how individuals—even those who had never studied music—could detect the end of a musical phrase because our brain interprets it as a type of uncertain event and directs its attention to trying to figure out *what comes next?* Another recent study found that our innate impulse to tap our feet or bop our heads along to music—what we (and scientists) call *groove*—may actually be rooted in our brain's predictive power. When researchers exposed individuals to a piece of music with a familiar but relatively unpredictable rhythm, they found that they moved their bodies in an effort to figure out the pattern of the beat. According to one of the researchers on this study, "The music requires us to move to be complete, in a sense." Our brains also use context clues and memory to fill in missing pieces of images that are obstructed from our

---

* This is of course extremely convenient from a biological standpoint, but also super annoying if you're on a diet or trying to hold off on indulging until later.

view. For example, if you're looking for a lost object in your home and see part of it poking out from under the couch, your brain will process the image of the full object so you know you've found what you're looking for.

Perhaps most telling, when left with nothing else to do, our brains default to thinking about the future—marshaling all the information available to try to make predictions about possible upcoming scenarios. Work by Joseph Kable at the University of Pennsylvania has identified a particular pathway of the brain known, aptly, as the default mode network (DMN) that activates "when you put people into a brain scanner and ask them to not do anything, to just sit there." In fact, the DMN is composed of two distinct but complementary parts, one that helps us to imagine an event happening and another that evaluates whether the imagined event is positive or negative. The idea that our brains *need* to process information at all times is known as the free-energy principle. Scientists believe that it's basically our brain's response to use it or lose it, the idea that if our brains had nothing to do, they would fall into disorder—much like an old barn, left unattended on an abandoned farm, slowly falls apart. Of course, any of us who have ever struggled with anxiety might argue that it's *thinking too much* that wreaks the most havoc. But I digress. Perhaps the DMN and the free-energy principle explain why our brains often seem to wild out when we're trying to go to sleep, rapidly creating scenarios in our head about what we have to do the next day, what will happen if this other thing happens, and how it's all going to make us feel. It might also help explain why we drift off into daydreams when we're not sufficiently focused on other things: We are using our spare cognitive energy to imagine what might happen in the future.

Knowing why and how our brains are wired for prediction, we can see why so many of us get frustrated with certain types of traditional therapy and self-help practices that focus only on the past or on the present. Thanks to the legacy of psychoanalysts like Sigmund Freud and Carl Jung, traditional talk therapy—which remains one of the most popular modalities practiced today—is focused on mining the past for answers about the present. According to this model, by uncovering how early experiences, especially those in childhood, affected the way we view the world, we can take steps to change those views if we want to. Before you can solve a problem, you need to identify it.

There is no doubt this is an incredibly valuable tool. When we understand why we are the way we are, we can start to question whether that way of being is suitable for our needs right now and going forward. We can investigate whether the stories we've been telling ourselves are true, and if not, how we might be able to identify the stories we want to tell. This is an essential component of self-awareness, which is critical for change to take place.

That said, simply understanding how the past has affected us doesn't help us change this for the future. No matter how crooked or ill-informed or harmful an adopted belief or behavior is, we can't simply flip a switch in our brains and fix it (oh, if it were that easy!). We must consciously and diligently work with our brain's natural chemistry to change its programming, effectively forcing our brain to unlearn what it's already learned and to substitute something new in its place.

Truth #3: The Brain Responds to Fantasy the Same Way It Does to Reality

Have you ever gotten angry by simply imagining an argument with someone? Felt anxiety bubble up in your stomach, your heart start to race, or your palms start to sweat so much that you begin to get mad at them for something they haven't actually done? Or have you ever felt a surge of pride and excitement at the thought of landing your dream job, even if you haven't applied for it yet? I've been known to get mad at my husband after having a bad dream in which he says or does something upsetting that he would never actually do in real life. The fact that I know intellectually and without a doubt that it's all in my head doesn't change the physical and emotional response I have. The feelings sometimes linger for hours after I wake up, and I—not to mention my poor patient husband—have to deal with it.

Our brains respond to vividly imagined scenarios in much the same way they respond to real-life situations. As a result, they send signals to other parts of the body to prepare it for the task it's expecting. In other words, the brain, in its talent for anticipation, tries to prepare you for future events that may never actually happen or are unlikely to happen simply because it anticipates they might. This explains why anxiety often feels so physically crippling: The brain, when flooded with images of stressful scenarios, is constantly triggering the rest of the body to go into its default stress response. Cortisol and adrenaline flood the body, inducing the heart to beat faster, blood pressure to rise, breath to speed up, and senses to heighten—all in an effort to prepare our body for fight or flight. In the face of imaginary threats, we become as revved up—and eventually exhausted—as we would if fleeing from a savage predator.

Fortunately, there is a way to direct the powers of our imagination toward much more productive pursuits through the process of performance-enhancing visualization. Over the past few decades, visualization has become increasingly popular among sports psychologists, who have put these findings to use by training their athletes to visualize possible performance scenarios so they can prepare for any eventuality—even something completely out of the ordinary. As long as you can imagine something happening, you don't need to actually experience it to prepare yourself mentally and physically for it. It has been well documented that Olympians like twenty-eight-time medalist swimmer Michael Phelps and four-time World Cup champion alpine skier Lindsey Vonn practiced visualization to enhance their techniques, and legendary tennis star Billie Jean King was practicing it back in the sixties. During the 2024 Summer Olympics, American gymnast Stephen Nedoroscik (aka pommel horse guy) gained fame, not just for his brilliant athleticism that helped the U.S. Men's team secure their first medal in sixteen years, but for his ritual of closing his eyes and visualizing his routine while he waited to compete. One study found that people who engaged in virtual workouts in their minds actually became stronger even though they hadn't performed the exercises with their bodies.

Sports is an ideal discipline in which to harness the power of visualization because it can be highly stressful and competitive, but it also relies on intense repetitive training in order to improve your skills. This makes it relatively easy to envision potential scenarios because even though the mechanics and patterns of any particular competition are unpredictable, the ultimate objectives, goals, moves, techniques, and situations are relatively predictable and repetitive. If you know the course of the slope down which you're about to ski, and you have a lot of past experience of skiing, you can visualize what it might feel like to actually ski down that particular mountain. You can even visualize possible—though unpredictable—scenarios like the direction of the wind, the roar of spectators cheering you on, your goggles fogging up or slipping off, etc. "[I tell my athletes to] strive for excellence because you're not going to be perfect," says Dr. Don Greene, a performance coach and sports psychologist who spoke to me on my podcast. Dr. Greene trains Olympic athletes and world-class musicians in visualization techniques as a way to prepare them for high-pressure (and often unpredictable) scenarios. "Something's going to come up with live performances or crowd noise. Or in an audition, the panel talking amongst themselves. Or in a concert, [the sound of] candy wrappers. You can't expect things to go well."

You don't have to be an athlete to benefit from the power of visualization. You can apply it to pretty much any goal you set for yourself, even those for which there are no traditional training programs. Want to stop yourself from raiding the fridge every night before bed? Or get over your social anxiety so you can relax at parties? Or become a more patient parent or partner instead of letting triggers get the better of you? Visualization can help. Science has shown that the act of purposefully imagining oneself doing something makes us more likely to actually do it, and the more we imagine that scenario, the more likely we are to follow through.

I use visualization with pretty much every client who wants to change an ingrained behavior or a strong (but not helpful) belief. By applying scientifically sound techniques in their particular circumstances, people can radically transform their behaviors, their outlooks, and most important, their self-perception. Visualization has helped my clients land their dream jobs, find romantic partners, and kick long-term addictions in favor of more health-promoting behaviors. By diligently working to picture themselves as the person they wanted to be, they prepared themselves to do the things they needed to do to actually *become* that person. In chapter 6, we'll talk more about how to use visualization to help improve your optimism practice and increase your ability to achieve your goals.

Truth #4: The Brain Likes to Believe What It Already Believes

In order to help us survive, the brain has to learn *a lot* of things. This includes basic biological processes we take for granted like how to breathe, how to interpret our senses, and how to interact with other people. It also includes more conscious processes like how to interpret the events and people around you, how to regard yourself and your place in the world, and how to amass the right knowledge and skills you need to achieve your goals.

In order to process this much information, the brain requires systems that make the learning process more efficient. It does this, first and foremost, by helping us remember what we've already learned so we don't have to constantly relearn it, but also by filtering out information that is not relevant to our immediate needs. We tend to think of the word *bias* as negative, but cognitive biases are not bad per se; they are just mental shortcuts. Unfortunately, sometimes the brain is *too* efficient at doing this, leading us to cling to false information and unproductive habits while ignoring information that could clearly benefit our survival. This leads to what are called *cognitive biases,* perceived flaws in our neurobiology that make us do a lot of things that seem irrational—and can be extremely frustrating—but are actually rooted in biological necessity.

One of the most pervasive cognitive biases is the confirmation bias. The confirmation bias explains why our brains tend to seek information that confirms what it already believes while filtering out information that, if accepted, would force us to reexamine those beliefs and most likely learn something new to replace it. In extreme cases, we see the confirmation bias at work with people who adopt extreme or irrational viewpoints that, to the rest of us, fall apart with the smallest amount of scrutiny or common sense. These people will ignore overwhelming evidence that contradicts their chosen belief system but point to arcane information, implausible theories, or dubious "patterns" to uphold their preexisting view of the world.

But you don't have to be a zealot in order to succumb to the confirmation bias. Every single one of us engages in this bias regularly—probably every day—without realizing it. The confirmation bias is a well-documented psychological phenomenon, and studies show that the average person is often loath to abandon their beliefs even when presented with reliable data proving them wrong. In one study, researchers asked participants to read examples of different fictitious firefighters with various levels of risk tolerance and success in fighting fires. They instructed participants to detect patterns in the story to determine what factors best determined how successful a firefighter was and also to explain why that might be the case. In some instances, participants were told that the firefighters with higher risk tolerance were more successful; in others, they were told the opposite—that the firefighters with *less* risk tolerance succeeded more often. After the study, researchers told some of the participants that the information they'd been given was false—that the correlation between risk and success did not actually exist in the data. And yet most of the participants clung to their original belief regardless of the original dataset they'd been given. Those who believed risk tolerance was positively correlated with successful firefighting continued to believe that was true, while those who believed more cautious firefighters were typically more successful also held firm. In each case, it seemed that the reasoning they had come up with to support their original conclusions (for example, that risk-tolerant firefighters would be more likely to run into a burning building or that risk-averse firefighters would be better adept at assessing the scene) was sufficient to support that conclusion in the absence of hard data. Not only do we believe what we believe, we rationalize those beliefs so they become even more believable—at least to us.

The confirmation bias shows up in small ways, like when we buy a new car and suddenly see that exact same make, model, and color everywhere even when we never noticed it before. Or when we have a crush on someone and suddenly every little thing we encounter reminds us of them. But we also do this when we seek out information that upholds our existing, most closely held beliefs, while dismissing alternate points of view. Social media harnesses the power of the confirmation bias by programming algorithms to feed users the same types of content again and again. We see a message we agree with and engage with it, so we see more messages reinforcing that belief while being spared most content that would challenge those beliefs so that we believe the original belief even more. Tech companies may have exploited this reality, but they didn't invent it.

We also fall victim to confirmation bias when it comes to our own self-image, continually accumulating evidence that supports what we think about ourselves—for good or for ill. Confirmation bias is the reason some artists focus on one negative review rather than a thousand positive ones or why we may dwell on that one time someone called us an asshole in traffic even if we're usually a courteous driver. It's also how we confirm the most closely held aspects of our identity—filtering information that proves we're bookish or irresponsible or the funny one or unlovable. These beliefs may also be based on bad, outdated, or incomplete information, but our brains cling to them because abandoning them would disrupt the normal flow of information.

If we want to change these beliefs, we need to actively change the way we process information, seeking evidence for the things we *want* to believe rather than letting the default process take over. I often have clients come to me who are holding on to deeply held problematic beliefs about themselves: "I'm not smart." "I'm not a good parent." "I'm not worthy of love." "I don't deserve to be happy." Many of them know rationally that these things are not true, but because their brains have been programmed—probably for decades—to seek out information that validates these false beliefs, they often default to them whenever challenges arise. A breakup is proof that they're a bad partner. Losing their temper with their kid is proof that they're a terrible parent. A negative performance review confirms that they're simply not that good at their job. When I work with these people, I know we have to rewrite the scripts they tell themselves, so I urge them to look for clues in their lives that actively debunk their false beliefs and then train them to pay attention to confirm the truth. It takes a lot of diligence and practice, but it works. We'll talk more about how to do this in chapter 4.

Truth #5: The Brain Is Wired for All Emotions

One of my biggest pet peeves is the media's obsession with stress. Yes, too much chronic stress is bad for you. It can cause all sorts of mental and physical ailments and lead to irrational behaviors that put us directly in harm's way. But what the hell are we supposed to do about that? Simply *stop being stressed*?! Have you been outside? Have you watched the news? Have you ever been frustrated or sad or lonely or angry? If we hadn't been reading these types of warnings about stress for decades at this point, I'd guess they'd all been written by AI. Stress is a natural response to the human experience, and yet we somehow believe that in order to thrive, we need to rid ourselves of it.

Yes, "positive" emotions like joy, contentment, excitement, and love are good for us. They make us mentally and physically healthier and promote decision-making and behaviors that lead to increased well-being. Anger, fear, grief, anxiety—all these "negative" emotions, when left unchecked, can make us emotionally and physically miserable.

But totally suppressing undesirable emotions is not only impossible but also not all that helpful. As human beings, we are *supposed* to feel all our emotions; we were designed that way. Every emotion we experience is a piece of information about what is happening and how we feel about it. Emotions help us learn and adapt to our environment by keeping our focus on the most relevant and urgent inputs and stimuli in front of us. Scientists have identified emotions' critical role in memory, decision-making, problem-solving, and social connection. The most basic emotions—such as joy, sadness, fear, anger, disgust, and surprise—develop by the time we're six months old as we adjust to and make sense of life on earth for the first time. Emotions that induce positive feelings—those like joy, pride, desire, and excitement—activate our brain's reward centers, thus motivating us to solve problems and take action. Without these emotions, we wouldn't be able to take the steps necessary to make life worth living; we wouldn't know how. Meanwhile, emotions like aggression, fear, and anxiety give us the tools we need to protect ourselves and our loved ones from perceived threats. Yes, even stress—the emotion we're so often told is a dangerous toxin that can literally *kill* you if you experience it too much—is essential for human survival. "Stress is what happens in your body when you need to adapt and respond to life," says Kelly McGonigal, author of *The Upside of Stress* and a researcher at Stanford University who has studied how to use stress as a motivator. When I interviewed her for my podcast, she spoke at length about how to use stress in a way that is beneficial without letting it overwhelm you. "There's something inherently problematic if you believe what happens in your body when you need to respond or adapt to life is toxic and the thing that is keeping you from being healthy and happy."

While, yes, difficult emotions can wreak havoc if left unchecked, when we try to ignore or suppress them, we disrupt an essential part of what it means to be human. A more optimistic approach is to accept and validate these feelings and experience and approach them with curiosity about what we can learn in these moments. This is how we become more resilient and self-aware—and therefore more able to navigate all of life's ups and downs.

In the following chapter, we'll talk more about how emotions operate and how to work with them to become more resilient, increase optimism, and motivate positive action toward achieving your highest goals.

Truth #6: The Brain Cannot Suppress Thoughts

Quick brain exercise: Think about elephants.

I imagine you just conjured a pretty typical image of an elephant: big, wrinkly, grayish brown, big trunk, tusks. Maybe it's bathing itself in a stream. Maybe it's a baby unsure on its new legs, stumbling over itself as it rolls down a hill trying to follow its mama. Or if you're a mom of small children like me, you might imagine a more cartoon-like version, like Dumbo or the character from the Elephant and Piggie series by Mo

Willems (a go-to classic in our household). Point is: It's fairly easy to picture elephants doing elephant things.

Okay, now, new task: *Stop* thinking about elephants.

Let me guess: You're *still* thinking about elephants? You weren't thinking about elephants two minutes ago and now you cannot stop thinking about elephants. Don't worry. This is completely normal.

Research into the brain shows that when we try to stop thinking about something, we end up thinking about it even more. This is why people on a diet tend to think about food even more than people who aren't on a diet: They're actively trying *not* to think about eating, so they want to eat even more. Or why alcoholics find it so hard to resist a drink even if they're trying to kick the habit. We know how hard it is to get rid of unwanted thoughts because, chances are, we've all tried to do it at one point or another. Ever had a bad day at work and just tried not to think about it? Or attempted to move on from the loss of a relationship by putting the other person out of your head? Or struggled to quiet negative self-talk by telling yourself you shouldn't think those things? We so often think there's something wrong with us if we can't control our brains. In fact, this is just how brains are.

Research shows that not only is thought suppression impossible, but it can actually backfire. When we try to suppress an unwanted thought, we usually end up thinking about it even *more*, especially if it's highly emotional or relevant to our lives. In fact, in what is, quite possibly, one of the cruelest ironies of human psychology, people who try to control their thoughts are at an increased risk of depression. This is why it's so difficult to change unwanted behaviors—because the mere act of trying to change those behaviors prompts our brains to obsess over them even more.

Fortunately, knowing this allows us to take an alternate, more effective approach. When we try to change a habit, thought, or behavior, we tend to focus on what we don't want to be doing anymore. "I want to stop drinking." "I want to stop eating so much." "I want to stop this negative self-talk in my head." "I want to stop making the same mistakes I do in relationships." "I want to stop being nervous in front of people." Instead of trying to change a behavior or a thought by *stopping* it, we need to focus instead on replacing those thoughts and behaviors with the ones we want to practice. Instead of saying, "I want to quit smoking," say, "I want healthy lungs." Instead of "I want to stop raising my voice with my kids," try "I want to help my kids make good choices by demonstrating patience and love." Instead of trying not to think about elephants, tell yourself to think about penguins instead. This subtle mental shift, combined with the predictive and imaginative power of our brains, can reinforce a new neurological pattern that over time will replace the intrusive thoughts and unproductive behaviors.

Truth #7: The Brain Can Change

Up until fifty or so years ago, scientists believed that the brain stopped changing as soon as we reached adulthood. They assumed that after about twenty years of intense learning and growing, the brain hits stop. No going back now, and you can't teach an old dog new tricks. While it's true that less mature brains have a much higher capacity for learning (thanks to an abundance of young, malleable brain cells), research over the past few decades has shown that in fact even when we reach adulthood, our brains possess an enormous capacity for growth.

This capacity is called *neuroplasticity*, meaning the brain's ability to transform itself in response to its environment. The brain communicates using neurons, specific brain cells that transmit signals to one another and to other parts of the body. Each transmission helps establish a series of pathways, which help facilitate the future flow of information so that learning becomes easier over time. It's like a highway system: Instead of having to forge your own path every time you need to get somewhere, you design a designated route to make it relatively easy to get where you want to go.

When we learn something new—something that disrupts the usual flow of information—these pathways shift, making it easier, over time, to adapt to this new way of thinking. This happens every time we learn something, from a new word to a new mathematical formula to a new skill to a new language. The more we reinforce this learning through repetition, the more encoded it becomes in our brains. This is why things that start off challenging get easier with practice—our brains have rewired themselves to make it so.

By the time we reach adulthood, we've programmed our brains with tons of information, having established the neural pathways for most of our thoughts and behaviors, through either conscious effort or unconscious learning. At this point, it becomes more difficult to change these pathways—but not impossible. Studies show that the brain continues to learn when exposed to novel situations and stimuli that force it to adapt. For example, when stroke victims suffer severe damage to a particular part of their brain, intact parts of their brains will, with rehabilitation and training, take over the functions that were previously lost. There is also evidence that the brains of Covid-19 patients who have lost the ability to taste and smell can regain these senses through what is known as olfactory training—essentially exposing the patient to strong scents that encourage the brain to relearn how to detect them. Deaf people develop certain types of better visual perception—such as motion detection and peripheral vision—as areas of the brain associated with auditory processing take on additional responsibilities for interpreting visual cues. Meanwhile, some people who lose their vision actually develop echolocation capabilities when their brains redirect the energy that would normally be put toward sight into improving their hearing. Brain image studies have revealed stark changes in the brains of people who learn a new language, memorize complex driving directions, and regularly play challenging games that keep their minds engaged.

When we understand how our brains learn, we can actively stimulate this process through specific interventions that promote neuroplasticity. These include things like maintaining a healthy diet, exercising, getting enough sleep, playing games, adopting a meditation or mindfulness practice, and learning new things. Later in the book, we'll explore how to use these and other practices to train the brain toward greater optimism.

Exercise: How to Change Your Mind

Want to practice changing your thoughts? Try these exercises as an experiment.

Under the Influence Game

This is not what you think!

Say out loud the first thing that comes to mind when you hear the following words. Say them in order before moving on to the next one.

Ocean

Salt

Deep

When people play this game, their responses to the second two words (in this case, *salt* and *deep*) are usually influenced by the first one (*ocean*). This happens because their brains have been primed to think about words associated with the first word and our brain works in patterns. The brain connects concepts automatically through what is known as semantic priming, meaning your last thought subsequently influences your next thought. If you want to think about certain things or be in a particular mindset—especially before important activities or scenarios—try priming your brain with similar thoughts beforehand.

Mental DJ Game (or Find Your Reset Song)

Think about something that makes you feel anxious or frustrated. Immediately after, play a song that brings you joy or elevates your mood or brings you peace. Time yourself for sixty seconds. How has your mood shifted? Now try a different song and see how quickly you can intentionally shift your mood and thoughts. You can reprogram your thoughts by activating the limbic system, which helps control your emotions and behaviors and your dopaminergic pathways, which help with motivation and reward-based learning.

Direct Your Own Mental Movie

You can change the emotional impact of your memories.

Recall a distressing, mildly negative (but not traumatic) memory from your past. It can be a situation, event, or conversation you had with someone else. Play it through your mind as if it were a scene in a movie and you are a character. Now rewrite the scene and redirect it. Change the language, make yourself react differently, change the soundtrack (or add one). Maybe turn it into a comedy by adding a funny twist or unexpected ending. Notice how your reaction to and emotions about the memory are different. The brain re-encodes memories every time you recall them, so you can alter your emotional associations by reimagining memories in different ways.

CHAPTER 3

"Good Vibes Only"

What the Cult of Positivity Ignores About Human Emotions

Ignoring what we truly and authentically feel does not make us stronger or happier; it only distances us from who we truly are.

Dana was a mother of two in her mid-thirties who had come to me through UCLA's psycho-oncology program. When I met her, she had just undergone a double mastectomy, completed radiation, and begun an aggressive course of chemotherapy to treat breast cancer. Like many of the patients I worked with through this program, Dana had tried basically everything she could think of to treat her cancer, maintain her physical health, and cope with the emotional fallout of her diagnosis. While her doctors at UCLA oversaw her surgeries, treatments, and screenings, she had also experimented with several alternative methods such as hypnosis, meditation, and dietary changes.

When she showed up in my office for our first session, I was struck by how fragile she looked. Her recent surgery, radiation, and ongoing chemo treatments certainly explained some of her physical characteristics—thin frame, hairless body, waxy and pale skin—but I immediately sensed there was something else going on.

"How are you feeling today?" I asked.

"To be honest, I'm really, really scared," she told me.

"Of course," I assured her. "It's totally normal to be scared when you receive a cancer diagnosis. I don't know anyone who *wouldn't* be scared."

"It's not just that." She sighed before continuing. "When my doctors suggested chemo, I really didn't want to do it. But they insisted it was the best option. They said if I didn't get it, the cancer would likely spread. When my family heard that, they basically forced me to say yes. We were all so scared, but I just decided to try every option available. If nothing else, I did it for my kids."

"That's understandable," I told her. A lot of cancer patients become so overwhelmed by the decisions they have to make that they defer to others for guidance—doctors, current or former patients, family members, or anyone who can provide even a morsel of insight, perspective, or expertise. "It must have been difficult to see the effect this had, not only on you, but the people around you."

"That's it," she agreed. "But now I worry I made the wrong decision. I'm worried the treatment might be making the cancer worse."

"What makes you think that?" I asked.

"Well, I started working with a healer that my friend recommended. She told me that by going through with the treatment, I am basically admitting defeat. She said that I wasn't trusting my body, which is perfect on its own, and was poisoning it and making things worse."

At this, my spidey sense started tingling. Years prior, when I was in high school and experimenting with various new age practices, I had had a similar experience with a spiritual teacher a friend had introduced me to. This person had told me pretty much the same thing as Dana's teacher had told her. "Your body is perfect just as it is," she said. "You don't need to alter or fix it in any way. Your body is a hologram that you create with your mind. Your physical body is nothing more than a projection of your thoughts. If you believe it is perfect, it is."

At the time, I believed her. And while I would never discount the existence of miracles (every day incredible things happen that even science can't explain), my thinking on the connection between our brains and our bodies had become a lot more nuanced in the time between meeting this teacher and sitting in front of patients like Dana. I also knew, having worked closely with oncologists and therapists in my role at UCLA, that while treatments like chemotherapy are far from perfect, chemotherapy is the best chance most cancer patients have at beating their disease. Accepting this reality was not "admitting defeat"; it was coming to terms with a difficult yet undeniable truth.

Still, I could see how conflicted Dana was. Scared and vulnerable, she was searching for some way to control a situation over which she had very little control. I couldn't just rattle off a bunch of statistics about remission rates; I needed to meet her where she was.

"Okay, so if this teacher thinks that chemotherapy will make your cancer worse, what does she think you should do instead?" I asked.

"She thinks the reason I'm sick is because of stress. That I've been so preoccupied raising my kids and worrying about their safety and taking care of my family that I was never fully present in my body and so invited the cancer in."

I detected doubt in her voice and sensed that Dana didn't fully believe what this teacher had told her, even though she wanted to. "Do you think that's true?" I asked. "Do you think you're responsible for causing your cancer?"

Dana slumped her shoulders forward and sighed. She cast her eyes down to the floor and started fidgeting with her hands. I could hear a quiver in her voice as she replied, hesitating, "Yes . . . Well, maybe . . . I don't know." She looked up at me, and I noticed tears in her eyes. "I have always been a pretty anxious person. I was always worried about the future, rarely relaxed or fully present in the moment. Having kids didn't make that any easier. She says I need to think positive. That I need to let go of the stress in my life so that my body can heal itself."

I felt so much empathy for Dana—and an enormous responsibility to help her in any way I could. Not only was she dealing with a life-altering diagnosis and the heavy emotions that came along with this, but now she was wrestling with the idea that perhaps her own mental outlook had somehow caused her to get sick. Her entire life had been upended, and now, in the midst of all of this uncertainty, she was conflicted about what she should do. Could she really be making herself sick by trusting her doctors' advice? Were the stress, anxiety, fear, sadness, and anger she felt about her situation making things worse? And if so, how could she possibly make herself *not* feel that way? Besides that, I understood why she felt so conflicted. Even as someone who has benefited from and is forever grateful for the help of modern medicine, I fully appreciate why someone would distrust Big Pharma and America's for-profit healthcare system. I can also understand—as someone who has long turned to alternative medicine and wellness practices—why Dana would believe that natural or homeopathic remedies were inherently preferable to the literal poison that is chemotherapy.

In her quest to cope with her diagnosis, Dana had wandered into the trap of toxic positivity. Toxic positivity occurs when someone attempts to diminish or disregard negative thoughts, feelings, and experiences—be it their own or someone else's—in favor of maintaining a cheerful, upbeat, and joyful disposition. Unlike real optimism, which acknowledges that difficult experiences—and the difficult emotions that accompany them—are a natural, necessary fact of life, toxic positivity disregards and vilifies these experiences as, at best, unhelpful, and at worst, destructive. In doing so, toxic positivity sets up an unrealistic standard of mental health: Not only *can* you feel happy all the time, but you should.

Optimism Versus Positivity

Dana was far from alone in thinking that by ridding herself of anxiety, stress, and other so-called negative emotions she could somehow rid herself of her disease. In my time at UCLA, most of the patients I worked with expressed some version of the same sentiment. Some, like Dana, felt that way because of particular spiritual beliefs. Others had simply picked this notion up from pop culture or a misinterpretation of the science around stress. There's no doubt that chronic stress can wreak havoc on our immune system, but as mentioned in the previous chapter, regular stress is an essential component to our biology that helps us plan for the future and respond to threats. While too much stress is definitely bad for health, if we eliminated stress completely, we could literally not survive.

This explains why toxic positivity is so, well, toxic: It implies that it's not only possible but preferable to eliminate certain emotions while disregarding the essential role they play in our lives. Instead of teaching us how to cope with reality and manage difficult emotions to our advantage, toxic positivity teaches us to fear them—which leads only to more stress and suffering. Toxic positivity forces us to disregard an essential truth of our shared humanity: Uncomfortable emotions have a lot to teach us, even if we dislike feeling them.

When Dana was first diagnosed, she no doubt felt a swirl of disturbing and stressful feelings: fear at the prospect of dying; grief for her physical health and the life she once had; anger at the universe or God or the bad luck that had made her sick; and so on. Instead of helping her process these feelings and reckon with her new reality, a teacher she desperately wanted to trust told her that she shouldn't feel the way she felt and that her very genuine emotions were actually bad and unreliable—in fact, likely to ruin her life. Instead of feeling validated or understood, Dana now felt guilty and ashamed for not being able to think positive or will away her bad feelings—which were, of course, normal. Instead of relieving some of her burden, this teacher left Dana with an even heavier weight on her shoulders and a sense that she was somehow responsible for this whole mess she was in.

To be clear, I believe this teacher genuinely wanted to help Dana. Having worked with similar practitioners since my early teens, I know that most of them choose their line of work because they have personally benefited from the beliefs and practices they espouse and feel called to share their knowledge with others who are experiencing pain. I assume that Dana's teacher had the best intentions; that she thought she was giving Dana the tools she needed to combat her diagnosis; and that she was offering Dana a real alternative to chemotherapy and invasive surgeries. Trust me, as someone who has dabbled in pretty much every alternative therapy known to humankind, I know that what might seem out there to one person could be the very thing that brings someone else the peace and motivation they need to get through another day.

I also know that you don't need to subscribe to any particular belief system in order to succumb to toxic positivity. Most of us, through one mechanism or another, have been taught to think this way because we've never been taught how to adequately deal with our most uncomfortable emotions. No one likes to feel pain, be it physical or emotional. In fact I would argue emotions can be an even more troublesome source of pain because so many of us feel guilty for experiencing them. If you have a migraine or sprain your ankle or cut your finger while slicing onions, you don't try to convince yourself the pain isn't actually all that bad or that if you just ignore it, it will go away.* And you probably don't tell yourself that you're stupid or silly for seeking treatment. You understand that pain is your body's way of alerting you to something important. So why do we treat our emotions so differently?

Emotions are extremely complex and powerful. We've all had experiences in which we've behaved in unproductive—even destructive—ways because we let our emotions get the better of us. We do and say things we don't mean. We ruin relationships and hurt the people we love. We turn to problematic coping strategies like drugs or alcohol to temporarily alleviate our suffering, even though we know they will cause more suffering later on. We retreat from the things and people that bring us joy.

The ability to respond to our emotions while keeping our undesirable or problematic impulses in check—what is known as emotional regulation—is a cornerstone of mental well-being. Meanwhile, emotional dysregulation—a state in which you are unable to manage your emotions in a way that allows for normal and productive human functioning—is a hallmark of many severe mental illnesses including depression, anxiety disorders, addiction, social phobias, panic disorder, post-traumatic stress disorder, and others. Knowing this, of course we try to exert control over our most uncomfortable emotions; we worry that if we don't, they'll take over and potentially ruin our lives.

We also know, of course, that optimism is determined, in part, by how

---

* Though several years ago I did work with a holistic practitioner who tried to get me to transcend my discomfort whenever I felt physical pain. I gave it my best shot and it worked—for about one second.

positively or negatively we frame the events that happen to us. As Martin Seligman, a leading expert on optimism and the founder of positive psychology, observed, optimistic people interpret negative events as less personal, permanent, and pervasive than pessimistic people do. Did you lose out on that job offer because you're unintelligent (personal)? Or nothing good ever happens to you (permanent)? Or the system is rigged against people like you (pervasive)? Or did you lose it because it wasn't the right fit for your skills? Or someone was more qualified? Or maybe you didn't prepare as well as you could have for the interview and can do better next time? In the former scenarios, a relatively pessimistic person blames forces beyond their control or internalizes failures to the point of abdicating responsibility. In the latter, a more optimistic person chooses to interpret their bad luck as an isolated event, one that they can work through, even if it doesn't feel good to do so. Optimism is an active response to life.

But there's a huge difference between positive *thoughts* and positive *feelings*. When something happens (aka a stimulus), our brains generate a thought about it based on instinct, our previous experience, or some combination of the two. That thought then elicits an emotion, which directs our brain toward a particular action. In other words, it's the *thought* we have about the event—not the event itself—that determines how we feel about it.

Event → Thought → Emotion → Behavior

For example, if we see a snake in the grass, we might immediately think, *That's dangerous!* Our emotion of fear would kick in and would in turn trigger our bodies to get ready for fight or flight. But if we pause and assess the situation, we may realize, based on experience, that it's a harmless garter snake that's probably more afraid of us than we are of it. Once the thought changes, the fear goes away, and so does our impulse to flee.

This pattern also explains why two people might react in a completely different way to the same event. For example, someone who has never been around snakes may be naturally more fearful of them (regardless of how dangerous they actually are) than someone who grew up in an area where they were common. Their different experiences trigger different thoughts about the same stimulus, which then elicit different emotions.

While you can train yourself to view the causes of a particular event more optimistically, and while doing so can help shift your emotional state to be more positive, it's not always possible—or even preferable—to do so. If we try to banish fear in the presence of a real threat (perhaps that snake in the grass is venomous after all), then we could easily end up doing things that are not in our best interests. All emotions, even the icky and unpleasant ones, are essential to our survival. They arise naturally and each one—even those we don't particularly enjoy feeling—serves a biologically determined purpose. We can choose how we respond to our experiences and try to change our perspective on the challenges that arise in our lives, but when we practice toxic positivity by denying, ignoring, or suppressing our authentic emotions, we are disregarding an essential part of our humanity.

This is what Dana was trying to do by talking herself out of the stress and sadness she was feeling about her diagnosis. She didn't *want* to feel this way, but she couldn't help it. Very few people could. But rather than giving herself the space and compassion to acknowledge her feelings and attempt to understand what those feelings were trying to tell her, she tried to bury them. And when she couldn't, she was left feeling even more stressed out and conflicted, even further from the peace and stability she was seeking. Her stress about her stress was making her even more stressed.

Remember Truth #5 about the brain: It is wired for all emotions. All emotions—both the fun, positive ones and those that cause distress and discomfort—play a role in building the human experience. They are vital to our survival, and short of manipulating our inherent neurobiology, we can't just get rid of them. Without them, our lives would be far less interesting and meaningful, and we would never be able to achieve the things we want to.

At the same time, just as it's impossible to suppress a thought, it's also impossible to suppress an emotion. Research shows that people who attempt to tamp down unwanted emotions end up feeling them even more acutely than those who allow themselves to acknowledge and express them. Not only does toxic positivity promote an unrealistic standard for our emotional well-being, but the practice can also make us feel worse by suggesting that if we can't control our emotions—if we dare to feel sadness or express anger or admit that we're stressed—then we are somehow deficient, unevolved, or unintelligent. People who practice toxic positivity typically do so because they have been taught that it's an effective coping strategy—usually by their families or communities, who often practice toxic positivity (or its cousin, emotional suppression) themselves. "Put on a happy face." "Good vibes only!" "Keep calm and carry on." "Look on the bright side." "Don't worry, be happy." These and other sentiments may seem innocuous enough. Who wouldn't prefer to feel happy rather than sad or love rather than anger or relaxed rather than anxious? But when promoted as a coping strategy, these maxims inadvertently encourage a culture of toxic positivity by implying that (a) it is always possible to control your emotions; (b) certain "positive" emotions are better and more productive than others; and (c) expressing "negative" or undesirable emotions is a sign of weakness or maladjustment.

The truth is, while we should all strive to foster a positive mindset, doing so at the expense of the full range of our emotional experience will make us worse off, not better. Studies show that people who practice toxic positivity experience even more negative emotions than those who don't and dwell on challenging or stress-inducing events more than others. As a result, they are prone to burnout, emotional suffering, and a general reduction in their mental health. They also have a more difficult time forming connections with others because their inability to process their feelings may cause them to overreact to challenges, both real and perceived, which may alienate those around them. Even if they somehow manage to hold all their feelings in, their inability to express vulnerability or open up about their emotional needs can make it difficult for them to form authentic connections with others. As a result, they may struggle even more to process challenging events because they lack a social support network to help them do so.

Once we know all this, the obvious question becomes: How do we cultivate optimism without veering into toxic positivity? More specifically, how do we make space for our emotions without becoming paralyzed by them? How do we adopt a positive outlook on the future while acknowledging the emotional realities of the present? How do we become resilient in the face of adversity while letting ourselves feel all the things we're supposed to feel? How do we get comfortable in that liminal space between initially experiencing an acute, painful emotion and the moment we've moved beyond it? To begin, we must first understand the role emotions play in our lives so we can better interpret what they're trying to communicate.

The Role of Emotions

Despite the fact that emotions have been with us since the dawn of human existence, scientists have only recently begun to fully appreciate their importance in our lives. Up until a few decades ago, most scientists believed that emotions were inherently primitive and irrational—an evolutionary holdover from our less advanced ancestors but fundamentally basic, wild, and unintelligent. For centuries, traditional wisdom held that because humans were gifted with logic, reason, and the ability to deduce meaning from multiple inputs in our surroundings, intelligent people should be able to use their sound judgment to control, inhibit, and direct their basest passions. According to this way of thinking, our intellect is what makes us superior to less evolved species. The more intelligent you are, the more mastery you can exert over your primitive instincts. This belief in part helps explain the rise of the positive thinking movement and of popular self-help culture; if you work hard enough and gain enough wisdom, you, too, can conquer your irrational self.

More recently, however, scientists have come to learn that emotions are actually extremely sophisticated and complex and that true well-being requires understanding what they have to tell us. While there is still debate among scientists about exactly what emotions are and how they work (from a neuroscientific perspective, it's a more complex subject than you might think!), there is no doubt that they are essential for our survival. Emotions help direct our attention to circumstances that are relevant to our well-being. They help us learn, remember, relate to others, predict the future, and make decisions in the present. Our most basic emotions—fear, surprise, anger, joy, sadness, and disgust—develop within the first six months of life.

Positive emotions motivate and inspire us to behave in ways that benefit our health and safety. Empathy promotes social connection and sharing resources; love allows us to bond with others and take care of our children while they're at their most vulnerable; excitement encourages us to plan for the future and accomplish goals; and so forth. When we lose the capacity for these emotions, we can find it difficult to put forth the effort required to get through another day.

But difficult emotions also play a vital role. Fear—our oldest and strongest emotion—helps us spot and respond to threats. Aggression helps us defend ourselves, our loved ones, and our resources from predators. Even anxiety—one of the most common and challenging emotions we can experience and the root of some of the most common mental disorders—serves a purpose. It allows us to effectively predict and prepare for potential future scenarios, and it also helps us determine what is important to us, since we usually feel anxious when something we care deeply about is on the line. We may not like the way these emotions feel at any given moment, and when left unregulated, they can wreak havoc on our lives and the lives of those around us. But we ignore them at our own peril.

Toxic positivity requires us to ignore some of our most powerful emotions, but science shows us that the more effective strategy is the exact opposite. In order to direct our behaviors, we need to heed our emotions, take the time to listen to what they are telling us, and use that information to guide our thoughts, decisions, and behaviors with an eye toward a positive future. Emotions draw our attention to things that are relevant to our well-being so that we can respond to them efficiently and appropriately. In the process they also help us learn how to spot cues in our environment and which responses to those cues yield the results we want. This is why we can recall emotionally significant events in our life—our first kiss, the loss of a childhood pet, a traumatic injury, the thrill of winning the state championships—but struggle to remember the mundane events of last Monday.

Emotions on their own are neither good nor bad, not positive or negative. The quicker we can accept this reality and quit shaming ourselves and others for feeling the way we feel, the quicker we can shift away from the cult of toxic positivity and toward a more holistic and humane approach to our lives. Real optimism encourages us to acknowledge and appreciate each and every one of our emotions for what they are: vital factors in our health, safety, and well-being.

The Only Way Out Is Through: How to Engage with Your Emotions to Enhance Well-Being

One of the defining characteristics of optimistic people is their ability to be resilient in the face of life's challenges. They don't fall apart or let their emotions get the better of them, but they also don't simply grin and bear it—tamping down their emotions and pretending everything is fine. When confronted with difficult emotional scenarios, optimistic people gather themselves up and move forward with intention, softness, and self-compassion. This quality is known as emotional resilience.

Toxic positivity promises a shortcut to emotional resilience by pretending that we can ignore uncomfortable emotions and be just fine. But as we've already demonstrated, not only is this impossible, but it also shuts down one of the main avenues we have for learning. When we ignore a vast subset of our emotional experience, we're basically closing the door to the knowledge inherent within that experience. Learning how to tune into that knowledge without letting our impulses take over is key in treading that line between optimism and toxic positivity.

Each one of us is born with an innate capacity for resilience, though how resilient we are is determined by a variety of factors—from how we choose to interpret the events that happen to us, to how well we regulate our emotional response to those events, to what social, physical, and communal resources we have at our disposal. The environment in which we grow up and the events of our childhood can also have a profound impact on our resiliency as adults. People who grow up in nurturing, stable households surrounded by caregivers who model resilience and emotional regulation are unsurprisingly more likely to learn emotionally adaptive behaviors than those who lack these early support systems.

Resilience is also dynamic. It can vary dramatically depending on what stage of life we're in or even what scenarios we face at any given moment. We can demonstrate amazing resilience, say, in stressful work scenarios but may have a more difficult time coping with interpersonal crises or family emergencies. For example, I am actually really resilient when a major emergency happens—like when I broke my jaw while riding my bike in the Hamptons after giving a talk out there—but I will almost have a panic attack if I realize I booked the wrong flight or missed an important deadline.

Crucially, though, resilience can be learned. No matter how resilient you are (or believe yourself to be) right now, you can always increase your capacity by actively choosing to engage in behaviors and adopt thought processes that increase your ability to cope with stress and disappointment. One of the best ways to do this is by harnessing the power of your emotions in a manner that helps identify and solve problems. This is an ongoing process. Even though you can never fully predict future events—let alone how you might respond to those events—you can draw on your experiences in the past and present to prepare yourself for whatever may lie ahead. In the process, as your capacity for resilience gradually increases, you will naturally become more optimistic because you will better appreciate the opportunity and lessons the future holds.

Acknowledge Your Authentic Feelings

The first step toward building emotional resilience is to accept and acknowledge all your emotions, even the icky and uncomfortable ones. When Dana first came to me, she was at war with her emotions because she had convinced herself that they were dangerous and unhelpful. Instead of validating her experience, one of the people she had turned to for guidance had dismissed and diminished it. As a result, Dana was left feeling even more confused: upset about the situation *and* upset that she was feeling upset. Realizing this, I knew the first thing I needed to do was to simply listen and give her the space to talk about what she was truly feeling. Of course, because I saw this woman was in pain, my immediate impulse as a highly sensitive and emotional person was to try and fix her; to tell her that she needed to let go of the guilt and shame she was feeling and that it was okay to be sad or stressed during a sad and stressful time. But of course, as a therapist, I knew Dana didn't need another expert telling her how to feel; she needed an empathic ear and a safe space to process her true feelings without feeling judged.

While it can be extremely helpful to work with a professional—or even just a trusted, empathetic friend—to do this, you can, with the right tools and a fair amount of practice, learn to do so on your own. The most important thing to remember is that you're only human. Have some empathy and compassion for yourself and try not to judge or rationalize how you're feeling, no matter how uncomfortable, confusing, or irrational you (or others) may try to tell you it is. Instead, give yourself permission to feel—just *feel*—whatever comes up for you at any given moment. Research shows that simply putting a name to your emotions—a process called *labeling*—or regarding them with curiosity and no judgment (for example, "I'm feeling angry in response to this text I just received from a good friend. Huh. Why?") can help with emotional regulation, cooling your nervous system so you can make better decisions without acting on impulse.

One of the most effective ways to process emotions is through writing. Several studies show that writing, even for just a few minutes at a time, about an emotionally resonant situation can help people alleviate stress and become more solution-focused and optimistic about the future. Although the style of writing matters less than the act of writing itself, one technique is to pretend you are writing a letter about your experience to a friend. Another option is to simply talk to someone you trust about what you're feeling. This could be a friend, a family member, a therapist, or someone who has experience going through something similar. Expressing your emotions to another person not only helps you process what you're feeling but can also increase your sense of resilience by reminding you of the social support network at your disposal. Articulating your feelings releases oxytocin (the love/connection hormone), which induces positive mood and can prepare you to take productive action. Humans are social creatures! Our capacity to bond with and relate to one another is *literally* healing!

If an emotion arises suddenly or unexpectedly, it might be difficult to detach yourself from it in this way. Our brains are so efficient that emotions often arise from unconscious thoughts or triggers that we can't immediately identify. Meanwhile, our bodies respond by releasing hormones that help us prepare for a particular physical response. This is true of all emotions, but when we experience stress, our bodies typically respond with the so-called fight, flight, or freeze response, pumping cortisol (aka the stress hormone) and adrenaline throughout our nervous system, which directs our attention to potential danger and, if necessary, prepares us to attack or run away. We're basically in a state of emergency, with all our mental and physical resources directed toward protecting us from immediate danger. But if you're not *actually* in immediate danger, being in this heightened state makes it hard to respond appropriately. When this happens, we need to signal to our bodies that we are safe and attend to our physical state before shifting to our mental or emotional one. Here are two of my favorite strategies for doing so:

3×3 Breath

Emotions often manifest themselves as physical sensations. For instance, whenever I am stressed, I usually feel tension in the back of my neck. Someone else might feel a lump in their throat, a knot in their stomach, or a tightness in their chest. Next time you are seized by an uncomfortable emotion, try to locate where this is showing up in your body. Once you pinpoint that location, focus on it as you take a deep breath and inhale oxygen into that space. Tighten the muscles in that area as you breathe in for a count of 3 and hold for a count of 3. Then release them as you breathe out for a count of 3. Do this three times or until you feel the tension slip away. You have successfully calmed your body down and brought your brain back to neutral.

Adult I Spy

When you're in fight, flight, or freeze mode or an anxiety spiral, your brain is solely focused on whatever threat it perceives in your environment. You can signal to your brain that you're not actually in danger by redirecting your focus to another, neutral object in your environment. One of my favorite ways to do this is by playing an adult version of the classic kids' game I Spy. Shift your attention to your immediate surroundings. What do you see, hear, feel, or smell? Identify these things by name without judging or telling a story about them. *I see a picture frame. I feel the breeze on my skin. I hear the sound of traffic.* Do this for thirty seconds and then notice how whatever stress you were previously feeling has subsided. I've found this works a lot like a reset button, and I used it frequently when I saw patients at the hospital who were dealing with anticipatory anxiety relating to upcoming surgeries or treatments.

Keep in mind that emotions are dynamic, not static. They ebb, flow, and change depending on time and circumstances. You might be feeling content and at ease when, out of nowhere, something triggers a wave of long-forgotten fury. Or you may feel like you're drowning in a wave of recent grief but surprise yourself by laughing at a joke you hear on a podcast. It's okay to feel whatever you're feeling, even if it seems inconvenient or inappropriate.

It's also okay—and completely normal—to feel multiple, seemingly contradictory emotions at once. For instance, someone caring for an ailing parent may mourn the loss of their loved one when they pass away while simultaneously feeling a sense of relief that they no longer have to take on the role of caregiver or the emotional labor of helping someone prepare for death. When we can embrace such emotional ambiguity, we open ourselves up to greater compassion and self-awareness.

Seek Authentic Perspective

Years ago, I had a client who had recently left her husband of several decades after learning he'd been living a double life and cheating on her for most of their marriage. When she came to me, she was understandably hurt, angry, scared, and humiliated. How could the man she loved most in the world turn out to be so untrustworthy? How could he treat her so horribly? How did she miss the warning signs? Would she ever be able to trust or fall in love again?

"Well, at least he didn't die," a well-meaning friend had said in an effort to comfort her. "Think about how much worse you would feel if the love of your life had just tragically died."

Unsurprisingly, this did not make her feel better.

Every time we tell ourselves (or others) that things could be worse or that "it's really not *that* bad" or that we should be grateful for what's going right instead of dwelling on what's going wrong, we are engaging in toxic positivity. We are dismissing our genuine emotions as illogical, misplaced, or exaggerated, and rather than make us feel better, doing so usually makes us feel worse by implying we're wrong for feeling the way we do or that we're guilty of being indulgent because someone else has it worse.

That said, there is a real benefit to trying to find a ray of light in dark scenarios. Research shows that the act of identifying the positive side of a negative situation can help us build resilience, identify solutions, and improve our overall mental health. The key here is that whatever silver lining you identify must be *real* and must actually make you feel better. The woman whose husband betrayed her did not find solace in her friend's assertion that at least her husband didn't die. She did, however, take great comfort in reminding herself that, frankly, he'd been a terrible partner all along. Long before she learned about his secret life, he was aloof, often dismissive, and frequently selfish. She never felt fully supported by him, and she rarely felt secure in the relationship. She had not wanted to admit this to herself when they were together, but now that they had separated, this fact provided her a much-needed sense of relief.

Let's not get it twisted: The pain she felt at her husband's betrayal was *very* real, and it was probably going to take her a long time to recover the sense of trust and openness that he had squandered. But by tapping into her optimism, she could see that one day (just not today) she would get over this loss because, well, what had she really lost after all? Plus, now that she was single, she could open herself up to new, more fulfilling relationships and spot red flags before they turned into larger issues.

If you're emotionally overwhelmed or in the midst of a major crisis, finding the light in the darkness may feel impossible. If that's the case, it can often be enough to reframe your situation as a challenge you can handle instead of a threat to your well-being or safety. Studies show that when prompted to frame an anxiety-inducing task as something they can manage, even people who score relatively low on general measures of resilience demonstrate a marked improvement in their ability to regulate their emotions and physiological responses regarding the situation. Another strategy is to remind yourself that no matter what the future holds, you will grow from the experience. If nothing else, the challenge in front of you is an opportunity to learn something about yourself or the world around you. By choosing curiosity in the face of fear, you open yourself up to those opportunities, some of which may come from unexpected places.

Scientists call this phenomenon the broaden-and-build theory of emotions. When we're confronted with negative emotions, our perspective narrows to focus on the threat (or perceived threat) in front of us. The emotions associated with stress typically correspond to one of a few extremely specific impulses. For example, if we're angry, we feel an impulse to lash out; when we're afraid, our instinct is to flee or freeze, etc. But research shows that positive emotions broaden our repertoire of possible actions so that a much wider range of options becomes apparent. We become more critical, creative, and capable of making sound decisions.

To be clear, the act of broadening your perspective does not mean you won't continue to feel crappy about whatever you're going through. As I mentioned, emotions ebb and flow. As long as you're facing a challenge, you can expect those emotions—even the really uncomfortable ones—to arise from time to time. Broadening your perspective by seeking positive emotions simply primes you to be better able to cope with those challenges in a healthy, productive way.

As a challenge, next time you're feeling anxious or low, try to find at least one thing to smile about every day. This doesn't need to be something epic or life-changing or ecstasy-inducing. It can be something as simple as getting lost in a good book or TV show. It can be calling up a friend to see how they've been. It can be the taste of your favorite sweet treat or a nice cup of tea—anything that shifts your attention to the good things in life. Pay attention to how these moments make you feel. Better yet, write it down so you can remember it for the next time you need a pick-me-up. I encourage all my clients (and pretty much everyone I know) to make a joy list. Just as you might add a song you like to a playlist, think of things that bring you joy and add them to an ongoing joy list. Whenever something new makes you smile, add that, too. I find that simply having a list of things that spark joy can help me get through even the toughest days. It's hard to come up with a joyful act when you're experiencing stress or fear or anger, so I keep my joy list on my phone's notes app to make it easier to access whenever I need.

Draw Strength from Your Past

If you've made it this far in life, you have most certainly overcome some shit. It might not be the stuff of bestselling memoirs or Oscar-winning dramas, but you have definitely had to face some obstacles in order to get to where you are right now. You have confronted your fears, reckoned with disappointment, failed, lost something dear to you, and pushed through anxiety, stress, and setbacks to accomplish something worthwhile and important. Whether you appreciate it or not, all these events have helped create your resiliency story.

When you're going through a difficult time, it can be useful to revisit your resiliency story to uncover the lessons you can take away from it. Think back on a time where you went through something similar. If your current situation feels new to you, then consider a time when you *felt* something similar. How did you respond in that scenario? What effect did your response have? Did your actions in that moment make you feel better or worse? Did they move you toward your goal or improve your sense of well-being? Or did they set you back? Even if you're not particularly proud of the way your past self behaved, you can draw wisdom from the memory by reflecting on what you might have done differently. For example, if you've ever gone through a devastating breakup, you probably felt in that moment that your life was over, that you would never get over it, that you would never love again. But consider where you are today. Have you moved on? Have you recovered from the despair you felt? Have you perhaps found love again? Even if you've never fully gotten over it, you survived, didn't you? And if you ever go through something similar, you know you will survive again. That doesn't mean the next time won't be painful or that you won't grieve the loss of your partner; it's just a reminder that this, too, shall pass and you will be okay because you have been okay before.

When Dio was going through treatment, my husband and I drew resilience from an earlier tragedy we'd experienced together. Before Jag was born, I got pregnant with a baby girl. Naturally, Alex and I were over-the-moon excited, but at the beginning of my second trimester, we found out the fetus was not viable. Anyone who has experienced a loss like this knows how absolutely devastating it is. At the time, it was the worst thing I'd ever experienced. But we got through it, and just a few months later, I got pregnant with Jag, which would not have been possible if the first pregnancy had made it to term. After going through that horrible experience together, Alex and I knew that we could do hard things. And as terrifying as it was to watch Dio go through what he did, I drew some comfort knowing that I had overcome something horrible once and I would again. I felt like I was in hell, but I knew it was a temporary hell. I would get through this—even if it was messy (which it was), even if it hurt (which it did), even if it changed me forever (which it did)—because I had to.

Limit Your Worry Time

I am, by nature, an extremely anxious person. As I'm writing this, I'm sitting here worried about *Star Wars*. A few weeks ago, my husband, Alex, and seven-year-old son, Jag, came down with a nasty cold. While they were quarantining together in a separate room by themselves to prevent the rest of the family from getting sick, they watched all three of the original *Star Wars* movies. Jag is—as you might expect—completely obsessed. Meanwhile, my first thought was *Should I be worried?* I don't know much about *Star Wars*, but I know there are light sabers and fight scenes and space monsters. Is he too young? I trust Alex's judgment, and as much as I want Jag to enjoy things, I know his brain is still developing and that the media he consumes can have a profound impact on him later in life. Do I let him watch the movies again? Do I let him watch the other films in the franchise? Do I now have to screen all those films and all the spin-off series to make sure they're okay?!*

Oh and, just recently, I saw a video on social media about a yacht that sank off the coast of Sicily, killing seven people on board for reasons authorities don't yet fully understand. I was actually in Italy when this happened, and I was on *several* boats while I was there (none of which were yachts, for the record, but *still!*). Could I have died while cruising the Mediterranean? If I ever go back to Italy, do I need to worry about getting on a boat or which body of water I go into? Does this have something to do with climate change? Was it just a freak accident? Should I just avoid all boats from now on?

Neither of these things are all that important to my life right now. The boat thing has absolutely nothing to do with my life right now, and anxiety aside, I do in fact trust my husband to not expose our kid to anything that would scar him for life. But I'm still worried. And as much as I tell myself to chill out, I'm probably still going to worry. And even when I stop worrying about the age appropriateness of *Star Wars* and private

---

* Update: I did in fact discuss my worries with my husband and we agreed that the original franchise is perfectly fine for a kid Jag's age.

yachts I've never been on sinking for dubious reasons, I'm going to find something else to worry about.

Because the brain is future oriented, I—and all human beings—are programmed to worry. Maybe you're not as worry-prone as I am, but you still worry. And chances are, you worry about stuff that isn't all that relevant or useful to you. While too much worrying can lead to burnout, we can't ever fully stop ourselves from worrying. So how do we manage all our worries without letting them overwhelm us?

The key is to set boundaries about what you worry about and when. I advocate a practice I call worry time, which is exactly what it sounds like: You set aside certain times of day to worry about certain things, and then you try not to worry again for the rest of the day. Here's how it works.

Worry Time

Step 1. Designate Your Time to Worry

Pick a time of day during which you have sufficient energy and won't be easily distracted. For me, I pencil in worry time in the mornings, right after I drop my kids of at school but before I get caught up with all my meetings and appointments for the day. Set aside no more than fifteen minutes. When starting out, you may need a few worry periods per day. Try one in the morning, one around lunchtime, and one toward the end of the day but well before you go to sleep. Don't let the total time exceed thirty minutes. Designate a place to worry that is not usually associated with rest or comfort. For example, an office or a coffee shop can work well, but your bed or family room is not ideal.

Step 2. Add Worries to a List

As you go throughout your day, pay attention to all the worries that come up and decide which ones can be saved for worry time. Obviously, some things require your immediate attention—especially in times of crisis—but not everything does. If something can wait, jot it down on your worry list and tell yourself you will think about it later. Good candidates for worry time include things that aren't of immediate importance or relevance to you but that you find yourself dwelling on throughout the day—like a troubling story about a humanitarian crisis or a new law that is going into effect. You can also include things that are important but not immediate (like calling your insurance company about a bill you think is incorrect or looking for a new job). I also recommend using this time for scrolling social media, which we know can induce anxiety, and reading or listening to the news.

Step 3. Prioritize

When worry time starts, go through each item on your list of worries and ask yourself, "Can I do anything to control or change this thing I'm worried about?" If the answer is no, ask yourself if you can let the worry go. If the answer is yes, make a plan to deal with it, either during your current worry time or at a specific point in the future.

This exercise may seem kind of silly at first, but studies show that setting boundaries around your time in this way can help people get comfortable with uncertainty and render them more capable of coming up with productive solutions for things under their control. I personally have found that the practice helps me feel less anxious over time; I can let myself worry in structured, productive ways instead of letting every worry that pops into my head sap me of my energy and attention.

The Weight of the World: Channel Anxiety into Activism

One of the questions people often ask me is "How can I possibly be optimistic when there are so many terrible things going on in the world?"

Life is stressful enough when we have only ourselves and the people around us to worry about. But in a world where we're constantly exposed to bad news and terrifying images from all over the globe, it is easy to despair about the future. Often it feels like we're carrying the weight of the world on our shoulders. How can we remain optimistic while reckoning with our current reality of increasingly destructive natural disasters caused by climate change? Or the human cost of war? Or rampant poverty in the same communities as unimaginable wealth? Or global pandemics? How can we maintain our own mental health when we know how many others are suffering? How can we work toward solutions when the problems seem so intractable and enormous?

When people ask me these questions, the first thing I do is remind them that it's in the darkest times when optimism becomes the most critical. Without a belief that things can and will get better, we lose the motivation to do the work required to actually make things better. Pessimism and apathy are not inherently more rational or realistic than optimism and faith; they're often just failures of imagination. There has never been an activist in history who did not believe that a brighter future was possible. When the actress and activist Sophia Bush was a guest on my podcast, I asked her to define what optimism means for her. Her answer sums up the necessity of optimism perfectly: "When I think about optimism, I think about it being the choice to seek hope, the willingness to identify whatever light there is despite how much darkness. The commitment to the justice of joy because joy is a right. Pursuing it, holding it, finding it, making space for it, that is a big part of justice work. When you can find or create justice and joy, that to me feels like a world worth being optimistic about."

Thankfully, you can apply many of the same tactics used to forge emotional resilience toward dealing with these feelings in productive ways. Here's how:

Stay Engaged

I know many people who, in an effort to protect their mental health, don't watch the news. "It's all bad, anyway," they say. "It's just too much." Turning off and tuning out may work as a short-term coping strategy. It can also be beneficial if you're dealing with a personal situation that requires your full attention, or even if you're just too depleted to take on additional emotional burdens at a given moment. But in the long term, disassociating from the world around you doesn't promote optimism; it promotes ignorance—and ignorance is *not* bliss. If you want to effect change, you have to stay engaged. You need to understand what's going on and why and question whether the systems, structures, and rules that govern our society are actually working. If you find yourself getting upset at something you see on the news or social media, take it as a signal that you care about it. Instead of looking away or stressing out, see if you can channel that energy toward learning more about the situation. It's amazing how much more empowered you feel when you take the time to educate yourself.

That said, of course, it's important to understand your limits and set boundaries so you don't become overwhelmed. Empathy is a valuable but finite resource, and as with any finite resource, you need to find ways to conserve it. Be strategic about how and when you engage with specific content. For example, I know a lot of people who avoid looking at social media or listening to the news in the evening hours before they go to bed. At the end of the day, we're usually mentally, physically, and emotionally depleted, and we're not going to be able to change the world while trying to get a good night's sleep. As an alternative, try scheduling time to think about these issues during your prescheduled worry time sessions. You can use this time to dive into the subject further or, if you determine it's important enough to you that you want to prioritize it in other parts of your life, to brainstorm things you can do to engage proactively.

Seek Inspiration

When asked about how to talk to children about the hard realities of life, Mister Rogers famously said, "Look for the helpers. You will always find people who are helping." There's a reason this quote still resonates with so many people: Not only is it inspiring in such a beautifully simple way, but it's true. While headlines and news feeds are usually dominated by serious, often devastating stories about wars, scandals, natural disasters, injustice, and all manner of tragedies that can make even the most optimistic person feel like crawling under the covers for days at a time, human beings are, as a group, extremely resilient, compassionate, and cooperative. No matter how dire a situation is, there is always someone who is trying to make a positive difference.

The next time you start to feel pessimistic about the state of the world, take some advice from Mister Rogers and look for the helpers. Studies show that simply observing an act of kindness can help boost our mood by releasing endorphins and neurotransmitters like serotonin, dopamine, and oxytocin, all of which trigger positive feelings and changes in the body. Better yet, do something kind for a stranger today. Research shows that the act of doing so not only boosts your sense of optimism but is also contagious, boosting the recipient's mood and attitude as well. The surge of positive feeling you receive from observing or performing a positive action can help broaden and build your perspective so that you can more easily focus on solving problems instead of stressing about them.

Engage in Purposeful, Positive Action

No matter how passionate you are about and engaged you are with a societal or existential issue, you're not going to solve the problem by yourself or all in one day. Knowing this, you might find it easy to get discouraged or feel like it's not worth taking action at all. What good could it possibly do anyway?

But every successful social movement has started small, and even seemingly insignificant actions can help lay the foundation for something bigger. Sharing a post on social media may help raise awareness of the issue or identify like-minded people within your social circle. Attending a protest or educational workshop can motivate and educate and make you feel like part of a larger community. Calling or writing elected officials can put pressure on the people with the power to effect immediate and direct change while helping instill a sense of civic engagement.

If you're not sure where to start, one strategy is to consider how to best utilize your personal skills, knowledge, talents, interests, and resources. Maybe you're not the type of person who is going to organize a march on the mayor's office—or maybe you are, but you lack the expertise and connections to do so. So consider what you are realistically willing and able to do. Can you donate money or other resources to a cause you care about? Provide professional aid like legal advice, copywriting skills, counseling, graphic design, or fundraising? Can you offer your home or office for a meeting? Or provide rides to an event for those who lack reliable transportation? For example, as a way to get more involved with the causes she cares about, the graphic designer and digital creator Manassaline Coleman harnessed her talent and passion for graphic design to create and post a guide to virtual protesting that quickly went viral, amassing more than two million views in one week. "I'm not someone that's really into politics. Design—that's really all I do," she told me when I asked her what she had learned from the experience. "This really showed me that . . . you don't necessarily have to go outside of what you do normally to make a change . . . If you have an idea, if you feel like whatever you can do is going to help, do that thing. Even if you feel like it's not that big of a deal, we need everyone. Everyone needs to play their role."

Spreading joy can also be a form of activism, especially when you do it in a way that feels authentic to you. As founder and creative director of Bob's Dance Shop, Vince Coconato, aka Coco, uses his passion and talent for bringing people together through dance to organize huge flash dance mobs and other performances, all with the goal of spreading joy, inspiring others, and promoting self-expression, self-acceptance, radical love, and creativity. "My passion and my skill set is building community and bringing people together," he told me in an interview for my podcast. "Bob's Dance Shop is a paradise for self-expression. . . . It's really, truly about bringing joy into a space and tapping into our inner child [because] we're all children that grow older, but we all just want to play. And that playful environment is really where we find the most authentic joy."

Embrace Discomfort

One of the biggest reasons people hesitate to get involved in social causes is out of fear. They don't feel qualified or skilled enough to get involved, or they're afraid of the consequences if they do. What if people judge them? What if they offend someone? Worse yet, what if they face material consequences like losing their job or their friend group? What if people threaten or hurt them? Even if they don't fear serious repercussions like these, they may still fear that their actions won't matter—that they'll be wasting their time and energy for no reason.

Taking even a small, purposeful action helps us overcome this fear. Either we learn that our fears were unfounded or exaggerated or we are forced to face our fears head-on. If our risk pays off—even if only by making us feel like we did something worthwhile—our brain's reward center lights up, releasing dopamine into our nervous system and motivating us to seek that feeling again. All of this creates a feedback loop that helps us learn how to spot risks and determine which are worth taking and creates neural pathways that give us the confidence to take on additional risks. As we become more confident and resilient, we can choose to take even bigger risks that promote bigger change, and we become more adept at managing the emotions surrounding those risks.

Next time you feel the weight of the world on your shoulders and feel like you're on the verge of succumbing to despair, ask yourself: "What would I do if I knew it would make a difference? What would I do if I knew things were going to turn out okay?" A small shift toward optimism can provide the motivation you need to take action. And who knows what might spring from that?

CHAPTER 4

"Therapy Fixes Everything!"
Taking Mental Health Beyond the Couch

Your brain is complex, adaptive, and extraordinary, but don't forget you are the one steering it.

When I was in grad school, one of my first therapy jobs was as an exposure therapy consultant for patients diagnosed with obsessive-compulsive disorder. Before I took this position, my primary knowledge of OCD came from movies and TV shows like *As Good As It Gets* or *The Aviator*. In the former, Jack Nicholson plays a cranky older man with OCD whose life is consistently interrupted, but never severely disrupted, by a series of odd but ultimately harmless tics, like avoiding cracks in the sidewalk or washing his hands with multiple bars of soap at a time. In *The Aviator*, Leonardo DiCaprio portrays Howard Hughes, a real-life sufferer of OCD whose disorder is presented as an unfortunate price to pay for outsize genius and ambition, not unlike a tortured poet or an eccentric artist with addiction issues.

The reality, of course, is much different than Hollywood makes it seem. OCD is an anxiety disorder in which one becomes hooked by an obsessive thought such as "I'm going to get sick" or "Did I turn the oven off?" and then must complete a particular compulsion, such as washing their hands a certain number of times or performing a specific gesture, until they can move on. Patients with severe OCD often struggle to hold down a job, interact with others, or complete everyday tasks because their obsessions and compulsions are simply too pervasive and disruptive.

This was the case with Monica, one of my first patients at the OCD clinic. Monica was obsessed with the idea that she could contract a deadly contagious disease any time she left her house. Even though she was extremely intelligent and well educated, she was so paralyzed by this fear that she rarely went anywhere, even to visit her family, with whom she had once been extremely close. She couldn't commit to a job. She had no social or dating life. Her entire world revolved around her disability. And make no mistake, even though it wasn't physical or visible, it *was* a disability.

By the time she came to work with me, Monica had been dealing with this condition for nearly a decade and had tried basically every form of therapy imaginable to treat it. Her symptoms had started showing up when she was a teenager, and she had worked with professionals to help her understand the root of her obsessions and attempt to deconstruct the irrational narrative that she was in constant, imminent danger of getting sick. And yet, despite all her efforts, she was still at the mercy of her illness. Even though she knew rationally that her fears were unfounded, and even though she desperately wanted to free herself of her compulsions, her obsessions continued to trap her in a cycle of thoughts, emotions, and behaviors that was making her daily life unbearable.

Through our program, Monica received a combination of talk therapy and exposure therapy. Exposure therapy is an extremely common method of treating OCD and involves exposing patients to the things that trigger their obsessive thinking and then helping them resist the urge to complete their compulsion. The therapist exposes the patient to the same triggers over and over and for longer periods of time and then works with them to deal with the anxiety that arises without actually completing the compulsion. Over time, as the patient gathers more and more evidence that performing the compulsion doesn't affect the outcome (that is to say, they don't get sick after touching a doorknob even though they didn't complete their compulsion of washing their hands repeatedly afterward), their obsessions start to lose power over their thoughts and behaviors and they stop feeling the need to perform compulsions at all. My job was to escort Monica to places she usually avoided—like public restrooms or crowded shopping areas—and have her touch surfaces that might harbor germs. It was stressful—often disgusting—work, and even though I knew the science behind the method, I couldn't help but feel a little sadistic as I forced this young woman to do things—including, on more than one occasion, touching a public toilet seat—that clearly upset her.*

One afternoon, I took Monica to a crowded coffee shop in Hollywood, an area I knew would be overrun with tourists and locals in the middle of the day. After we spent some time inside the café, during which Monica was exposed to various triggers, we walked outside and immediately heard the familiar wail of police sirens coming up the street. Within seconds, about ten police cars stopped right in front of where Monica and I had been standing, and an officer jumped out of his car and began shouting through a bullhorn. "Everyone get down on the ground and remain calm! There are reports of an erratic individual with a weapon in the area. We need to secure this location."

As I lowered myself to the pavement, I looked over at Monica, expecting her to be in a full-blown panic. Not only was there potentially someone dangerous on the loose—certainly a good enough reason for anyone to freak out—but we were lying face down on one of the most traversed sidewalks in Los Angeles. She seemed dazed but otherwise okay. After several agonizing minutes, the cops gave us the all clear. As I stood up and dusted myself off, Monica looked at me with a flash of panic in her eyes. "Did you see blood back there?" she asked.

I looked around to see if I had missed something. "Blood? No. I didn't see any blood."

"Not here. Back there," she corrected. "When we were leaving the coffee shop, I thought I saw something red on the doorframe. Did you see it? I think you might have touched it. Do you remember touching it?"

I was stunned. We had just experienced a very real potentially life-and-death situation, and Monica did not seem to have even registered it

---

* I have a strict rule that I will never ask a client or patient to do something that I wouldn't do myself. These days I would never touch a public toilet seat or ask a patient to do so, but I was a lot less anxious about germs and health when I worked with Monica.

had happened. She was so hooked by her own obsessive thoughts that she literally could not see past them to her own reality. For a young psychology student like me, it was a profound lesson in just how powerful—and debilitating—our thoughts can be.

The Power of Thought

Even if you have never experienced a mental health condition as crippling as Monica's, chances are you can still appreciate the power of obsessive negative thinking. If you've ever struggled to break a habit (or start a new one), abandon a persistent but unhelpful belief, shift an interpersonal dynamic between yourself and another person, or generally try to change in any way, you know that the process is incredibly difficult.

In my years working with clients, I encountered plenty of people with severe mental disorders or illnesses like Monica—people who came to me with a particular diagnosed condition with specific symptoms and behavioral tendencies. But I also encountered plenty of others who didn't meet the criteria for an official diagnosis. These were people with successful careers, stable families and relationships, active social lives, and generally a lot of ambition, talent, and drive. And yet they also struggled with self-defeating thoughts and behaviors that got in the way of their leading their optimal lives. The power of thought unites us—and doesn't discriminate.

As I worked with these people, I began to notice several patterns. First, many of them had already tried therapy and came to me with a lot of insight into why they were the way they were and did the things they did. They understood why they might have developed certain behavioral or coping patterns or certain core beliefs and emotional tendencies, but they struggled to change them. They had done a ton of work to develop a deep self-awareness and a desire to change and had reached the stage of "Now what?" How could they channel this knowledge into becoming the person they most wanted to be?

I also noticed how much of the work they had done was focused on their past, even though their concerns were lodged primarily in the future. They spent much of their time thinking back on earlier experiences, trying to determine how they could have responded differently. But when a similar situation presented itself, they defaulted to old patterns and behaviors. I began to wonder what might happen if they redirected that energy away from what had already happened toward preparing for what might happen next. How could they take advantage of their brain's natural inclination to prepare for the future by looking forward instead of back?

Finally, when it came to the question of "Now what?" most of them focused solely on what they wanted to change about their lives. They wanted to manage anxiety, get healthier, be more productive, become more present and less anxious—all sorts of things. They'd spent a ton of time and energy thinking about what they lacked or what wasn't perfect or where they fell short, and yet they spent very little time thinking about the things that were going *well* for them. They had a vision for who they wanted to be but didn't fully appreciate who they were *right at this moment*. Their desires and concerns were of course valid, and in some cases they were actively interfering with their ability to live a full life. But it struck me as unfortunate and incredibly demotivating that they could not celebrate and value their lives in the present.

I was called to psychology because I knew firsthand what it was like to struggle with these same issues. Although I'm fortunate to never have experienced a debilitating mental illness, I know what it's like to get stuck in old patterns and habits. I know what it's like to feel like something is missing from my life or that I could be doing more to make it better. And I'm certainly not immune to the pressures of our modern life: the constant stress, the ever-present comparisons, and the never-ending demands on our attention. I know what it's like to search and search for answers and not be able to find them, and I certainly know what it's like to worry. I empathized deeply with every single one of my patients and clients.

But, after several years of doing this work, I also knew that I *did* have answers that I didn't have before and that I could use my knowledge and experience to help others in a way that resonated with me—and hopefully them. I realized that if I wanted to help these people change, I needed to take a step back and reframe the work we were doing together. First, I needed to make them believe—*truly believe*—that they were worth the effort required to change. When we focus on our shortcomings, we can begin to believe that change is impossible—or that even if it is possible, we don't have what it takes to achieve it. By contrast, when we pay attention to the areas of our personalities and lives in which we can take pride, we start to refocus our energy toward productive change.

Change may arguably be the most difficult state a human can be in, yet it is entirely inescapable. Change is difficult for every single one of us, but it's possible if you can focus on what your life might look like in the future—after the change is complete. In order to put forth the effort required for change, you need to know—*really know*—just how much more favorable your life can be if you commit to it. Remember that one of the key differences between optimists and pessimists is that while pessimists overidentify with self-limiting beliefs and allow past mistakes to inform their judgments about their futures, optimists stay open to the potential that things can be different. Where pessimists see their wins as flukes and failures as immutable truths about their character, optimists take ownership of their successes and draw on innate self-esteem to fuel efforts toward achieving their goals.

Today I call my approach to client interventions *self-worth work*. The process draws on principles of various traditional therapy modalities with the goal of giving people the tools necessary to unhook from their self-defeating thoughts so they can—systematically and consistently—shift their behaviors toward ones they deem more desirable. Ultimately, my goal with any client is to help them achieve self-mastery—the ability to regulate their thoughts, emotions, and behaviors in ways that align with their goals. I don't want them to leave my office feeling temporarily unburdened by their problems but then get stuck the next time they find themselves in a situation that triggers their old thought patterns and habits. I want them to be not only *aware* but also *empowered*. I want to help them, but I never want them to depend on me for help. Of course, this process is easier said than done. It requires a lot of work alongside an understanding of how the brain creates thoughts, how those thoughts direct our emotions and behaviors, and what is *really* required to change.

To be clear, I am still a massive fan of traditional therapy. Many of my clients have benefited from working with a professional to identify and challenge unhelpful patterns, and my process is rooted directly in several therapeutic modalities, especially cognitive behavioral therapy (CBT), one of the most well-known and effective interventions for people struggling to shift unproductive behaviors. I don't consider my work a substitute for this type of work, especially for those (like Monica) who have received a clinical diagnosis and require specialized or intensive treatment. Instead, I consider self-worth work to be a future-directed, neuroscience-backed, goal-oriented complement to traditional therapy that is specifically focused on the question of "Now what?"

Later in this chapter, I will explore the root of my methodology and provide tips and exercises for individuals to begin engaging in their own self-worth work. But first let's take a moment to explain the role our upbringing and belief systems play in creating our unwanted thoughts in the first place.

What Makes a Thought?

Why is it so hard to change a thought? Why do we continue to think and do things we don't want to do? Why is it so difficult to unlearn something even if you know it's not true?

For starters, our thoughts are rarely neutral; they include judgments and explanations for what is happening in your environment and why. Taken together, these thoughts represent your belief system: a set of rules, assumptions, and cause-and-effect statements you have learned over the course of your life that help you explain why the world works the way it does and what your role is within it. Starting from birth, we form beliefs as a way to help us make sense of the world around us. As we interact with our environment, witness events, and observe the behavior of others, our brains begin to spot patterns and assign cause and effect to various stimuli and outcomes so we can process information more quickly in the future. We touch a hot stove and learn to avoid it going forward—or at least make sure it's off. We watch our caregivers embrace another person and come to believe that person is safe. Our teachers scold us for talking during class, and we learn to keep quiet (or at least be more discreet when we want to gossip with a friend). Our brain creates these beliefs because they help us process lots of information quickly, which in turn allows us to conserve energy for other things, make decisions efficiently, and avoid danger. They also help us pick up cultural cues and traditions and adopt social norms.

Over time, we start to receive and process increasingly complex information about ourselves, all of which helps us to form beliefs about our self-image and role in society. We receive feedback on our strengths and weaknesses and which of our personality traits are desirable and which are not. We might be praised for being a good student or constantly reprimanded for being disruptive, so we form beliefs about what this means for our standing in the social order.

The process of belief formation is extremely efficient and necessary for our survival. Without it, we would have to constantly analyze and interpret information from our surroundings as if we'd never encountered it before. But that efficiency sometimes comes at the expense of accuracy. When our brain processes information quickly, it often leaps to conclusions based on incomplete or even incorrect information. As a result, we end up forming beliefs that may not be rooted in reality and may in fact be detrimental to our overall well-being. For example, you may assume someone is trustworthy because they appear or dress a certain way, but your brain is actually just taking a shortcut to that conclusion. Most rational people know that you can't judge a person based on the way they look or the clothes they wear, and yet we judge people this way all the time.

What's more, research shows that, starting from the time we're infants, humans are much more likely to pay attention to and remember information we perceive as negative, threatening, or unpleasant than we are information we perceive as positive or affirming or that sparks feelings of contentment and joy. This is known as the negativity bias, and it explains why we so often get caught up in beliefs and emotions that don't ultimately benefit our lives and mental health. It explains why we tend to dwell on unpleasant experiences or focus on undesirable traits in ourselves and others. It explains why we ignore ten glowing performance reviews but agonize over a single critical one. It explains why we take criticism personally but dismiss compliments as undeserved. It explains why we notice the person sulking in the corner of the party we're throwing but barely pay attention to the dozen or so others clearly having a great time. We are wired to focus on potential threats—real or perceived—while neutral or positive information demands relatively little of our attention.

"[Our brain is like] Velcro for bad experiences, but Teflon for good ones," psychologist and meditation coach Rick Hanson told me when I interviewed him for my podcast, *Looking Up*. "Our ancestors needed both to get carrots and avoid sticks," he explained, describing the evolutionary necessity of finding food while avoiding mortal danger. "If you fail to get a carrot today, you'll have a chance to get one tomorrow; but if you fail to avoid that stick today . . . no more carrots forever." In other words, our brain is primed to spot and respond to perceived threats more readily than it is to focus on neutral or positive inputs, because in general avoiding threats is more important for our survival.

This also explains why we so often get hung up on negative thoughts about ourselves and our experiences. We focus on what's wrong with our lives rather than what's right because we unconsciously believe that fixing a problem is a good use of our time, energy, and attention, even if that thing prevents us from savoring the good things we already have. The negativity bias is also why we tend to believe negative feedback more than favorable feedback, compare ourselves unfavorably to others, and judge ourselves (and others) harshly for mistakes.

This focus on the negative has a direct impact on our mental and emotional well-being. In the last chapter, we examined the powerful role emotions play in our lives. But emotions do not exist without thoughts. Even our most basic and seemingly inescapable emotions require some sort of thought in order to arise. Seeing a tiger crouched in the bushes waiting to make you its lunch does not by itself induce the emotion of fear. What makes you afraid is the thought that this tiger is a dangerous predator poised to attack and potentially kill you. The thought signals to your body that you should be afraid, which then triggers the fight, flight, or freeze response as you prepare to respond to the threat in the way you determine is most likely to help you survive.

Throughout our lives, every single one of us acquires a different set of thoughts and beliefs that then influences our emotions. This is why two people can have vastly different reactions to a similar situation: Their different belief systems lead them to interpret the scenario in a different way. For example, if you believe that you are not very capable or that you constantly have to prove your worth through your efforts, you may interpret constructive criticism from a boss to mean that you are terrible at your job and possibly at risk of getting fired. Meanwhile, someone else may view the same criticism as an isolated incident and an invitation to do better next time because they believe they are skilled and hardworking and that they add value to their work and team.

In each case, different beliefs give rise to thoughts that trigger different emotions within the scenario. The first, criticism-sensitive individual may feel ashamed, upset, angry, afraid, anxious—some generally awful combination of uncomfortable and stressful emotions. As a result, they may not be able to focus on their work, may not be as present with their team or others around them, or may possibly resort to coping mechanisms like withdrawing, spiraling, or self-medicating. By contrast, the latter person may walk away feeling neutral, if not pleased, by the interaction.

The relationship between our thoughts, emotions, and behaviors is the foundation of cognitive behavioral therapy, a popular therapeutic intervention developed in the 1960s that works to shift individuals' behaviors by targeting and changing the thought patterns that trigger them. A CBT-oriented therapist working with someone who is sensitive to criticism, like the person in the above scenario, would work with that person to systematically challenge those beliefs so that, over time, the patient learns to think in a different way. The more they challenge their existing unhelpful beliefs, and the more evidence they gather in favor of a more optimistic way of thinking, the easier it becomes to distance themselves from their old beliefs and choose a different path. So the next time they're faced with criticism and recognize the old familiar bubble of anxiety forming in the pit of their stomach, they can recognize it for what it is—the result of an old thought pattern—and choose to look at the situation differently. If they do this enough and they like the results, they'll eventually stop defaulting to the unhelpful belief at all, effectively replacing the old belief system with a new one.

Of course, as we know, shifting these beliefs is incredibly difficult because the brain likes to believe what it already believes. Many of our most intractable beliefs were formed early in childhood and reinforced by years of learning. By the time we are self-aware enough to recognize that these beliefs may not be working for us, the neural pathways our brains have developed to help transmit and process information have become like a well-worn path through a dense forest. We formed that path because it was initially the most readily available based on the tools we had at our disposal. Now that we recognize that the path doesn't take us where we want to go, we need to form a new one. But it's going to take a different set of tools—not to mention a whole lot of effort—to do so without veering back to the original path.

How to Change Your Thoughts

Okay, so now we know why it's so difficult to change our thoughts and behaviors, even if we desperately want to and know they're not based in reality. Fortunately, in this case, difficult does not mean impossible. It *is* possible to change your thoughts, beliefs, and behaviors—as long as you take into account how the brain works. In order to create real, sustainable, permanent change, we need to actively rework the neural pathways our brain uses to process information so that it automatically selects the pathway we want instead of the former default. This is how the exposure therapy (which is a version of cognitive behavioral therapy) I used with Monica works. By consciously and systematically exposing Monica to things that normally cause her brain to light up with the obsessive thought of "I'm going to get sick," we forced her brain to notice how she did not in fact get sick. Trying to convince her brain of this without actual proof was never going to work; her brain needed to actively engage in the dreaded scenario in order to neutralize the perceived threat. The more we did this, the more solid the new neural connection became, so that over time her brain chose the more neutral, realistic reaction of "I am safe" to counter her obsession that she would get sick.

While this or a similar type of therapy might be warranted in cases of severe mental distress or diagnosed conditions, there are ways you can train your brain to be more optimistic and unhook from unproductive thinking without the aid of a professional. We do this by employing techniques that complement our natural brain chemistry and human tendencies.

Recognize Cognitive Distortions

The negativity bias, discussed above, is an example of one of the many types of cognitive distortions our brains often employ in an attempt to filter and process information. In its ever-present quest for efficiency, our brain resorts to these distortions in a way that generates unhelpful—and usually untrue, or at least exaggerated—thoughts that keep us stuck in cycles of negative thinking and self-talk. Knowing this, one of the first steps toward unhooking from these thoughts is to take a moment to stop and recognize when a cognitive distortion may be at play.

Below is a list of common cognitive distortions. Using the example mentioned above of someone getting a lackluster performance review, let's see how they manifest themselves, and notice how many of them overlap with the 3 Ps of optimism versus pessimism: pervasiveness, permanence, and personalization.

Black-and-white thinking. Thinking in absolute, all-or-nothing terms that lack nuance or shades of gray: "I must not be a good employee."

Jumping to conclusions. This one is pretty self-explanatory and happens when we use limited information to make assumptions about a situation: "My boss hates me."

Fortune-telling. Another form of jumping to conclusions, this happens when we use limited information to predict the future, often negatively: "I'm going to get fired."

Personalization. Blaming yourself for unfortunate events: "I am a drag on my team and this company."

Should-ing. This happens when we make statements about what we *should, ought to,* or *must* do: "I should work harder and put in more hours."

Mental filtering. Focusing on a single piece of negative information to the exclusion of all positive evidence that may be to the contrary: "One person gave me some critical feedback on my presentation, which means I did a bad job—even though multiple people praised my efforts."

Magnifying the negative and minimizing the positive. The flip side of mental filtering, this is when we acknowledge positive experiences or information but minimize their importance: "My previous good performance reviews were flukes."

Overgeneralization. Making sweeping statements about circumstances based on isolated events: "I'm not cut out for this role. I'll never succeed."

Comparison. Comparing ourselves, usually unfavorably, to others based on limited perspective about their circumstances: "My colleagues are more confident and intelligent than me."

Emotional reasoning. Assuming that if we're feeling a certain way, we must have a reason for feeling that way: "I feel like my boss wants me to quit. I can sense it."

Catastrophizing. Assuming the worst-case scenario: "If I lose this job, I won't be able to find another one. No one will want to hire me!"

Labeling. Assigning judgments or qualities to ourselves based on isolated events: "I'm not talented."

The fallacy of control. This happens in one of two ways, where we believe either we are in complete control of our lives or we lack control completely. Neither is true; we have control over some things and none over others: "The universe is working against me."

The fallacy of fairness. Judging our situations based on perceptions of justice or fairness: "It's not fair! I can never catch a break."

The fallacy of change. Believing that we can change other people through our actions: "If I have a more positive attitude, I can get my boss to respect me more."

The need to be right. People who struggle with perfectionism often resort to this distortion and have a difficult time admitting when they're wrong or made a mistake: "Perhaps if I explain myself, my boss will see that their interpretation of my performance is incorrect."

Heaven's reward fallacy. The belief that through hard work and sacrifice, you will get the reward you deserve: "If I just keep my head down, I'm sure to get that promotion."

Disqualifying the positive. Consider this one a cousin of the distortion of magnifying the negative. This happens when we discount positive information as irrelevant to explain a situation: "My success to this point has been due to luck."

You don't necessarily have to identify *which* cognitive distortion you're resorting to at any given moment—especially since we often engage in more than one at a time. But next time you find yourself explaining a scenario using broad, exaggerated negative language, try to pause yourself long enough to consider that your mind may be playing a mean trick on you. Recognizing what's happening is often sufficient to disrupt your thought patterns and begin to shift them toward a more useful approach. Which brings us to the next step . . .

Seek a Different Framing

We rarely have access to all the reliable information we need in order to determine why things happen the way they do. And that's fine, because life is rarely so cut-and-dried. Multiple things can be true at once, and many of life's events happen for reasons that have nothing to do with who you are as a person. So next time you find yourself caught in a negative thought loop, ask yourself whether there might be a way to frame your situation differently from the one you're currently using. For example, if you receive a bad performance review, instead of telling yourself that you're not talented or smart enough and will likely lose your job, you may choose to view the negative feedback as constructive criticism. Instead of "My boss thinks I'm terrible," maybe consider "My boss wants me to succeed and gave me this feedback in the hopes it will help me improve." Did you have a disagreement with a friend or a loved one? Instead of "They just don't like me, and I'm a terrible friend," try "They feel comfortable being honest with me about their feelings and want to strengthen our relationship." Even something as simple as "Maybe that person was having a bad day" can help ease the frustrating self-talk and promote a more optimistic way of viewing the situation.

Another strategy is to question the accuracy of your perception. What evidence is there for your reasoning? What evidence can you marshal against it? For example, those coming to terms with a less-than-stellar performance review may remind themselves that every previous review has been positive. Or they might consider the fact that they recently moved into a new, more challenging role and are still learning the ropes. They might also look back on the review itself, paying attention to the positive, supportive feedback their boss gave them and not just the critical notes.

Tell a Different Story

In addition to searching for alternative explanations for a situation that is causing you stress, you can also shift your language to be kinder and more optimistic. How can you tell the story you're telling more gently? How can you be more compassionate to yourself? For example, instead of "I'm a failure," try "I'm disappointed with the way things turned out" or "This was a setback, but I will have more opportunities to succeed." Instead of "I'll never find love," try "I am opening myself to love but haven't found it yet." Instead of "I'm an awful parent," try "I lost my patience today, but I will be more mindful tomorrow." Subtle shifts like these can alter the associations your brain makes and put you in a more optimistic, solution-oriented frame of mind.

Stay in the Moment

If you're having trouble reframing or retelling a more positive story about your situation, one technique is to simply refocus your attention through a simple mindfulness practice. Much like I recommend playing Adult I Spy when you're hooked by a negative emotion, you can do something similar when you are trying to unhook from a thought. The brain has only so much capacity; it can't really focus on more than one thing at once. By redirecting your attention to your senses and identifying what is going on right now in your environment, your brain will not be able to dwell on what's bothering you. It's a healthy, simple distraction.

Another one of my favorite tactics is the "twelve-second scheme," which I borrowed from Dr. Rick Hanson. According to him, it takes only about twelve seconds for neurons to form new connections with each other. That's right, you can literally rewire your brain in less time than it takes you to respond to a text message or reheat a cup of coffee. How incredible is that? You can now put this knowledge to work the next time you find yourself spiraling into an anxious or negative thought loop. Pull yourself back from the edge, take a deep breath to get centered, and focus on something positive. It can be something that is taking place around you—maybe you're stuck in traffic but a song you love comes on the radio, or maybe you're frustrated with a coworker but take a moment to focus on a picture of a loved one you've placed on your desk. If nothing in your environment is doing the trick, think back to a happy memory that always brings a smile to your face. Now, focus on that positive thought and the feelings it evokes for at least twelve seconds. How do you feel now? Better, right?

Building an Optimistic Mind

In addition to the above tools, which are useful when you find yourself dealing with specific negative thoughts or challenging situations, you can take steps to cultivate a more optimistic mindset when things are going well. As humans, we tend to focus on the things that need fixing, so when things are moving along smoothly, we tend to adopt an "if it's not broke, don't fix it" mentality. But taking the time to practice optimism during these times can help you cultivate a more generally positive mindset that you can then lean on during times of stress. Think of it like taking your car for an oil change or getting an annual physical: preventive care can help you stave off and prepare for a crisis later on.

Relish Moments of Joy

One of the main downsides of our inherent negativity bias is that we are programmed to direct our attention to negative, threatening, or upsetting information but *not* uplifting, empowering, or positive information. The same resources we direct toward assessing and responding to threats are not automatically directed toward moments of joy, pleasure, and pride. However, we can train our brains to pay closer attention to positive emotions and events, thereby systematically redirecting our attention toward things that can help promote a sense of optimism.

Try this exercise the next time you experience a moment of joy. Set a timer for sixty seconds and use that time to focus on what you're feeling. Take the time to bask in the good feeling. Pay attention to your surroundings to help solidify the memory. Next, write down what triggered the experience so you can revisit it later. Add it to the joy list we talked about in chapter 3. This doesn't have to be a life-altering or major event. It could be something as simple as a pleasant conversation with a stranger that made you smile, taking a few minutes to lie down and do absolutely nothing, or belly-laughing at a joke your friend told. The next time you're feeling stressed, drained, or down, turn to your joy list and see what you can pull from to refocus your mood.

"We have to see the good facts, then we have to feel them," says Dr. Rick Hanson. "And then third, [we need to] really take them in." Engaging in the mindful, joy-solidifying exercise described above can help us do just that. "Attention is at the front end of who we are becoming," Hanson says. "If we're not able to establish sustained present-moment awareness—which is the standard definition of mindfulness—we're not masters of our own house because our attention keeps getting dragged here and there."

Acknowledge Your Strengths

When I started working one-on-one with clients, I noticed how they seemed very comfortable and adept at talking about the things in their lives that they wanted to change. This was especially true of those who had been to therapy or tried other self-help interventions in the past. They had a keen understanding of their weaknesses, but when asked to identify their strengths, they seemed less assured. In some cases, this was because they were dealing with low self-esteem and simply couldn't look past what they considered to be their failings to appreciate all the things they had going for them. But even those who were aware of their accomplishments, skills, and admirable qualities felt uncomfortable naming and embracing their strengths.

We'll talk more about how to cultivate deeper awareness of your strengths and the positive aspects of your life in the next chapter, but for now I encourage you to try accepting your strengths as an exercise toward building a positive mindset. Having trouble? Try this exercise:

Discover Your Strengths

Step 1. Take Your Strengths Inventory

Take a moment to reflect on times when you have felt truly engaged and successful. Answer these questions:

- Which activities make you lose track of time?
- When have you received compliments on your skills or abilities?
- What do friends, colleagues, or family members often ask for your help with?

Step 2. Look at Your Network

Ask three people in your life (colleagues, family members, or friends) what they think your top three strengths are. Do you notice any common themes? Do certain strengths come up more than once?

Step 3. Put Your Strength in Action

Review your reflections and feedback and identify one strength that stands out. How have you used this strength in the past? How can you intentionally apply it to a challenge or goal this week?

By the time you end this exercise, you should have a clear sense of what you naturally excel at and how you can leverage it in your daily life.

If people consistently ask you for advice, that's a sure sign they trust you, think you're a good listener, or respect your opinion—perhaps all three. Maybe your more obvious strengths fall more into the realm of skills rather than qualities: You're an excellent cook or a great driver, have a facility for languages, or are good at remembering personal details about people. After you've identified your strengths, pay attention to when you receive feedback that validates those strengths. Remember: your brain has the capacity to focus on only so many things. Why not focus on what's going well?

Set Goals

Life gets overwhelming and stressful when we feel we're not in control of our circumstances, and this can trigger anxiety that just makes our moods worse. If you find yourself up against a specific challenge, hooked by negative self-talk or anxiety, or generally struggling to stay motivated, one way to refocus your attention is to set small, specific, and achievable goals. Research shows that simply having and working toward goals promotes greater well-being by helping people more actively engage in their lives and feel a sense of purpose.

Importantly, these goals need not be huge, long-term, or even that impressive. As long as they are achievable and aligned with your goals, they can help shift your thinking and improve your sense of optimism. In fact, even if you ultimately hope to achieve a large goal, it's important to break it down into smaller milestones so you don't become demotivated. After all, before you can run a marathon, you need to be able to run a mile. You also need to be honest and gentle with yourself about where you're starting from. I once worked with a woman who wanted to start exercising to increase her health and vitality. But she was so out of the habit of regular exercising that the mere act of getting to the gym felt overwhelming. So we started by setting a goal of having her lay out workout clothes every night before bed so she would see them when she woke up first thing in the morning. Then we set a goal for her to put them on. Then we set a goal of having her park farther away from store entrances when she went shopping so she'd be forced to walk a little bit. Over time, she was able to walk for twenty minutes around her block three days a week. After she started doing that consistently, she added two virtual at-home weight-training classes per week, and after that she started going to a cardio class at a local gym once a week. Sometimes the best way to start a big goal is to just simply prepare for it—like by literally putting your pants on!

When to Seek Interventions: The Case of Trauma

The above tools are great for people who are dealing with natural everyday thought patterns or cognitive distortions, but those experiencing trauma or severe mental illness may not be able to unhook or alter their thinking without first addressing the root cause of their problematic thought patterns. If any of the following describe you, I encourage you to seek professional psychological help:

- You're experiencing symptoms of one or more diagnosable conditions as described in the *Diagnostic and Statistical Manual of Mental Disorders*.
- You're engaging in behaviors that are causing harm to yourself or others and/or are unable to take care of yourself.
- You are experiencing thoughts of suicide.
- You're struggling with addiction (substance abuse, chronic gambling, sex or porn addiction, etc.).

In addition, I always encourage people to pay attention to signs of trauma. In the past few years, the word *trauma* has become something of a buzzword, with seemingly everyone on social media discussing their various traumas, both big and small. I am not a trauma specialist, but as a psychologist, I do worry that the term is often overused and misunderstood, so I want to take a moment to discuss trauma in the hopes it will help people recognize when they may be experiencing it and could benefit from some additional help or resources.

Trauma is defined as overwhelming emotional distress that results from a specific event or series of events and interferes with an individual's ability to cope. People experiencing trauma often feel unsafe in their environment, may be triggered into emotional distress by an event that reminds them of the original traumatizing event, and may perceive that something bad can happen to them at any given time. Common traumatic events include sexual or physical assault, military combat, loss of a parent in childhood, war, natural disasters, and sudden loss of a loved one, among others. Less understood or discussed sources can include childbirth, minor traffic accidents (even those that don't result in injury), life-threatening illnesses, toxic relationships (even in the absence of abuse), chronic loneliness, and bullying. Signs that someone is experiencing trauma include:

- Flashbacks about, reliving, or dwelling on the traumatic experience
- Insomnia or trouble sleeping
- Nightmares
- Difficulty recalling specific details of the traumatic event
- Difficulty concentrating or thinking clearly
- Avoiding the location of the traumatic event
- Being easily distressed by things that remind you of the traumatic event
- Isolating from friends and family
- Physical symptoms like frequent headaches, stomachaches, digestive trouble, or a racing heart

If you are experiencing one or more of these symptoms, consider reaching out to someone who specializes in trauma therapy and post-traumatic stress disorder (PTSD). There are several well-known interventions for PTSD, most notably cognitive therapy (a kind of cognitive behavioral therapy), eye movement desensitization and reprocessing (EMDR) therapy, and family systems therapy. EMDR involves working with a specialist to move your eyes in specific patterns while you process memories of a traumatic event. It is a relatively new (developed in the late eighties) but highly effective therapy based on the theory that our brains store normal and traumatic memories differently. Through this different storage system, our brains attach novel experiences that remind us of the traumatic event to the trauma itself, causing us to recall the memory in a way that triggers panic, fear, and anxiety. Family systems therapy, as its name suggests, involves individual members of a family working together to understand how their dynamic has impacted one another's lives. This is especially useful when trauma occurred within a family as a whole, perhaps because of a pattern of abuse, addiction, or the mental illness of one or more family members. Take the time to research which methods might work best for you and seek professionals who specialize in the most effective treatments.

Toward an Optimistic Future

Our brains are extremely powerful, but so are we. When we understand how they work and how to change them, we can redirect that power toward cultivating the thoughts, behaviors, and eventually lives we want. It takes effort and practice and, most important, a belief that change is possible. A sense of optimism that the future can be better than it is now—possibly even better than we can currently imagine it.

Take Monica. After the incident outside the café, I knew we had our work cut out for us if we were going to help her detach from her obsessions and compulsions so she could lead the full life she so desperately craved. We kept at it and set a realistic but major goal. Before her OCD became severe, Monica's family had established a tradition of gathering at her parents' house every Friday night and watching a movie together. At some point, Monica had stopped attending, so we set a goal for her to be able to start going again—and actually relax.

She did it. After a few months, she was able to attend her first Friday movie night in several years, and she made a point of going back each week. Not only that, she took a job as an administrative assistant at a childcare facility—a true breeding ground for germs!—and was able to start dating again. What once felt impossible for Monica became possible. What is possible for you?

CHAPTER 5

"You Can Have It All!"

How the Impossible Ideal of "Balance" Hampers Optimism

You can have it all—just not all at once.

Around the time my oldest son, Jag, turned eight months old, my career started to take off in ways I had been striving toward for years. I had earned my PsyD in 2011, just five years before I got pregnant, and had decided to forgo the traditional route of becoming a licensed clinical therapist in order to launch my own practice and personal brand. I wanted to reach as many people as possible, and doing things my own way seemed like the most logical step. In addition to working one-on-one with individual clients, I was partnering with corporate teams, major brands, and media outlets and had even signed on as the head of business development for a new online-therapy app (several years before the pandemic of 2020 made such apps popular). Because I had been so sick throughout my pregnancy, I had barely been able to function, let alone work, but after several months settling into new motherhood (and recovering from an emergency C-section), I was eager and excited to get back to my career. I had always known I wanted to be a mother, but I had also always known that I wanted to work. And as I entered this new stage of my life and career, I felt confident I could do both without compromising how well I did either.

I had plenty of reasons to believe this was true. It was 2017, and women everywhere seemed freshly motivated to pursue their ambitions just as energetically as men. On social media, they shared family photos next to professional achievements and marathon times, captioning these milestones with #*girlboss* and *Nevertheless, she persisted*. They marched by the tens of thousands demanding equal pay for equal work, better maternity leave and healthcare, and safe working environments in which they could pursue their dreams without threat of harassment. Maybe I was just paying closer attention at this time now that I was embracing my new identity of working mom, but even though the idea that women could have it all had been around for decades, it felt more potent than ever. It seemed like everywhere I turned, I encountered another interview with a high-profile politician, a celebrity, or some other accomplished woman offering advice on how to ascend to the heights of your career while still making it to your kids' piano recitals, consuming an all-organic home-cooked diet, hitting the gym four times a week, and having passionate sex with your partner on the regular.

Through all of this, one word kept coming up again and again: balance. "Yes," they said, "you *can* have it all. You just need to figure out the right balance." "Balance is key." "I couldn't do it until I found a sense of *balance* in my life." I didn't pause to consider what having it all actually meant or that the concept of balance implied perfect equilibrium, which is incredibly difficult to sustain. All I knew was that I had worked too hard and come too far in my career to slow down now. After all, if all these other amazing women could do it, so could I. Why should my career have to suffer because I had a kid or vice versa? All I needed to do was to strike the right balance and all would be fine.

Dear reader, it was not fine.

If you haven't figured it out by now, I am more than a little prone to anxiety. I'm definitely an overachiever and something of a perfectionist, and when I'm focused on something, I can become hyper-fixated on making sure it turns out exactly how I envisioned it. This isn't true in every area of my life, but it is definitely true when it comes to my health and my kids, and this became all too apparent when I became a mom for the first time.

Like all parents, I wanted to bond with my child, and I decided—for some reason that now escapes me—that one of the best ways to do this was to exclusively breastfeed Jag. No formula, no pumping—just my body and whatever nutrition it had to give. I also determined that I should be the only person to put him to bed or wake him up. Apparently, being a good, present, nurturing mother meant being the only person my baby saw when he woke up or drifted off to sleep. This was fine in the first few months, during which I spent most of my time at home, but as I started to ramp up professionally, I somehow convinced myself that nothing needed to change. I made sure to schedule meetings and events around Jag's sleep and feeding schedule so I could always be the one to feed him and put him to bed. *This is it!* I thought. *Balance!*

I managed to pull this off—mostly—until one day when I was scheduled to speak on a panel on the opposite side of Los Angeles. After the panel, I told the organizers I had to take care of something at home but would be back in time for the networking session that started in an hour. I rushed out to my car, hopped on the 405, and arrived at home just as Jag was waking up from his afternoon nap. After a quick nursing session, burp, and diaper change, I handed him over to our nanny and sped back to the hotel where the event was taking place. As I walked into the ballroom for the networking happy hour, one of the organizers waved me over. I assumed she wanted to introduce me to someone, but as I approached, she pulled me aside and whispered, "Deepika, you might want to go to the bathroom. The buttons on your shirt are very crooked and some are undone."

After the initial shock of embarrassment wore off and I discreetly made my way to the ladies' room to fix my shirt, I had a moment of clarity: If this was balance, then I was about to tip all the way over.

The Trap of Impossible Balance

There is absolutely nothing wrong with wanting to squeeze the most out of our one precious life. It is entirely human—and the essence of optimism—to strive for things that bring our lives meaning, connection, and joy. For many of us, this includes doing work that fulfills us (whether we're paid for it or not), forming strong connections with people we love, staying healthy and vigorous, and making time for hobbies, rest, and other leisurely activities.

The problem starts when these natural desires morph into an anxious quest to do, attain, and achieve as much as possible and we start to believe that becoming the best version of ourselves requires doing specific things in a specific way. When we start to believe that a fulfilling life requires an envy-inducing career, six-pack abs, a passionate sex life with a devoted partner, two to three Instagram-worthy vacations a year, a packed social calendar, an immaculate, well-appointed home, and maybe a couple of well-behaved, exceptional, and intelligent children, we risk losing sight of what we *really* want and need. And when we start to believe that we can have it all as long as we figure out a precise strategy for maximizing our time and energy, we quickly fall into the trap of perfectionism, which often impedes our ability to live life authentically and, yes, optimistically.

We know intellectually that perfection is not possible, but in a society that praises productivity and hard work and celebrates achievement over enjoyment, it's easy to internalize the message that we are somehow falling short of our potential if we're not constantly striving. This is why I dislike words like *balance* and *having it all*. For starters, no one really knows what this language means, but it implies that there is some ideal way to live, that there are things we all want in life, and that it is possible to have them all as long as you go after them with all you've got. The reality is that time is short, energy is limited, and even if you're the most disciplined person on the planet, something is bound to go wrong—throwing whatever precarious balance you may have achieved off-kilter. Under these circumstances, we can end up placing unnecessary pressure on ourselves to get back into balance, trying to juggle a bunch of competing demands on our time in an effort to live life to the fullest.

Meanwhile, we are regularly exposed to scenes from the lives of people we barely know or don't even know at all, which makes it incredibly easy to start comparing ourselves to others. Of course this is human nature; it's one of the ways we try to determine where we fit in our social order so we can make decisions about where to invest our time, energy, and other resources. Before the rise of mass media, that social order was usually limited to the people we saw every day—our family and neighbors and some prominent people in our community. Since, with some exceptions, people who live near one another tend to have similar means and lead similar lives, this meant the opportunity to compare yourselves to others was relatively limited.

Today, however, every headline about this celebrity's postpartum bounceback or LinkedIn post about that college classmate's impressive new job or Instagram reel of some random acquaintance's epic food tour in Tokyo provides a chance for you to compare your life—usually unfavorably—to theirs. As anyone who has experienced this phenomenon knows, this constant upward comparison can quickly become overwhelming and, on our worst days, more than a little depressing. Of course, when all you see are the highlights of someone's life, any comparison you make will be incomplete and probably inaccurate, because you don't have a full set of facts. You see a promotion announcement, not the hours of overtime this person put in working under an abusive boss and the toll it took on their mental health. You see perfectly curated photos of Japanese sushi parlors, not the fact that it's the first proper vacation this person has taken in years and they banked all their PTO to make it possible. As a good friend once put it, "You see the highlight reel, not the *real* reel."

We already know, of course—from personal experience and through scientific research—that excessive social media use promotes social comparison, which can increase feelings of anxiety and depression and affect our general sense of well-being. We tend to view our lives negatively in comparison to others, even though we know intellectually that we're not seeing the whole story. As a result, we feel dissatisfied, stressed out, and envious.

Our constant exposure to other people's lives can leave us thinking we want things that aren't actually that important to us. At the same time, we're also being fed a steady diet of messages that lead us to believe that all of us should want the same things. We see people being celebrated for rising to the top of their careers and think, *In order to earn respect, I must work just as hard and strive to reach the same level.* We see a colleague's engagement photo and worry, *Am I a loser because I'm single?* We see some TikTok influencer's morning routine and wonder, "Should I start waking up at five a.m.?" This happens for all of us, but it seems especially prevalent in the lives of parents, particularly mothers. There is so much pressure on mothers to be perfect, and because no parent *really* knows what the hell they're doing, especially at first, many moms tie themselves in knots making sure they feed their kids the "right" things, send them to certain schools, enroll them in enriching extracurricular activities, and spend a certain amount of quality time with them every day. The prevailing mindset could even lead you to believe you need to exclusively breastfeed your baby even if that means fighting LA traffic for several hours one afternoon only to arrive at a professional event looking like you forgot how to dress yourself. Imagine that!

On the surface, our constant striving to have it all and our unending quest to balance it appears to be a sign of unbridled optimism. After all, in order to reach your potential and realize the life you want, you have to believe it's possible—and you have to put forth effort to get it. In actuality, of course, it's a recipe for disappointment, burnout, and an inauthentic life because we constantly feel that if we're not engaged in something productive or steadily progressing toward some worthwhile goal, we are somehow selling ourselves short. When we subscribe to someone else's definition of success, we lose our ability to make decisions. After all, when we do this we are essentially outsourcing our instincts to others—often strangers—who have no idea what is best for us, and as a result, we suffer. Nearly half of American workers report feeling overwhelmed, stressed, and unfulfilled by their work, and roughly 20 percent of the population suffers from an anxiety disorder. Parents, meanwhile, have become so stressed that as I was working on this book, the U.S. surgeon general issued an advisory declaring parental well-being a public health issue and calling on governments, communities, and institutions to intervene to help support parents while they do the "sacred work" of raising children. The reason? In our highly competitive society, parents feel increasing pressure to provide their children with resources, activities, and support to help them get ahead in life as compared to previous generations. Among the general population, but especially among young women, people who compare themselves unfavorably to others report lower self-esteem than those who don't engage in such comparisons.

So how do we lead big, bold lives without having to become masters of our own high-wire balancing act? The key is to remember certain truths:

1. *You can have it all, just not all at once.* In order to resist the pressure to have it all, I like to think of my life as a series of different seasons. Different seasons have different priorities, and what makes sense for one season may not be feasible in another. For example, if you're early in your career, this may be when you prioritize work. You're laying the groundwork for your future career, putting in extra hours, and driving yourself hard so you can set yourself up for success. Later on, however, you may lack the energy to go so hard and decide to explore other interests. Or perhaps you start a family and simply don't have the time to work around the clock like you used to.

When my sister and I were young, my mother chose to stay at home full time while my father worked. She poured all her time and energy into making sure her kids had the best lives possible and were set up for success. Because my dad worked long hours and often traveled, she didn't have a lot of time for herself. Today, however, now that all her kids are grown and out of the house, she travels every chance she gets. Every time my father has to schedule a trip for work, she tags along, often extending the trip so she can make the most of it. Travel was always a goal for her, and now that her season of stay-at-home motherhood is over, she can enjoy this new pursuit as much as she wants.

2. *"Having it all" means different things to different people.* Just because something brings joy to someone else doesn't mean it will bring joy to you. My cousin, for example, is a stay-at-home dad, despite the fact that this is still extremely uncommon, and even well into the twenty-first century, men still feel a ton of pressure to be the breadwinner. One of the best ways to resist comparison is to get clear with yourself on what *you* really want and ignore what everyone else is doing. Not only will this make it easier to make choices about how you spend your time, but it will allow you to avoid the misery of constant comparison.

3. *Empowered choices require boundaries and sacrifice.* Once you've figured out what having it all means for you, you need to figure out a system for getting it. This requires setting boundaries around the things you want to prioritize in this season of your life. We often think of boundaries as tools to fence us off from what we don't want to do or what doesn't otherwise serve us. But a boundary can also require you to sacrifice something you may otherwise want in order to protect something else. Just last week, I was invited to fly to New York to appear as a guest on a popular talk show. Normally, I would have jumped at the chance. It would have been a nice boost for my career, and it would have allowed me to further a relationship with an outlet that could potentially invite me back in the future. Unfortunately, my husband was already scheduled to travel at the same time, and the invite came only a few days before I would have had to leave, leaving us with insufficient time to find someone to watch the kids. When we first became parents, Alex and I established a rule that, unless we could arrange childcare with a trusted family member well in advance, one of us would always try to be home with the kids. If this had been a once-in-a-lifetime opportunity, I might have tried to make it work, but in this case, I decided to put my kids first and reluctantly declined the offer. It was disappointing, but I took comfort from the fact that I had made the choice willingly and honestly and in line with my values and needs. It was a far cry from my trying to commute back and forth across the city so I could breastfeed, and it was a lot more sustainable and affirming.

Purpose over Productivity

The secret to a fulfilling life is not to cram your life with pursuits society deems worthy of your time, nor is it to achieve a certain number of goals or milestones. Rather, it's to prioritize the activities and relationships that give your life a sense of meaning, contentment, connection, and pride. To do this, it helps to connect (or reconnect) with your sense of purpose in life—the unifying theme that connects your most worthwhile pursuits—and then prioritize that purpose in all you do. Research shows that people who feel a keen sense of purpose in their lives experience better mental and physical health and live, on average, longer than those who don't. Purpose helps prevent stress and burnout and makes it easier for people to make decisions about how to spend their time and energy in ways that improve their sense of self-worth, autonomy, and overall well-being.

There are many ways to go about identifying your purpose, and if you've ever engaged in any spiritual or religious practices (or even if you've participated in certain types of workplace or leadership training in recent years), you might already have some experience with these exercises. My favorite method, however, is the Japanese practice of finding one's *ikigai* (pronounced *ee-key-guy*). The word originated in Okinawa and dates back over a thousand years to the Heian period in Japan. It is a combination of the words *iki* (meaning "life") and *kai* (meaning, essentially, "fruitfulness" or "the result of effort") and roughly translates into "reason for living." In Japanese culture, ikigai can describe multiple things, including activities that bring life meaning, the motivation to fulfill that meaning, and the general sense that one's life has meaning. Basically ikigai is what we may call purpose or our reason for getting out of bed in the morning. The concept is so central to life in Japan, and in Okinawa in particular, that it is credited as one of the reasons people in that region tend to live longer, on average, than people in most other parts of the world. Several scientific studies have found that those who practice ikigai experience better physical health outcomes, including speedier recoveries from surgery, a lower risk of disability as they age, improved immunity, and an increased chance of recovering from a heart attack or other cardiac event.

I first discovered ikigai in the early 2010s, not long after I started grad school. I had always been drawn to Japanese culture and had even spent three months traveling around the Japanese countryside when I was in my early twenties. At the time, I was (like most twenty-somethings) more than a little directionless, definitely searching for meaning and purpose or, as I might have put it at the time, an answer to the question "What the fuck am I supposed to do with my life?" After earning my bachelor's degree in sociology, I experimented with a few career paths (among them a brief but fun stint at a punk rock record label and a brief, interesting, but not as fun stint at an investment bank), but nothing called to me. I quit my banking job and decided to take a hiatus to the Far East. While there, I learned about the *moai,* an Okinawan tradition in which young children are organized into small social support groups that meet regularly (up to a few times a week) and continue to gather until the members are well into old age. Originally designed to provide communal financial support, the groups also foster a sense of camaraderie, shared purpose, accountability, connection, and intimacy. I was struck by the pervasive energy and optimism within these communities; it felt like nothing I had experienced back home.

So when I decided to pursue a psychology degree shortly after, I was thrilled when I came across the concept of ikigai, which seemed to explain why the Okinawans all seemed to have a clear sense of purpose and belonging. I was so thrilled, in fact, that I started to make all my friends and family members take ikigai assessments whenever we got together. You know how some friends read one another's horoscopes or take personality quizzes? It was like that, but we were trying to uncover one another's purpose in life. Later, when I started my own practice, I incorporated ikigai into my work with individual clients and, eventually, with my larger group corporate clients, who were interested in how the concept could be applied to the workplace.

The process of discovering your ikigai is relatively simple, but you will benefit from taking your time with it. Ikigai is also not static. As you move through the seasons of your life, I recommend revisiting this exercise periodically to make sure you're investing your time in the right activities. I like to do this once every season of the calendar year because I find it's a nice way to check in with myself and assess my priorities for the coming months. It can also be a fantastic exercise to do with others, particularly those with whom you work or interact closely (for example, romantic partners, business partners, or even kids if they're old enough to understand the concept).

You arrive at your ikigai by first identifying four different types of activities as they apply to your life:

1. What you are good at
2. What you love
3. What you can get paid for
4. What the world needs

After that, you look for places where these activities overlap with another one. Each pairing represents one of the four facets of your life:

1. What you are good at + what you love = your passion
2. What you love + what the world needs = your mission
3. What you can get paid for + what the world needs = your vocation
4. What you're good at + what you can be paid for = your profession

Finally, you identify a word or phrase—typically a verb—that your passion, mission, vocation, and profession all have in common. This is your ikigai. Examples might be "to teach," "to inspire," "to heal," or "to connect." Mine at the moment is "to guide."

If it's helpful, you can think of your ikigai as a series of concentric circles like the one on the next page.

"You Can Have It All!" 115

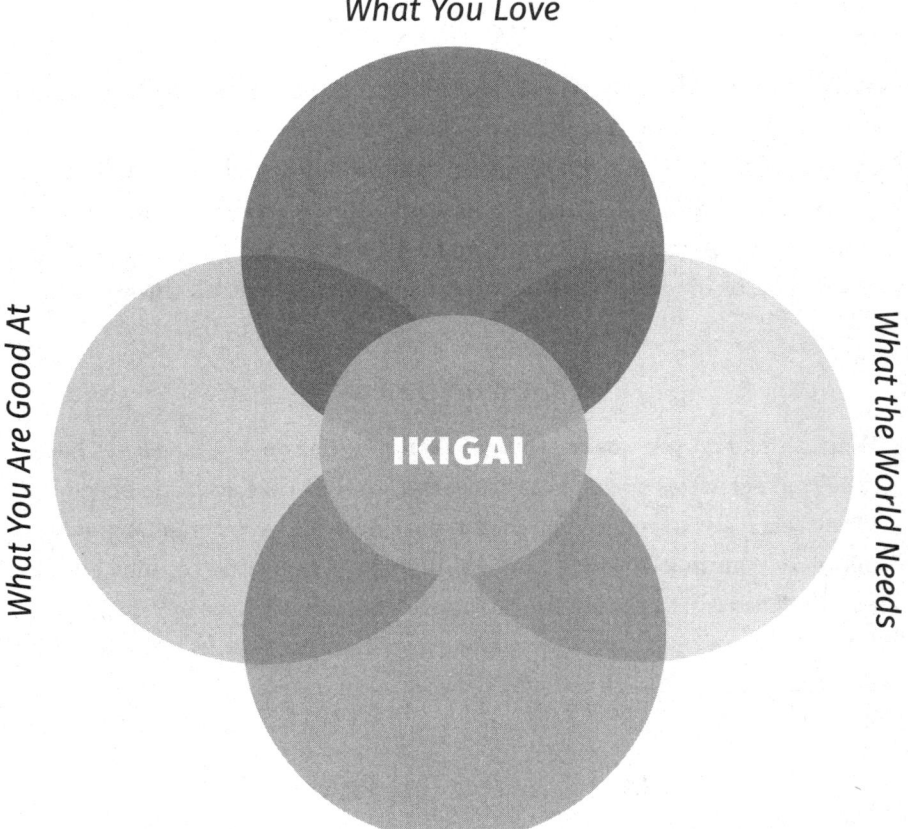

Let's walk through each of these steps together. If you get stuck or want to explore your ikigai a little deeper, there are several books and online resources available to walk you through the process. You can also ask friends or trusted loved ones for feedback, as it can be clarifying to get an objective perspective on something that is otherwise so personal. For each of the following categories, write down as many things as you can think of—the more the better. And don't worry if something seems odd or far-fetched; you never know where a worthwhile idea might come from.

What Are You Good At?

What skills or strengths do you have? These can be hard skills like graphic design or coding, or they can be soft skills like empathic listening, gift giving, or storytelling. Think of things you list on your résumé or that people have praised you for or given you positive feedback on in the past. What do people ask for your advice or help on? What have you studied, trained in, or practiced for many hours or years? Write all these down.

What Do You Love?

What things do you absolutely love doing? What do you never get bored of? What activities do you get so absorbed in that time seems to speed up? What relaxes you, makes you feel a sense of pride or accomplishment, or improves your mood? These can be things you do every day or only once in a while. They can be things you do for work or things you do purely for pleasure. They can be things you do alone or with other people. (Optimist Pro Tip: Add these things to your joy list so you can refer back to them easily!)

What Can You Get Paid For?

What do you currently get paid to do or what have you been paid to do in the past? What skills do you have that you could get paid for if you decided to? What could you get paid for that you've been interested in learning, even if you haven't learned it yet? What skill could you monetize if you developed it further? Some people find this question tricky because it's often difficult to see what marketable skills we have if we haven't ever been paid to use them. In that case, think of what you've seen other people get paid for or ask for suggestions from friends, colleagues, or anyone else whose opinion you trust.

What Does the World *Need*?

What changes do you wish to see in your community or society as a whole? What do the people around you need? What do you care deeply about? What keeps you up at night? If you could snap your fingers and change one thing about the world, what would it be?

Once you've completed all four lists, compare them to see where they overlap to identify your passion, mission, vocation, and profession. In some cases, you might identify something that falls into all four categories. For example, maybe you're a highly skilled and passionate environmental lawyer. Law is a skill, a passion, and something you can get paid for, and the world could certainly use an advocate to fight on its behalf. In this case, your ikigai might be "to advocate." In other cases, however, you might need to get a bit more creative. For example, maybe you're passionate about music, but you have no skill for writing or performing it. However, you're highly adept at connecting people and believe strongly in early childhood music education. Maybe your ikigai ends up being something like "to connect," "to inspire," or "to facilitate." Whatever word or phrase you arrive at, you should connect with it and feel that it accurately represents your goals and values.

Create an Ikigai-Centered Life

Once you've done this exercise, the next step is to assess how much you are actually practicing your ikigai in your daily life. This is where the real clarity starts to happen. You'd be surprised how many people can't name a single thing they do on a daily or weekly basis that brings them joy or a sense of purpose. They're so caught up with what they think they *should* do or what they feel they *have* to do that they have completely deprioritized the things that are most important to them.

Take some time to analyze how you spend your time. What things are you prioritizing and what are you not? Is there a way to start incorporating more of the things you love and care about into your life, even if it's just for a few minutes at a time each day or a couple of times a week? Are there activities you can incorporate into your existing daily tasks—the things you do for your job, as part of raising your children, or even as you go about your daily errands, chores, and other otherwise mundane tasks? Specifically pay attention to ways you can practice your ikigai—your life's deepest purpose, your reason for living—but also pay attention to ways you can create simple moments of joy in your life. Refer back to the joy list you started creating in chapter 3. What items on it have you not been prioritizing lately? How can you start to prioritize them more?

In addition, pay attention to things you're doing that are detracting from your joy and purpose. What things are creating unnecessary stress? Could you change how you perform them or how often you do them so they take up less space in your life? Could you outsource or ask for help with them? Could you cut them out altogether? For example, maybe you've decided you need to be home in time to have dinner with your kids every night, but it's cutting into your productivity at work in a way you're not comfortable with. How would missing dinner once a week or a few times a month impact your life—and your kids? If you decide it's necessary to put the extra time in at the office, perhaps you can figure out a way to do so that doesn't interfere with dinner by, say, working from home after they go to bed. Or if that's not possible, making up the missed face time at the dinner table in other ways (for example, making them a special breakfast on the weekends or taking charge of the bedtime routine). Likewise, maybe you pride yourself on keeping a spotless home. (I don't, lol. I wish I did, but I just don't.) Could you tolerate a little bit of dust and clutter for the sake of more time to relax in the evening? The point is, we often do things because we get in the habit of doing them or because we think we *should* be doing them. But there are very few things in life you absolutely have to do *right now*. Consider the pros and cons of doing these activities versus replacing them with something more life-affirming.

Here are some questions to help you incorporate your ikigai into your life:

- What activities do I do on a regular basis that help promote my mission, vocation, and/or profession?

- What activities do I regularly engage in that don't bring me joy? Of these, which are essential and which could I do less of, outsource, or stop doing altogether?
- What skills could I develop in order to further my ability to perform my ikigai?
- What is something I keep saying I want to do but don't? How important is that thing to my overall sense of well-being and purpose? If it's important, how may I start incorporating it more into my life?
- With whom do I most enjoy spending time? How much time am I spending with them? On the other hand, are there people I spend time with who are draining my energy? Can I spend less time with them? If not, how can I shift the relationship so it works better for me?
- What do I spend most of my hours each day doing? Is it fueling my ikigai? How might I shift the way I perform this activity so that it better reflects my ikigai? If that's not possible—if the thing I spend most of my time doing does not bring me a sense of purpose—what can I start doing so that one day I no longer have to engage in this activity?

When you start to examine how you spend your time, you will immediately notice how you might spend it more wisely to further your goals and purpose. In addition, you will notice how many opportunities you have to reallocate time from some nonessential or unpleasant task. Keep in mind, too, that the shifts you make don't need to be drastic. You don't need to quit your day job, change careers, go back to school, or move to a different city in order to live a life in line with your ikigai. Even small, incremental changes can help boost your mood and sense of optimism and get you in the habit of noticing opportunities to expand your life when they present themselves. Developing self-awareness is 90 percent of the battle.

An important note: your ikigai does not have to be the same as what you do to get paid. As a millennial, I was raised to believe that it was possible—and preferable—to get paid for work that you enjoyed, was aligned with your values, and gave your life meaning. I am fortunate that the work I do to help support myself and my family does exactly that, but I also recognize that this is a privilege not everyone has. Sometimes a job is just a means to a paycheck—*and that is totally fine*. We live in a world where you have to make money to survive, and it's extremely difficult to focus on filling your life with happiness and purpose when you're just trying to make rent and put food on the table. Not enough people talk about this. We can't all just follow our bliss at any given moment in time! If you are at a point in your life where you have to work a job you don't particularly love in order to pay the bills, you are not failing or falling behind or wasting time. You are simply in a season of your life where you need to prioritize financial solvency—and there is incredible purpose in this fact alone. There are also plenty of ways to weave your ikigai into your life without regard for financial compensation. In fact, one survey found that less than a third of Japanese people considered their work to be central to their ikigai. You can volunteer, teach, or simply exercise your skills and passions in your day-to-day life and interactions.

If you eventually want to get paid to do work that is personally meaningful to you, you could consider starting a side hustle that combines your passion and marketable skills. You'll be in good company; in recent years roughly 40 percent of Americans report having a side hustle that they use to earn additional income, and 41 percent of Americans with a side hustle said they started it as a way to spend more time doing things they enjoy. Or if you need to develop your skills before you can get paid for the work, you could experiment with new hobbies as a way to practice. Maybe the effort will eventually develop into a lucrative full-time business; maybe not. As long as you are living intentionally and prioritizing the things you hold dear, it doesn't matter how much, if any, money you make from the endeavor. All that matters is that you are reclaiming a sense of self and living your life authentically.

Create Healthy Boundaries

Over the past few years, the term *boundary* has become extremely popular as more and more people take to the internet to discuss the ways they try to protect and improve their mental health. And as with most therapy lingo that enters the mainstream lexicon, the word is frequently misused and misunderstood.

In terms of mental health, a boundary is essentially a rule that guides how someone engages with the world, other people, and themselves so they can preserve their physical, mental, and emotional safety. It is often used in the context of trauma treatment, interpersonal conflicts, and the management of certain psychiatric disorders so that individuals dealing with these issues can recognize and avoid situations that may lead to problematic thought loops or behaviors. For example, a victim of a violent crime may set a boundary to limit or avoid exposure to violent imagery or content. Likewise, an individual may cut off contact with an abusive parent, or if they want to preserve the relationship, they might set a boundary that they will immediately end an interaction if the parent begins behaving in a certain way (for example, drinking alcohol, raising their voice, or using insulting language).

Boundaries can be useful in less extreme circumstances as well. After I gave birth to Jag, my emotions were all over the place. I'm extremely emotionally sensitive in the best of times, but during this period, I could not tolerate even the slightest bit of sadness. I fast-forwarded through sad scenes in my favorite movies—or avoided watching them altogether. I limited how much news I consumed because every depressing headline triggered a spike in my anxiety. As I moved out of the postpartum phase and my hormones started to regulate, I eventually relaxed that boundary, but it was a useful tool when I needed it and helped me become much more in tune with my feelings and emotions. Depending on what season of life you're in, you may find such boundaries useful in preserving your energy and fostering an optimistic mindset.

It's also critical to set boundaries as a way to protect your time and energy so you can live life according to your *ikigai*. You may, for example, set a boundary of not working past six p.m. so you can spend uninterrupted quality time with your family or partner. You may limit your engagement on social media so you don't accidentally get sucked into a spiral of negative comparison or toxic content. You may also reevaluate your relationships and set firm boundaries around how you interact with certain people. For example, maybe a friend of yours loves to gossip, but talking about other people in this way leaves you feeling icky and depleted. You don't need to stop hanging out with this person altogether, but you can be honest with them about your feelings and ask that they avoid gossiping with you in the future. A good friend will learn to respect this boundary—and if they don't, well, it may be time to reevaluate the relationship.

However, boundaries are *not* an excuse to simply refuse to do things you don't want to do—or to act like an asshole by justifying selfish behavior. While it's one thing to abandon tasks, events, and relationships that don't bring value or joy to your life, the things and relationships that *do* bring meaning into your life usually require you to occasionally do things you don't always enjoy. As I said earlier, empowered choices require boundaries *and sacrifices*. Protecting and nurturing the things you hold dear will often require making difficult decisions. For example, you may not love your significant other's best friend, but you will likely need to at least tolerate them at least once in a while. Perhaps (*gasp!*) you could even try to find at least one thing you appreciate about them. A little effort can go a long way toward showing your partner you care about their happiness.

Similarly, you can't expect every moment of every day to be filled with excitement and meaning. Sometimes shit just has to get done. Some days you'll hit a career milestone before an intimate date night with your partner and after working on your novel and volunteering for the ASPCA. Other days you'll spend waiting in line at the DMV, answering mind-numbing emails, and listening to your five-year-old drone on about Pokémon while cleaning up the mess they made in the living room. And yet there is purpose to be found in all of it; even the mundane can sometimes hold meaning.

CHAPTER 6

"Just Ask the Universe!"

A Science-Based Guide to Manifesting Your Dream Life

The moment we believe our path is ours to shape is the moment we become strong enough to walk it.

When I was in my late teens, a friend introduced me to a married couple—we'll call them Joshua and Evelyn—who worked as respected spiritual teachers and healers in my community. This was before I'd started studying psychology, but I'd been fascinated by spirituality and new age self-help culture since I was thirteen. Yes, when most of my friends were listening to NSYNC or Britney Spears on their Discmans, I was listening to books on tape about vibrations in the universe and forms of meditation.*

One of the earliest concepts I encountered was the Law of Attraction and, along with that, the practice of manifestation. Anyone who has read the mid-aughts bestseller *The Secret* or has practiced positive psychology is likely familiar with these ideas. Basically, the Law of Attraction posits that the energy we put out into the world through our thoughts, feelings, and behaviors reflects back on us in the form of either positive or negative energy from the universe. If we think positively, good things will happen; if we think negatively, we invite misfortune into our lives. Simple as that.

---

* Okay, yes, I did listen to music, but I was way more into the Smiths, Nirvana, and Garbage than boy bands. Let's just say I had a lot of feelings as a teenager.

The skeptic in me wasn't 100 percent convinced that I could somehow control the universe with my mind. But I loved the idea that we could create our own reality and that our thoughts could have a direct and profound impact on our lives. I wanted to learn more, so when a friend told me about Joshua and Evelyn, I trusted they could help.

I was immediately taken in by their presence. Both of them radiated positive energy in a way I could literally *feel*. They exuded a profound sense of calm and seemed to walk through life with a lightness that even a self-proclaimed spiritual skeptic could envy. Curious—and eager to learn—I asked them how they did it. How were they able to operate at such a high existential and emotional level? And how could I do the same?

"You must start by eliminating the negative from your life," Joshua explained. "Manifest only the positive, and you will attract only the positive to you. Focus solely on what you *want* to have happen, not the alternative. When you manifest the positive, there is no room for the negative in your life."

"For instance," Evelyn chimed in, "we do not lock the doors to our home because we have manifested a life of safety and comfort. Locking the door would invite negative energy into our home by suggesting that we are in fact not safe. We know the universe will keep us safe, not a locked door."

I have to admit, I raised my eyebrows at this a little bit. I lived in a relatively safe beachside suburban town around LA, but it seemed that leaving your door unlocked would invite more trouble than locking it just to be safe. Then again, was that just my negative energy getting in the way of my true desire? Maybe if I redirected my thoughts toward accepting the Law of Attraction as true, I could harness the power of the universe to my benefit. What's the worst that could happen?

A few weeks later, I was with our mutual friend when they got a call from Joshua. There was an emergency: An intruder had broken into their house. He and Evelyn had been robbed.

The Misinformation About Manifestation

I'm willing to bet that you are at least somewhat familiar with the concept of manifestation. Even if you're not a spiritual searcher, self-help aficionado, or follower of new age thinking, all you'd have to do is take a stroll through the home goods section of your local Target (or pretty much any department store) to see what I mean. Notice all those decorative wall prints imploring you to "Radiate Positive Energy" or coffee mugs promising that "The Universe Will Provide"? Those are borrowing the language of manifestation—repackaged for the modern everyday consumer. The practice of manifestation has been around since the early 1800s, but has gone mainstream in the twenty-first century thanks to a combination of self-help culture, social media, and the increasing popularity of spiritual movements that aren't tied to any particular organized religion.

I totally understand why people are drawn to the practice. We all have dreams and hopes for our lives. We're all on journeys of self-actualization and improvement. Who wouldn't want to believe there was some cosmic life energy surrounding us that could help us achieve our goals while simultaneously improving our mood and emotional well-being? And besides, how often do we give ourselves permission to *really* think about what we want most out of life? When was the last time you sat down and *dreamed* about the future you want to create for yourself? When was the last time you gave yourself permission to fantasize about what life would be like if you could have everything you wanted?

Trust me, I get it. I first learned about the idea when I was thirteen and came across a copy of *The Law of Attraction* by Esther and Jerry Hicks, a couple who first articulated the idea in the terms we take for granted today. For many years in my teens, twenties, and even into my thirties, I was a devout practitioner of manifestation. Maybe it's my Indian heritage (though my family isn't all that religious), but I liked the idea that the energy we put out into the world would reflect what we took out of it.*

There's just one problem: Most conversations about manifestation (particularly on social media, where anyone can call themselves a guru) disregard the crucial *next* steps. You cannot simply *think* your way to greatness. Or true love. Or wealth. Or happiness. You cannot prevent bad things from happening to you just because you will it to be so. You must back up your desires with practical actions that will improve your odds of reaching those desires. At the very least, you must lock your doors if you want to reduce your chances of getting robbed.

It's this disconnect between intention and action that bothers me about so many modern manifestation practices. Sure, some people are just lucky, and fate, the universe, or just fortunate circumstances conspire to help them accomplish things the rest of us only dream about. But even when these people credit positive thinking or manifestation for their success, they often leave out the diligence, grit, and shifts in mindset that were also required to get there. There is great power in the promise of manifestation. As we've already discussed, science has proven a direct link between what we think, how we feel, and how we behave. This is what the practice of real optimism teaches us: In order to achieve our highest goals, we must first believe that they are possible; that good things *can* happen, even if life is not always as rosy as we'd like it to be. Even if you think the idea that we can manifest our reality is hocus-pocus, research shows that it's not *all* nonsense. In fact, manifestation may be an essential first step toward reaching your loftiest goals.

If we want to turn our greatest fantasies into reality, we need to understand what happens in this middle part. How do we stop dreaming and start doing? That's the question this chapter will answer.

---

* I was less on board with some of the more supernatural aspects—for instance, that all the concepts the Hickses were writing about had come to them via a collection of spirits named Abraham who used them as conduits to deliver their message to humans. That seemed a little out there to me.

You Don't Always Get What You Want, but You Usually Get What You Expect

Whenever I speak to a roomful of people, I like to perform a little thought experiment that was inspired by a conversation I once had with an old supervisor of mine. "Who here would like to win the lottery?" I ask. Inevitably, most, if not all, of the people in the audience raise their hands. I'm not surprised.

"Okay, now keep your hand raised if you've purchased a lottery ticket in the past week?"

Inevitably, most, if not all, hands go down. I am equally unsurprised.

I've never met anyone who doesn't say they want to win the lottery. But I also know very few people who consistently buy lottery tickets. Why? Because the odds of winning the lottery are extremely small—and everyone knows this. They know that they won't win the lottery unless they buy a ticket, but most of them would rather spend their money on something else that is more likely to pay off even when the fantasy of winning the lottery is indeed quite sweet.

This is not my way of telling you to play the lottery. (I mean, go ahead if you want to, but the odds of winning are close to one in 300 million, which means you're more likely to become an Olympic athlete or have identical quadruplets than you are to win, but it's your money.) It *is* my way of illustrating a logical fallacy we as humans are all prone to: the self-fulfilling prophecy.

Chances are you've heard this phrase, but did you know it describes a documented psychological phenomenon? The term was coined by psychologist Robert K. Merton in 1948 to describe the process by which people make choices that reinforce their expectations even (and often especially) when those actions sabotage their desires. Think of a time you have set a goal or intention for yourself but then backed out because you thought, *What's the point? It's never going to happen anyway.* Ever passed up the opportunity to apply for a job because you thought you were underqualified or that the field was too competitive for you to stand a chance? Ever blown your budget on something frivolous because you couldn't imagine ever having enough money to take that dream vacation or finally afford a down payment on a home? These actions undermine your ability to achieve your goals, and yet we all take them every single day.

Our inclination to create self-fulfilling prophecies points to a truth about the brain that explains why so many people fail to realize their goals—and why common manifestation practices often fall short of expectations. If you don't *believe* the reality you want is possible, you are less likely to perform the actions necessary to make it possible. On the other hand, when you believe that you can attain a goal, you are more likely to put in the work to reach it, even if it's difficult or takes a long time. Chance and circumstance might still get in your way, and life doesn't always turn out the way we want or prepare it to. But when we believe—*truly believe*—our destiny is in our hands, we naturally become more equipped to face it. This is optimism at its essence.

Of course, changing your beliefs is easier said than done. (Just ask anyone who has been in therapy!) But it *is* possible. The tricky part is that it requires more than desire and a positive attitude. It requires dedication, patience, self-awareness, and a healthy dose of practicality combined with the hope that change is possible. In short, optimism backed up by action. A form of manifestation I call evidence-based manifestation provides a science-based mechanism through which anyone can shift their most deeply held beliefs. I developed this practice through years of studying the brain and working directly with clients who told me about the lives they wanted but kept undermining their ability to get it because their actions did not align with their desires. To illustrate, let me tell you a story.

Evidence-Based Manifestation: How to Visualize the Life You Want Without Any Help from the Universe

"I want to be in a relationship, but I get so nervous in social situations. I just don't know how to approach people."

I sat across from my patient, Jake, a forty-something gay man and recovering addict who had come to me for help managing his depression and social anxiety. It was 2008. I was halfway through my first practicum year as a graduate student in the clinical psychology program at Cedars-Sinai Medical Center, and Jake was proving to be one of my toughest patients to date.

More than anything, Jake wanted to be in a committed relationship, but he struggled with severe self-esteem issues and negative core beliefs about himself. "I don't love myself," he had told me. "I don't believe I'm worthy of anyone else's love or affection." Jake was extremely self-aware and understood that his negative self-image was impeding his ability to connect with others. In some cases, he was actively sabotaging his own chances of success.

For example, a few months before he started working with me, he attended a seventies-themed costume party that a friend of his was throwing. He told me that large social engagements often triggered his anxiety, but he was committed to putting himself out there and trying to meet new people. In keeping with the theme, he picked out a flashy metallic gold shirt—something he knew would attract attention—and attended the party. As he mingled with the other guests, some of whom he knew, others he didn't, a few people complimented his costume. This helped ease his nerves a bit, but then he spotted a "very successful and very handsome" member of his social circle. When he went over to say hi and hopefully strike up a conversation, the guy looked over Jake's outfit and exclaimed, "Oh wow! That is *some* shirt!"

Another type of person would probably have interpreted this as a neutral comment, perhaps even a compliment given that this *was* a costume party and Jake had, as the saying goes, understood the assignment. Jake, however, was mortified. To him, his acquaintance may as well have laughed at his face and said, "What on earth are you wearing? You look ridiculous!" His interpretation of this guy's intention—correct or not—was enough to send Jake rushing for the nearest exit. He immediately went home and hadn't gone to a bar, party, or other social engagement since. It had been three months.

Jake was never going to meet Mr. Right if he didn't leave his house once in a while. But despite our work together and Jake's increased awareness of his false core beliefs, and even though a relationship was what he wanted most, he couldn't get out of his own head. His anxiety had hijacked his brain, so he automatically went into social situations with a pessimistic attitude: "I am not worthy of love, so everyone here is bound to reject me!"

Regular talk therapy had helped Jake figure out why he was so socially anxious, but try as he might, he couldn't break himself of the habit of retreating whenever he perceived the slightest threat of rejection. I decided to try a different approach.

As part of my graduate work, I had been studying the power of visualization—the act of intentionally imagining yourself in various scenarios as a way to prime your brain to respond when those scenarios occur in real life. Sports psychologists had already been using visualization techniques to help athletes improve their performance for several years, but there was ample evidence that an average person could apply the same techniques to everyday scenarios. What did Jake have to lose?

"Jake," I said, "I want you to visualize what your life would look like with the romantic partner you've always wanted. Can you describe that for me?"

Jake looked at me like I'd asked him to strip naked and run down Santa Monica Boulevard. "What?" he asked, looking puzzled and more than a little concerned. "How am I supposed to do that?" I realized my mistake. Jake fundamentally didn't believe that he was worthy of love and therefore couldn't even *imagine* a world in which he was in a loving relationship.

At our next session, I decided to try a different, more subtle—and perhaps slightly more manipulative (but in a good way!)—tactic. "Jake," I said after we exchanged the usual pre-session pleasantries, "who is the first person you are going to tell when you meet the man of your desires and are in a loving relationship?"

"My mom," he responded immediately. No hesitation. No worry. No overthinking. I kept going.

"Great. Where are you when you are telling your mom about this new relationship?"

"In her living room."

"What does her living room look like?"

"Um, there's a gray chenille couch that we usually sit on. Sunlight is coming through the vintage curtains . . ."

We kept on like this for a few minutes. I asked Jake to describe more and more details, and he began talking about the smell of his mother's lasagna and the color of the paint on the walls. The more he rooted himself in that specific space and situation, the more he was able to pretend he was actually there. He told me about the dog he and his future partner would share and the feeling inside him that came from being in a relationship full of mutual respect, trust, and love.

I could tell that Jake left that session feeling a little lighter, a little more optimistic about his romantic prospects. His breakthrough was small, but it was a breakthrough nonetheless.

As Jake and I worked together over the next several months, we continued to work on his visualization skills. I could see him becoming more confident and relaxed as he visualized this new life for himself and started taking the actions necessary to make that life a reality. About eight months after we started this practice, Jake was back in my office. "I met someone," he said.

"What?!" I exclaimed, almost spilling my tea. I knew he was making progress, but even I didn't expect our work together to pay off *that* quickly.

"Yeah," he said, settling into the couch and smiling to himself. "I hit it off with this guy while I was out with some friends one night. It's obviously too early to tell if he's the one, but it felt good to connect with someone. It's still terrifying, but it's better than being scared at home alone."

Jake's issues with his self-esteem and anxiety were certainly more severe than the typical concerns we all have when trying to date. But his story showcases how powerful our minds can be when we direct them toward our desires with intention, patience, and focus. Jake went from avoiding all social interactions to opening himself to a serious relationship within just a few months. And he did it by training his brain to visualize a reality he previously never thought possible. Here's how.

Why Visualization Works

The tool I used with Jake is known as sensory-based visualization, and it is exactly what it sounds like: a method in which someone engages all their senses in order to visualize a particular scenario that they would like to see come true. In the process, what may start as a seemingly impossible dream begins to take shape as a potential—perhaps even likely—reality.

At first glance, this might sound just as farfetched as manifestation. (The words even sound similar!) But scientists have been studying visualization as a tool for self-improvement for years. Research shows that those who practice intentional visualization perform better under pressure (across a wide variety of activities and fields) and are generally happier and more optimistic about the future. World-class athletes, like the Olympic swimmers Michael Phelps and Katie Ledecky, and successful businesspeople like Oprah Winfrey and Spanx founder Sara Blakely have gone on record to say that visualizing has helped them achieve many huge milestones throughout their careers.

Like manifestation, visualization promises to help you achieve the outcome you most desire by first conjuring a detailed picture of it in your mind. But the similarities basically end there. While advocates of manifestation hold that you can *will* something to happen (or not happen) simply by wanting it enough and putting positive vibes out into the universe, visualization uses the brain's natural chemistry to methodically shift your beliefs to ones that are more in line with your intentions. In this way, it acts as a tool to increase optimism, priming your brain to act in ways that better serve your goals, instead of undermining them.

Visualization works because it honors several truths about human psychology and the brain.

1. Our brains are biased toward what we already believe

As we've established, our brains are extremely efficient. From the time we are born, they constantly collect and process information in order to help us make the decisions that are most likely to help us survive. Unfortunately, this efficiency sometimes leads to glitches, especially when it comes to abstract concepts like interpersonal relationships or self-esteem. When we receive inputs—from our parents, from society at large, from our peer group, from our own limited observations about how the world works, etc.—we can start to believe things that are, at best, false and, at worst, destructive. We see how this bias can work against us when we witness (or practice) discrimination based on irrelevant details or make assumptions about how a situation will play out before gathering all the facts. In our own lives, this bias is what leads to self-fulfilling prophecies. If we believe an outcome is unlikely to happen, we are less likely to perform the actions necessary to achieve that outcome, even if our belief is based on bad or at least incomplete information.

Take Jake.

Jake's core belief that he was unworthy of love was deeply ingrained in his psyche. He knew intellectually that this was not the case because he did in fact have friends and loved ones who cared about him. He knew that everyone was worthy of love and could recognize the qualities he brought to a relationship, especially after years of therapy and counseling. But, at some point in his life, his brain had been programmed to believe that he would never find his soulmate. And if this was never going to happen, why would he put himself in situations that would just make him feel worse? He was stuck in a self-fulfilling prophecy, making decisions that consistently undermined his ability to get the thing he said he wanted most in the world.

No one likes to be rejected, so we try to avoid it as much as possible. The difference between a socially adept person and someone like Jake is that the former believes that social interactions are an opportunity for both rejection *and* acceptance. Most of us are optimistic that even though we might not hit it off with everyone we meet, we will connect with some people, and some of those will go on to become close friends or partners. We are willing to take the risk of rejection in the hopes that it will pay off.

Jake, for whatever reason, had come to believe that acceptance was impossible. This belief led to him being incapable of putting himself in situations that might lead to rejection. What's more, the results of his actions confirmed his false belief. To his biased brain, the fact that he wasn't meeting people proved that he never would. This is how self-fulfilling prophecies work: we believe something to be true, we make decisions that align with that belief, and as a result, we make the thing we believed to be true *come* true.

2. We can shift our beliefs by shifting our attention

If you're reading this book, chances are you know what it's like to be caught up in your own self-fulfilling prophecy. You harbor beliefs that you know are irrational, but when confronted with a situation to challenge that belief, you freeze or resort to default patterns that only reinforce what you already believe. You are sure that you're not qualified for a job, so you get anxious and screw up the interview—and don't get the job. You think your crush is out of your league, so you avoid them in social settings and thus never form a relationship. You believe you're not the type of person who will ever be wealthy, so you don't negotiate your salary or create a savings plan—and thus always feel financially insecure. You tell yourself to snap out of it, that if other people can achieve their dreams, then why not you? But you're stuck.

Sensory-based visualization helps us shift these beliefs by allowing us to create scenarios in which we can experience what's possible in a safe, controlled environment. When we visualize the outcome we want and imagine ourselves in that scenario, our brains gather evidence that that outcome is possible. As discussed in chapter 2, when sending signals to the rest of your body, the brain does not distinguish between fantasy and reality. When we *think* about doing something, our brains respond as if we're actually doing it. When we visualize a scenario that in real life would elicit a particular emotion, we experience that same emotion just as intensely. When Jake visualized how content and at ease he would feel in a loving relationship, he actually began to *feel* contented and at ease.

But how did this actually shift his beliefs? Scientists believe the answer lies with mirror neurons. Neurons carry information between your brain cells, allowing you to process information, make decisions, and perform all the bodily functions you barely think about as you go through your day. They are the messengers of the brain. Mirror neurons are specialized neurons that activate both when individuals perform an action and when they observe someone else carrying out that same action. Scientists believe mirror neurons are involved in a number of sophisticated functions that we as humans perform, including empathy, imitation, and learning. They also play a key role in the brain's ability to anticipate and understand the actions of others.

When an individual engages in visualization, they activate the same mirror neuron pathways in the brain as when they perform the action in real life. This activation helps to strengthen the neural connections associated with that action, which can lead to improved performance when the person actually completes that action. This is why visualization has become such a popular method in sports psychology. When gymnasts visualize themselves running through a perfect floor routine or quarterbacks visualize themselves executing the perfect play, their bodies fire the same signals they would if these athletes were actually performing those actions. The more they visualize, the stronger their neural connections become, and the more prepared their body will be to perform on the big day.

In Jake's case, his visualization shifted his focus from the embarrassment he felt at the party toward a scenario in which his dream of falling in love was realized. As a result, his body sent signals to his brain that this scenario was possible. The more he focused his attention on this visualization, rather than on his memories of rejection, the more Jake's core beliefs changed and the more he was able to come up with solutions and actions in line with his goals.

3. The familiar is more powerful than the abstract

Common manifestation practices usually encourage us to imagine the most perfect life for ourselves, even if it bears no resemblance to our current reality. But what if, like Jake, it's difficult for you to conjure this image because it seems so far out of reach? How can you predict how you'll feel in a scenario when you can't even visualize the scenario?

The trick is to start with the familiar. When we visualize ourselves in a familiar setting, we take advantage of the memories, associations, and emotions our brains already associate with that setting, thus improving our ability to connect the visualization to reality. By describing how it would feel to tell his mother about his new relationship, Jake could pull from other memories he had of sharing good news with her. He could imagine how it would feel to sit on her couch because he already associated the couch with certain feelings. Not only that, he could draw on sense memory to elicit even more physical responses: remembering the smell of her lasagna could make him salivate; remembering the feeling of the couch fabric could trigger his mind to believe he was actually sitting on it; and so on.

The more you practice visualizing yourself in a familiar setting, the more your brain will associate that setting with the feeling you're trying to elicit. For example, living in Los Angeles, I work with a lot of actors. Obviously, the main goal of any actor is to land their dream role, and usually that requires a lot of auditions. If you try out for enough roles, you quickly become familiar with the audition rooms at each of the main studios (they're basically all the same). So when an actor client comes to me for help preparing for a big audition, I usually guide them through a visualization in which they perform the audition exactly as they want it to go while paying attention to the specific sensory surroundings. What is the temperature in the room? Are there any ambient noises? What color are the walls? What does it smell like? What do the casting directors' voices sound like? If there is a bathroom on the way to the audition room, I have them visualize walking into it, standing in front of the mirror, and taking a deep breath. Then when they actually show up on the big day, they can reenact this moment—precisely as they visualized it—and prompt their brain to prepare for what follows. Every bit of information helps the brain prepare them for the actual audition day.

4. We can hope for the best but must prepare for the worst

When I was actively practicing manifestation, one of the most common pieces of advice I got was to never, under any circumstances, let *any* negative thoughts enter my mind. By imagining what might go wrong, or so I was told, I would invite unwelcome energy into my life, thus undermining my pull with the universe.

Even if you believe that the energy you put out into the world comes back to you, there is no denying that sometimes, no matter how optimistic you are, bad things happen. But the best way to handle life's challenges isn't to ignore them, but to prepare for them. This is how we build resilience. This is how we do the hard things we must do to create the lives we want.

This may seem counterintuitive (especially if you've been schooled in the good-vibes-only theory of manifestation), but if you're practicing visualization in an effort to change a belief or behavior or to realize an important goal, you must incorporate the challenges you will inevitably face into the visualization itself. By doing so, you prepare yourself mentally and physically to meet those challenges if, or when, they arise.

Several years ago, I worked with a client who was recovering from alcohol addiction. As part of her recovery, she needed to learn how to resist alcohol in a world where she was consistently tempted by it. Not only did she have to learn how to turn down a drink when offered one, she also needed to reprogram herself to resist temptation when confronted with a trigger that had previously set off her desire to drink.

In crafting her visualization practice, not only did we have to set a goal of her being sober, healthy, and energetic, but we also had to train her brain to respond the way she wanted it to whenever she was tempted. I had her visualize scenarios in which she came home after a long day at work, tired and desperately craving something to help her relax. We walked through the feelings of anxiety and temptation she would likely experience and then imagined scenarios in which she chose to do something else instead of pouring herself a drink or heading to her local bar.

I had her describe other activities that made her feel relaxed and secure—things like talking to a friend or exercising outdoors. As she visualized herself choosing those activities in moments of temptation—including how great she would feel about herself afterward—it became easier for her to make those choices in real life. We also practiced visualizing all the fulfilling things she could do without alcohol in her life—a reality she had always had trouble internalizing because of the hold her addiction had on her mind. This combination of hyper-specific, scenario-based visualization with the projection of a positive future for herself helped to provide her with the motivation and strength to give up alcohol for good.

When we consider these four truths together, we see how visualization and this process of changing our brains can help us manifest what we want, not through magical thinking, but by altering our mental processing to help us make better choices. While it's worthwhile to work with a professional coach or psychologist who specializes in visualization (especially when you're first starting the practice), here are some tips to practice on your own.

Visualization for Beginners

Step 1. Set a positive intention

Start by figuring out what you want your visualization to help you do. This can be something specific and immediate like "I want to deliver a great presentation at the annual corporate meeting next week" or "I want to run a six-minute mile." Or it can be something bigger and more amorphous, like Jake's desire to enter into a serious romantic relationship. It can also be about changing a core belief about yourself, such as "I want to feel more confident in social situations" or "I want to be kinder to myself."

Regardless of what kind of intention you set, be sure to articulate it in positive, not negative, language. The brain can't think in negatives. If you try to imagine *not* doing something, the brain can only imagine you doing that thing. It's the classic "Don't think about an elephant" trick. What are you thinking about right now?

If you're trying to eat more healthfully, say, "I want to choose foods that make my body strong and healthy," rather than "I want to stop eating junk food." If you're trying to become a more relaxed parent, say, "I want to speak gently and supportively to my kids. I want to be calm during times of conflict," instead of "I want to stop yelling at my kids." You will keep this intention at the center of your mind during the rest of this exercise, as you visualize yourself becoming the kind of person you want to be.

Step 2. Center your body and your mind

Find a place relatively free of distractions so you can practice your visualization without interruption. You want to be able to lose yourself in your visualization as much as possible, to feel like you're *really* there. Any disruptions or distractions will make it that much more difficult to stay focused on your thoughts. The more you practice this visualization, the easier it will become to tap into it in any given moment, even if you're in public or an otherwise chaotic setting. For the purposes of creating your visualization exercise, however, you want conditions to be as perfect as possible.

Don't forget to establish your visualization vibe. If certain sounds, scents, or sensations help you relax, feel free to use them. Research has proven, time and again, that scent can affect us at a neurological level. If you've never experimented with scent before, try lavender or jasmine, which are incredibly soothing. Another option would be to practice your visualization outside. Studies show that spending time in nature, even if it's just a local park or your backyard, can help improve our sense of well-being. Ultimately, though, if something works for you, don't worry too much about the science behind it; make this time and space your own.

You can sit or lie down for this exercise—whatever is more comfortable and grounding for you. Once settled, try to relax your body and calm your mind as much as possible. I always start my clients off with some deep-breathing exercises accompanied by a full-body muscle relaxation scan. I prefer to start at the bottom of the body, with the toes and feet followed by the legs, and work my way up, but you can start from the top if that feels more comfortable for you. Squeeze each muscle group as you inhale and then release it as you exhale. Continue this with each muscle group up or down your body until you've relaxed everything. Doing this forces you to shift your attention away from any racing thoughts you may have and toward what you're doing with your body.

Try not to let your mind wander away from the present moment, but go easy on yourself if it does. This is a judgment-free zone; negative self-talk will only increase your anxiety and interfere with what you're trying to accomplish. If you get distracted, simply take a moment to recognize what's happening and gently redirect your thoughts back to the exercise. Continue to breathe deeply.

Step 3. Select a setting for your visualization

Often when we try to picture the lives we want, we attempt to conjure the image of an idealized setting—a beautiful dream house overlooking the ocean; a renovated apartment in Paris; a chalet in the Swiss Alps. Basically, something out of *Architectural Digest* or *Condé Nast Traveler*. While these settings can be useful when trying to conjure a place of serenity or inspiration in order to relax your mind, for the purposes of this exercise, it's best to pick a setting that you're familiar with. Science tells us that visual imagery doesn't work if it lacks an element the visualizer doesn't feel is true. When trying to program a specific feeling or action or challenge a limiting belief, you'll find it more powerful and beneficial to imagine yourself in a mundane, familiar setting—a place you visit frequently. Remember, the goal is to get your brain to associate your visualization with reality and with the specific feeling or goal you're trying to achieve.

If you're visualizing for a specific event, imagine the setting in which you will be performing that event: the conference room where you'll give the presentation, the track on which you'll run the mile, etc. If the goal is more nebulous or not bound to a particular time and place, select a familiar place in which you can imagine this future version of yourself. This is what Jake did: He had no way of knowing when or where he was going to meet the love of his life—or what that person would look like—but he knew he would want to share the happy news with his mother. Maybe, for you, you'll imagine your favorite date spot or the day you bring your new partner home to meet your family.

If your goal is more about improving your feelings of self-worth, pick a setting in which you spend a lot of time. If they are struggling, I usually advise clients to imagine themselves in their shower. It may sound silly, but think about it: You spend *a lot* of time in the shower, and it's a place usually free of distractions where you can let your mind wander and relax. It's also full of sensory information: the sensation of the water on your skin, the smell of your shampoo, the color of your soap and the tiles on the walls. The shower is where people go to retreat, even if just for a few minutes. Who doesn't feel better after taking a shower?! When you pick a place like this for your visualization and then imagine yourself feeling the way you want to feel in that setting, you will start to associate that setting with that good feeling. How awesome would it be to experience a sense of self-love and gratitude every time you took a shower?

Regardless of the setting, try to visualize as many specific details as possible and engage all your senses. What do you feel, smell, taste, see, and hear? What is going on around you? The more details you can incorporate, the more effective the visualization will be.

Step 4. Walk through the scenario in your mind

Once you've visualized the setting and engaged your senses, walk through the specific actions you will take in that scenario. If you're focused on something that requires practice or rehearsal, imagine yourself performing each step (for example, each step forward as you run around the track or the exact words you want to say in the tone you want to say them during your presentation). If your goal is more abstract, imagine how you would want a hypothetical scene related to this goal to play out. Try to be as specific as possible about what you want to achieve and why you want to achieve it in order to craft a clear mental image for your mind to build on. For example, if your goal is to improve your feelings of self-worth, think about what you stand to gain by achieving this goal. Maybe you feel your lack of self-worth has made you more susceptible to being talked over at work. In that case, you could visualize a scenario that might arise at work in which you are self-assured and feel powerful in the knowledge you are sharing with your team. Imagine making the choices you *want* to make in this scenario instead of the ones you *usually* make.

If you're focused on an external goal, like acing that audition or presentation, picture yourself performing it in the third person. As mentioned, when we observe someone performing a task, our mirror neurons fire the same way they would if we were performing the task ourselves. In doing so, we come to associate ourselves with those actions. And when we associate ourselves with a specific identity or action, we are more likely to follow through on actions that support that identity.

Meanwhile, if your intention is more inward-focused and designed to help you shift your self-regard and identity, picture yourself in the first person. Experiencing the visualization from the perspective of your own body makes it easier for you to conjure the feelings when you find yourself in the setting your visualization takes place in.

Important note: Do not try to script out a conversation or interaction with other people as part of your visualization. People are unpredictable. Instead of rehearsing what exactly you'd want to say or do if someone behaved in a particular way, focus on the emotions and demeanor you want to convey in the moment. For example, "During the job interview, I will put my best foot forward and be calm and at ease." If you try to control too much of the scene, it's easy to become frustrated when (inevitably) things don't play out exactly as you imagined.

Step 5. Visualize what could go wrong

Once you've walked through the ideal visualization, switch it up by imagining various scenarios that could disrupt your flow. What if you get a cramp during your run? What if it starts to rain? When I work with my actor clients, I get them to visualize what might happen if they are disrupted during an audition. What if the casting director sneezes? What if other people in the room are whispering to each other? What if someone drops something? What if someone opens the door and interrupts you? What if you suddenly feel sick? Remember to be realistic; you don't need to visualize everything going wrong at once (for example, someone else in the room has a coughing fit, the fire alarm goes off, and you suddenly have to pee all at the same time). With each scenario, practice various versions of your visualization and incorporate these not-so-ideal scenarios one at a time. By preparing for problems in advance, you'll be better prepared when something deviates from the best-case scenario—and you're less likely to get thrown off.

Step 6. Repeat as necessary

Once you have come up with your visualization, try to practice it as often and for as long as you need it. There's no exact number of repetitions that will magically transform your sense of identity and possibility, but if your visualization is tied to a specific, time-bound goal, I recommend shorter (less than five minutes), more frequent (twice a day) repetitions. If your goal is more long term and abstract, you may try longer (fifteen to thirty minutes) sessions that are less frequent (maybe once a day to start, then less frequently once you've become more comfortable with the practice). This frequency can help you avoid burnout or monotony all while rewiring your neural pathways to solidify what was once a fantasy into a possibility in your mind.

The more you practice visualization, the more natural it will start to feel, and you will be able to tap into the visual imagery and the emotions it elicits whenever you need. And the more you practice the behaviors associated with the visualization, the more they will become a part of who you really are, leading you one step closer to becoming the person you most yearn to be.

Imagine Your Best Possible Self

In addition to using visualization to help them achieve specific goals, many of my clients find it helpful to practice a longer, all-encompassing visualization that touches on many aspects of their aspirational life. One of the best-researched exercises in positive psychology is imagining your best possible self. If you're new to visualization or meditation, it can be helpful to have someone walk you through this practice at first. If that's not an option, or if you'd rather practice on your own, consider reading the prompts out loud into a recording device and playing them back to yourself as you work through the exercise.

To prepare, set aside at least twenty minutes and find a quiet, comfortable environment in which to practice. Sit or lie comfortably and use whatever techniques you need to relax your mind and ground yourself. Close your eyes and take a few deep breaths to bring your mind to your center.

Scene Setting: Pick a specific date sometime in the future, preferably at least five years from now. Envision the details of this day: the date, the season, the weather. Are you at home, work, or a special place? Take note of the people around you. Who are you with on this significant day?

Positive Surroundings: Engage your senses to visualize a positive atmosphere. What do you hear, see, feel, smell, taste? Warm sun on your skin? Birds chirping or pleasant laughter? A delicious smell or soothing texture?

Achievements and Milestones: Now picture yourself achieving specific goals by this date. These could be personal, professional, or both. What is something you keep saying you want to do or change about your life? Imagine how you feel in this future moment knowing you have succeeded. Do you feel proud? Joyful? Fulfilled?

Strengths and Qualities: Take a moment to focus on the strengths and qualities that have led you to this point in your life. Embrace the confidence, resilience, and determination that have been your companions on the journey.

Positive Relationships: Visualize the positive relationships around you. Whether you picture yourself surrounded by family, friends, colleagues, or other members of your community, sense the support and connection you feel with them. Feel gratitude for the relationships that have played a significant role in your success.

Anticipation for the Future: Imagine the positive momentum you've built and the exciting possibilities that lie ahead. Embrace a sense of anticipation and optimism for your future beyond this date.

Gratitude and Reflection: Take a moment to express gratitude for the present and the journey that brought you here. Reflect on the steps you've taken to reach this point.

Bringing the Vision Forward: When you are ready, open your eyes. Now you can carry the positive energy and motivation from this visualization into your day. Consider jotting down any insights or intentions inspired by this exercise. Writing is a great tool for solidifying your intentions and bringing them forth into reality.

Repeat this visualization as needed, adjusting the details when necessary to align with your evolving vision of your best possible self.

CHAPTER 7

"Believe in Yourself!"

A Scientific Approach to Creating Affirmations That Actually Work

When we gather real evidence of who we are, belief in ourselves begins to feel less like a reach— and more like a return.

"I know I'm not attractive, and that's why I am single. I've known it my entire life."

Priya was an attorney in her late twenties. After graduating from a prestigious university and an Ivy League law school, she had joined one of the top corporate law firms in LA and had quickly earned a reputation as a rising star within her field. Her ambition and intelligence radiated off her, and she was extremely confident in her career.

But as she sat across from me at one of our first sessions, she looked deflated and withdrawn. A few months before we started working together, Priya's boyfriend had broken up with her. Within a few weeks, she heard through mutual friends that he was dating someone else—a gorgeous aspiring actress with quintessential Hollywood looks. Priya had never been confident in her appearance, and to her, this blow served as even further confirmation of what she'd always suspected—she simply was not good looking enough to attract, let alone keep, a partner.

This belief did not start with her ex, of course. As a kid, Priya had always been praised for her studiousness and intelligence, but never for her looks. Her older sister, meanwhile, had been homecoming queen at their high school and was constantly told how beautiful she was. The girls quickly adopted identities as "the smart one" and "the pretty one"—identities they both carried well into adulthood. "Thank goodness you're smart," an aunt had once told Priya. "Your sister has her looks to go on, but you have your brains."

It was clear that her insecurity about her appearance was wreaking havoc on Priya's well-being. As much as she excelled and took pride in her career, she desperately wanted to fall in love and find a partner but felt like she couldn't compete in the looks-obsessed dating scene of Los Angeles. "I feel like every single person I meet here is so far out of my league," she told me. "No one wants to date someone just because they're smart.

"I know, intellectually, that I'm not hideous," she conceded. "I mean, I don't stop traffic, but I've dated people before. And yeah, I occasionally get complimented when I dress up or do my hair nice. But I just can't help but compare myself to everyone I see. And when I do that, I always fall short."

Priya told me that before she started working with me, she had used affirmations as a way to try and shift her perspective about how she looked. Every night, just before bed, she wrote in her journal *I am beautiful. I am attractive. I am beautiful* in the hopes that simply reciting these phrases again and again to herself would help her feel more confident in her appearance. She wasn't alone. This was the mid-2010s, and countless self-help books and guides suggested the practice of reciting affirmations—short, positive phrases designed to challenge negative thoughts and self-perceptions—as a way to boost confidence and self-esteem. Online, in magazines, at wellness retreats, and even in therapy, it seemed like people were encouraging one another to start a daily affirmation practice. "Stand in front of a mirror and recite three positive affirmations every morning! I am confident! I am beautiful! I am strong!" "Write your affirmations on Post-it notes and stick them above your desk or wherever you can see them throughout the day." "Keep a journal where you write down your affirmations every night before bed." If you were at all interested in self-help at this time, you definitely encountered advice like this at some point.

I myself had practiced affirmations from the time I was a teenager. I learned about the practice after reading books like *The Law of Attraction* and others about positive thinking and manifestation. At first I was completely sold on the idea. I believed wholeheartedly in the power we had to change our thinking, and this seemed like a simple but effective way to focus the mind toward what you wanted and away from all the distressing and troubling thoughts that were distracting from your true potential. Plus, whenever I recited affirmations like "I am worthy" or "I am divine," I felt better—calmer and more connected to myself and the spiritual world.

But as I got older and my life got more complex, I noticed that the practice seemed less and less powerful. My doubts really began to surface in my mid-twenties when I was diagnosed with an autoimmune condition that caused a variety of physical ailments, including stomach and digestive issues and inflamed joints. In search of anything that could help me manage or eradicate my symptoms, I called an advisor—someone I frequently turned to when I wanted help dealing with some personal or emotional issue—for guidance. "This is a story you are making up about yourself," she told me when I mentioned my diagnosis. "Your body is a hologram. It is not real. You are projecting your story onto it. You need to remind yourself that you are healthy. Your body is perfect just as it is."

Desperate, I tried to do just that. I stood in front of a mirror, took a deep breath, and recited: "My body is perfect. My body is healthy. My body is perfect." And yet all the while I could feel a pang in my gut that seemed to be saying, "Um, no, I'm not. Please pay attention to me!"

Of course the physical reality of chronic disease is much different from a subjective belief like "I am unlovable" or "I am unattractive." Still, the experience left me with the nagging sense that something was off. Either I wasn't doing affirmations correctly because my doubt was getting in the way of my belief (which just made me feel guilty and ashamed) or maybe the approach I'd been taught to self-affirmation wasn't as useful as I'd been led to believe.

It wasn't until grad school, however, that I fully appreciated why this was. As I learned more about how the brain worked, I came to appreciate

Truth #4: The brain likes to believe what it already believes. The brain spends all its time trying to gather and interpret information so it can help us make decisions about how to operate in the world. As it gathers this information, it starts to form beliefs that may or may not be 100 percent accurate. But in order to maintain the brain's efficiency and maximize its limited resources, these beliefs become shortcuts to interpreting information that then reinforces those beliefs so that they become even stronger. As a result, when we're confronted with information that challenges these beliefs, our brain's natural inclination is to reject it because the act of changing that belief would require gathering additional information and processing it differently—all of which requires effort and forces us to question what is real and what is not. The brain does not like this uncertainty, so if we want to change a long-held and core belief, we need to consciously put in the effort to do so; this won't happen automatically.

Knowing all this, I immediately recognized the potential flaw in Priya's plan to improve her self-image. Every time Priya recited or wrote down the affirmations "I am beautiful" or "I am attractive," her brain immediately interpreted them as irrelevant and baseless lies. All her life, Priya had amassed evidence that supported the belief that she was unattractive. Simply telling herself the opposite was not going to convince her otherwise. Doing so was the equivalent of telling someone that the sun does not exist. Without concrete, reasonable evidence that the bright yellow ball you've seen in the sky your whole life is just a figment of our collective imagination, you're simply not going to change your mind.

"When you tell yourself you're beautiful, do you believe it?" I asked her.

She paused for several seconds before replying. "No," she said simply. "I don't believe it."

I share this story not to suggest that affirmations are bad or a waste of time. In fact, plenty of scientific evidence exists that shows how affirmations, when practiced correctly, can have a profound positive impact on our outlook, self-image, and even behaviors. Research shows that people who practice self-affirmation exhibit signs of reduced stress, are more effective at coping and problem-solving, and are more optimistic in their assessment of life's challenges, viewing them as obstacles to overcome instead of threats to their identity. Affirmation practices have been shown to improve academic performance among minority groups, health behaviors among individuals who are informed of risk factors regarding their lifestyles, and interpersonal relationships among romantic partners. However, in order to ensure your affirmations are effective in promoting the positive changes you seek, you need to respect the way your brain processes information, forms beliefs, and changes, and you need to tailor the practice so that it is specific and authentic to you. Only then will your brain start to believe what you're trying to tell it.

How Affirmations Work

No one knows the exact origins of our modern-day version of affirmation practice, but the general process has existed in one form or another for as long as human beings have been able to string thoughts together. You can see versions of it in ancient mantra and meditation practices from Eastern philosophy and religion and even in the French Enlightenment philosopher René Descartes's famous musing, "I think, therefore I am." In the early 1900s, the French psychologist, pharmacist, and hypnotist Émile Coué introduced a concept he called autosuggestion, which historians often credit as the earliest iteration of our modern notion of affirmations. According to Coué, most of human behavior and belief was driven by unconscious thoughts that happen automatically and often outside our perception. However, if we want to shift our perspective, we can do so by actively suggesting new conscious thoughts to ourselves, thoughts that with careful repetition would gradually replace any undesirable unconscious ones—and thus transform our reality. "Every thought entirely filling our mind becomes true for us and tends to transform itself into action," he wrote in his book *Self Mastery Through Conscious Autosuggestion*.

Reality, Coué believed, was basically the result of imagination; so long as you could imagine yourself doing something that was within the realm of possibility, you could make it happen. In this way, Coué was basically advocating an early version of positive thinking and its more scientifically sound successor, positive psychology. "So when you wish to do something reasonable, or when you have a duty to perform, always think that it is *easy,* and make the words *difficult, impossible, I cannot, it is stronger than I, I cannot prevent myself from* . . . disappear from your vocabulary; they are not English. What is English is: 'It is easy and I can.'"

Although some of his beliefs were radically pseudoscientific (such as his assertion that one could cure any physical ailment through the sheer power of autosuggestion), you can hear echoes of Coué's beliefs in books like *Think and Grow Rich* by Napoleon Hill and *The Power of Positive Thinking* by Norman Vincent Peale, two wildly influential and popular titles from the early twentieth century that are often credited with giving rise to the modern self-help movement. Coué's book also features a ritual affirmation practice that resembles much of what we see in self-help books and on social media feeds today. "Every morning before rising, and every night on getting into bed, [one] must shut his eyes . . . and then repeat twenty times consecutively in a monotonous voice, counting by means of a string with twenty knots in it, this little phrase, 'EVERY DAY, IN EVERY RESPECT, I AM GETTING BETTER AND BETTER.'" Sound familiar?

Even when we don't adhere to a specific, conscious affirmation practice, human beings constantly practice affirmations without realizing it. Whenever we hype ourselves up before an important event or performance or try to rid ourselves of negative thoughts, we are effectively affirming ourselves. "You got this!" "I am prepared." "I can get through this." We tell ourselves these affirmations in anticipation of some stressful or potentially threatening event without thinking too much about what we're trying to do.

There's a reason we do this. Scientists call it *self-affirmation theory.* Originally coined in the 1980s, this theory holds that all human beings have an innate sense of self that they want to view as essentially moral, worthy, and competent. Whenever something threatens that sense of self—say, a romantic rejection or a failing grade on an exam—we immediately try to protect it by countering the negative feedback with positive statements that reaffirm it. For example, after a devastating breakup, we may remind ourselves how much our friends love us or how many desirable qualities we bring to our relationships. After a poor exam result, we may remind ourselves of other areas in which we excel.

Importantly, psychologists who study self-affirmation theory assert that the process is not about positioning ourselves as perfect or superior to other people, nor is it about trying to convince ourselves that we excel at any one specific thing. It's about reminding ourselves that we are generally good people who are consistently doing our best to be seen as such. It's also not simply about trying to earn praise or recognition but about feeling that we behave in ways that actually *deserve* praise and recognition.

What this means is that we don't need to feel great about ourselves in every domain of life in order to have generally high self-esteem and an optimistic outlook concerning our place in the world and prospects for the future. For example, studies show that when presented with threatening information in one area of your life (like that failing grade), you can reduce the impact that information has on your sense of self by affirming your qualities in a completely unrelated area. (E.g. "I am well liked by my peers and am adept at putting people at ease.") In other words, Priya didn't need to try and convince herself that she was physically beautiful in order to believe she was worthy of love; she simply needed to bolster her belief in the qualities she already knew she had.

It is also critical that affirmations must feel authentic and specific to the individual using them. In one study, researchers asked participants to repeat generic phrases like "I am lovable" to themselves and then report on how it made them feel. They found that the individuals who had previously ranked high in self-esteem felt marginally better after the affirmation practice, while those with low self-esteem actually felt *worse*. "Repeating positive self-statements may benefit certain people, such as individuals with high self-esteem," wrote psychologist Joanne Wood, who led the study, "but backfire for the very people who need them most." The reason, researchers speculated, is that, for people with low self-esteem, positive statements that don't feel accurate or meaningful to them don't change their deeply held beliefs about themselves but simply remind them of all the ways they feel inadequate. In this way, affirmations can basically trigger confirmation bias as our brains naturally seek out evidence to confirm what it already believes.

That said, there is ample evidence that genuine, tailored positive affirmations can help boost people's moods and overall sense of self and even influence subsequent behavior. For example, in one study African American and Latinx seventh graders who were asked to write about their most important values at the beginning of the academic year performed better throughout the term than peers who were *not* tasked with this exercise, thus reducing the achievement gap that typically exists between minority students and their peers by roughly 40 percent. The results were even starker for students who had previously earned relatively low GPAs. Researchers suggested that the mere act of affirming their values and sense of self allowed these students to better cope with the perceived threat to their identity that exists in the pervasive societal belief that Black and Latinx students perform worse academically than white ones. What's more, despite the relatively brief nature of the intervention, the positive effects persisted for two and sometimes three years after the students had engaged in the affirmative exercise. This finding suggests that affirmations can create a positive feedback loop: The affirmation leads to a desired result, which serves as an additional affirmation, and so on.

In another study, participants were asked to rank their most important values prior to being shown messages that warned of the risks of sedentary behavior and promoted increased physical activity. Later, while undergoing an fMRI brain scan, some participants were asked to reflect on their most important values, while others were told to think about their least important values. Those in the first group showed increased activity in the reward and valuation systems of the brain and subsequently engaged in more physical activity than those in the latter, control group. The mere act of reflecting on their core values and affirming their self-worth inspired them to take better care of their physical health. The impact of affirmations on physical health has been confirmed by several other studies, showing that people who affirm their identities prior to receiving potentially threatening health information (for example, the dangers of smoking or excessive drinking or the risk factors for developing diabetes) are more open to receiving such information and subsequently altering their behaviors to align with the recommendations of medical experts.

Affirmations can also change the way we relate to one another. Couples who affirm one another regularly, even in the midst of conflict, feel more stable in their relationships and supported by their partners. Affirmed individuals are less defensive in negotiations and are more open to receiving information about people or a group of people they may have previously seen as a threat. When we feel comfortable and confident with our sense of self, we feel less challenged by outside forces, including other people.

The factor all these studies have in common is that the affirmation practices that researchers assigned to participants focused on what each individual deemed most important and already believed about themselves. The simple act of reminding them of their own unique identity—the things they felt made them special—was enough to bolster their self-esteem and sense of optimism. This unfortunately is what most popular affirmation practices miss; they assume a broad one-size-fits-all approach that for most people who are struggling with their self-image feels like trying to wear a coat that's two sizes too large: It doesn't feel right and becomes more of a burden than a benefit.

The Seven-out-of-Ten Rule to Make Affirmations Work for You

Knowing all this, we can see why generic affirmations and blanket statements often don't work to change our beliefs about ourselves. Unless we already believe what we tell ourselves to be true, it won't align with our identity and reality, so our brains essentially view it as irrelevant. However, this is exactly why an affirmation practice rooted in one's authentic experience can be so powerful; it helps reinforce what we already know.

This is how I decided to approach Priya's conundrum. Although she didn't believe she was beautiful in the broadest sense of the word, clearly she had enormous self-esteem in other areas of her life. If I could urge her to tap into those areas instead of focusing on what she felt was missing in her life, perhaps we could shift her perspective and, as a result, her expectations for her love life.

"Okay, so you don't believe you're beautiful. That's okay. What things *do* you like about yourself? It doesn't have to be physical," I asked.

"Well, I know I'm smart," she said. "I'm focused. I'm disciplined. I get things done. My colleagues respect me. I'm meticulous; I catch things that other people miss."

"That's great. Those are all qualities anyone would be proud of. What about aspects of yourself that don't have to do with your professional life?" I asked.

Priya considered for a moment. "You know, I really like my laugh. People have told me I have a great laugh." She smiled, clearly reflecting on a time when she'd received this feedback. "And I guess—it's kind of silly—but I think I have really great hair."

"That counts!" I said, pleased that Priya was able to appreciate things about herself that weren't just about her intellectual capabilities. "How do you feel when you say those things? Do you believe those things when you say them out loud?"

"I do," she said. "I mean, sometimes I doubt myself, but mostly I do."

After that, I asked Priya to write down some of the statements she had come up with. We then went through each one, one by one, and ranked how much she believed them on a scale of 1 to 10, with 1 being "I don't believe this at all" and 10 being "I believe this fully and wholeheartedly." By the end of the session, Priya had identified five or six affirmations that felt true to her, and I encouraged her to use those going forward in her nightly affirmation practice instead of generic statements like "I am beautiful." She did, and after about a month, she had also identified additional statements that she felt represented her best qualities and core values, so we had about a dozen affirmations to work with. After a few more weeks, I asked her how she was feeling about the exercise. Had she noticed any changes in her life?

"I feel more confident and self-assured generally, even at work," she told me. "I was always confident in my ability to do my job, but because I didn't feel great about myself in other areas, I realize now that I often kept my head down and tried not to draw too much attention to myself. This was fine in school, where all that mattered was how I did on tests and assignments, but it's definitely been a challenge since I started working. The field is so competitive and you really need to promote yourself and get people to notice you if you want to get the best opportunities. I've been speaking up more in meetings, sharing my opinions and offering my perspective. I think people are taking notice. I've been getting more feedback, and people are seeking me out for help on projects. It feels good. I generally feel good, and you know what? I don't focus so much on my appearance anymore."

We can all take a lesson from Priya's experience. Even if you don't suffer from the low self-esteem that Priya and Jake (whom we met in the last chapter) did, most of us, at some point or another, are prone to getting hooked by negative thoughts or feedback that threaten our self-image. By refocusing our attention toward evidence that affirms our identity, we can break this cycle and gradually become more self-assured. Here's how.

Remember the Seven-out-of-Ten Rule

From what I've observed, you don't have to believe in a statement 100 percent in order for it to work as an affirmation. As long as it *mostly* feels true for you, it's enough to work with, and your brain will start to seek information that confirms it. A good rule of thumb is to rank how much you believe in your affirmations on a scale of 1 out of 10, and practice only the ones you rank a 7 or higher. Maybe there are times when you've doubted the veracity of a certain statement, but overall you feel pretty confident in saying it out loud. When you don't believe something fully, it's like trying to make your brain do a 180-degree turn while going 100 miles an hour down the highway: You simply can't change course that quickly without running into some serious issues. You first need to slow down and change direction. That's what the Seven-out-of-Ten Rule is about. It's also why statements like "I am beautiful" didn't work for Priya, but a statement like "I have nice hair" did.

The mere act of stating something that you identify as true or mostly true focuses your attention toward that thing and away from whatever troublesome thoughts or information you may be trying to process. Studies show that when given the opportunity to affirm one's values, either before or after receiving a negative evaluation on a task, people tend to spend less time and energy thinking about the bad news than they would otherwise because their brains become focused on another, more pleasant thought. If you consistently tell yourself "I am a good friend" or "I am an effective negotiator"—and your brain believes it—you will unconsciously start to seek information that confirms this existing belief until you feel it even more fully.

Be Specific

It's much easier to identify with specific affirmations than generic ones because you can more easily point to evidence that the specific is true. If you say something like "I am a good person" or "I am lovable," you may start to dwell on evidence to the contrary. Maybe you once betrayed a close friend's confidence or have been consistently unlucky in love and so don't believe those broad statements as much as you want to. But when you drill down to the core beliefs that might support these assertions, you can narrow your focus to things the evidence supports. For example, instead of "I'm a good person," you might say, "I am an empathic listener and supportive friend." Instead of "I am smart," you may try, "I am inquisitive" or "I am good at analyzing facts." Doing this also helps you identify moments where you can demonstrate these qualities, thus reinforcing the belief even further.

Uphold Your Values

In chapter 5, we worked on identifying your ikigai—the thing that gives your life a sense of meaning and purpose. While performing this exercise, you had to identify things important to you, some of which could be described as your core values. Values are what you deem most important to a meaningful life. They are the things you focus on and want to uphold, and they likely also describe what you value in other people. Examples include (but are certainly not limited to) justice, honesty, family, compassion, curiosity, loyalty, wisdom, and faith, and they can manifest themselves in different ways. For instance, someone who values honesty makes a habit of telling the truth and being open with people, even if it's uncomfortable or inconvenient, while someone who values curiosity is diligent about seeking out new information and asking questions to fully understand a subject they're interested in. People typically value multiple things, but it can be helpful to identify your top five or six most important values so you can better maintain them and use them to guide decision-making. For example, someone who values achievement and recognition may make a vastly different decision about their career than someone who prioritizes personal expression and creativity.

When developing your affirmation practice, consider how you have demonstrated your core values in the past and how you *want* to demonstrate them going forward. For instance, if you value friendship, you may say something like "I value my friends by making time for them and listening to them when they need me" or "I consistently affirm and support my friends." Reminding yourself of your values, as the studies referenced earlier in this chapter show, is a powerful reminder of who you are as a person and can serve as a buffer against assaults to your ego.

Make Affirmations a Habit

Timing is key to helping affirmations stick. Studies show that affirmations are most effective before one is exposed to a threatening scenario or piece of information or immediately after (before one has had a chance to respond negatively to the situation). Knowing this, I recommend a daily affirmation practice so that you get in the habit of consistently affirming yourself—even if you're not currently struggling with a specific negative thought pattern. The great thing about affirmations is that they don't require a lot of time or energy and you can practice them anywhere. I like to practice them first thing in the morning, which can help set the tone for my day, and right before I go to bed at night, which helps refocus my brain before bed and relieve stress. In the morning, try reciting your affirmations while you get ready—maybe in the shower or while getting dressed. I like the process of habit stacking, in which one forms a new habit by doing it alongside other habits they already perform regularly. Maybe you can recite your affirmations while washing your face, making your morning coffee, or walking the dog—whatever helps you make the practice part of your daily routine. At night, I like to write things down in a journal, as this is also a good time to write about moments in your day that supported your affirmations and in which you acted in line with your core values.

Revisit Your Core Beliefs Often

Think about what core beliefs you've been carrying around and trying to shift. Perhaps, like Priya, you believe that you are not physically attractive. Or maybe you feel unworthy of love or untalented in most areas of your life. You may not be able to flip these assertions around overnight—perhaps even ever—but chances are you can find evidence that refutes them. For example, when I first asked my previous client Jake what he liked about himself, he was unable to think of a single thing. But as we worked together, he started paying closer attention to moments in which he felt good about himself. For example, he noticed that he felt good whenever he interacted with his niece and nephew; he enjoyed playing with them, and it was clear the feeling was mutual. Jake was then able to identify with the affirmation "I am a good uncle," which in turn made it easier for him to identify the ways in which he was lovable. By the time we finished working together, he still wasn't confident stating the blanket affirmation "I am lovable," but he was also no longer confident saying the opposite; there was just too much evidence to the contrary, and at this point, the idea that he was unworthy of love did not hold as much power over his psyche.

The same thing happened with Priya. The more she called out attributes about herself that she liked and the more confident she became overall, the harder it became for her to say "I am not beautiful" and believe it. Her affirmation practice had shifted her brain's belief system—with minimal focus on her most persistent and bothersome beliefs. As you practice your affirmations, check in with yourself regularly to question your old beliefs. How do you feel saying them now? Have they lost some of their power over you?

Connect with Others

While self-affirmation is a useful tool, you can also use affirmations to help bolster the people around you and improve the quality of your relationships. If you're familiar with the five love languages, you've heard about "words of affirmation." But regardless of whether you or your partner identify this as your love language (or identify with the concept of love languages at all), literally all relationships can benefit from consistent affirmation between partners.

Because humans are social creatures, our sense of self-worth is intrinsically tied to how others perceive us. When we feel like that worth is being challenged through either direct feedback (such as being openly criticized) or indirect feedback (such as the person you're on a date with yawning when you tell them a story about yourself), we can become defensive or put up barriers that impede effective communication. Studies show, however, that when trying to resolve conflict with your partner, you can help reduce tension and build trust and openness by affirming their positive qualities.

This need not be a formal practice like your self-affirmation routine in order for it to be effective. It does, however, need to be consistent, specific, and genuine. We often take for granted that people know how much we care about them, but given that we are all prone to focus on what's going wrong in our lives, it's easy to lose sight of the good. We all know what it feels like at the beginning of a romantic relationship or friendship; we consistently give and receive feedback to the other person about how much we enjoy their company and admire and respect them. But the longer the relationship lasts and the less novel your interactions become, the easier it is to slide into comfortable routines that lack spontaneity and this feeling of constant affirmation. Combine that with the regular stress of life, not to mention the routine conflicts or misunderstandings that arise in long-term relationships, and you find yourself in a situation where both parties may begin to feel insecure about their standing with each other.

In order to avoid this, look for opportunities to affirm your loved ones and remind them how much they mean to you. Of course, it's always nice to hear "I love you," but it's often even more meaningful to point out what in particular you love about that person. You might tell them how much you appreciate the way they listen or never fail to make you laugh. You might acknowledge the work they put into to a specific effort or task—or even just how much they clearly care about your relationship. Psychologist, author, and marriage counselor John Gottman calls this process "sharing fondness and admiration" and describes it as one of the fundamental building blocks couples need in order to establish a sound, long-lasting relationship. Don't worry if this feels awkward at first. When I started to do this with my husband, he would look at me, laugh hesitantly, and say, "Are you being serious right now?" We had been stuck in our comfort zones and routines for so long that I assumed he already knew all the things I valued about him, but when I started to actually point them out, he thought I was being sarcastic or making a joke! But that's okay: His reaction just showed me that I needed to start affirming him even more.

I see this come up a lot with couples, especially those in long-term relationships. It's actually kind of heartbreaking. More often than not, whenever I'm working with a couple and ask one partner to say out loud what they think the other person loves about them, they can't answer. We so often take for granted that other people know how we feel about them, but everyone needs reminding sometimes, and it can be a truly beautiful way to reconnect with someone and reaffirm your bond. Also, research shows that when we affirm someone else's positive qualities, they tend to lean further into those positive qualities, essentially making even more of an effort to live up to your opinion of them and their sense of self. It's a win-win!

If you have kids—or young people in your life with whom you are close—you can also use affirmations with them. One of the great things about using this practice with kids is that they are usually more prone to believe positive affirmations than older people. They haven't yet had many blows to their ego, and their brains are a lot more malleable than those of adults. Some of my favorite kid-friendly affirmations include:

I can do hard things, and I will keep trying.
I am important and my voice matters.
I love myself just the way I am.
I am unique, and that makes me special.
I am kind, smart, and loved.
I am a good friend, and I treat others with kindness.
I believe in myself and am proud of who I am.

Choose Your Words Carefully: Shift Your Language to Boost Optimism

While affirmations are an excellent way to focus your attention on your most positive attributes so you can boost your self-esteem, you must also pay attention to how you talk to yourself throughout the other 99 percent of your day. Doing so can make a huge difference in how you look at the world, and you may be surprised by how much your language is causing your perspective to be more pessimistic than you'd like it to be.

If you were raised in a certain generation, you probably grew up hearing the phrase "Sticks and stones may break my bones, but words will never hurt me." Mostly used as a way to dismiss playground bullying and to buck up a kid's confidence if they were being teased, this oft-recited phrase conveyed that, unlike physical violence, words can't hurt people, so it's best to just ignore them and move on with your life. Unfortunately, this is simply not true. Anyone who has ever been called a nasty name or, worse, a slur, or has spent hours analyzing the tone of an email or text knows that words do indeed have an immense power to wound—and the way we use them matters.

In fact, thanks to researchers who study the intersection between psychology, culture, cognition, and language, we know a lot about how language impacts our perspective and the way we interpret the world. Did you know that the language you speak can impact the way you interpret direction, count, mark the passing of time, and relate to other people? Words are not simply our way to communicate what we observe in the world; they can also change the very nature of those observations in the first place.

What's more, the words we use can literally induce pain and affect our physical state. Several studies have shown that the mere act of being exposed to pain-related words or imagery can mimic or magnify the experience of actual pain stimuli. In one study, participants who were primed with pain-related words like *excruciating* and *grueling* while being asked to perform a simple task showed elevated activity in the areas of the brain that process pain. In another, subjects who were exposed to pain-related or otherwise negative words while being given a mild electrical shock reported more intense pain than those who were exposed to neutral or positive words. Meanwhile, the language that doctors, caregivers, or other health professionals use with patients can influence their recovery times and their overall experience with their condition. For example, patients suffering from musculoskeletal issues report faster recoveries and better long-term outcomes and are less prone to disability when their doctors use neutral, positive, and plain language to describe their conditions. This is as compared to patients whose doctors use the overly scientific, often confusing and foreboding language that is often taught in medical school. Similarly, people who struggle with mental illness or addiction often avoid seeking treatment when exposed to stigmatizing language about their condition because they are ashamed to associate themselves with it. By contrast, when caregivers use neutral, person-first language (for example, "a person suffering from schizophrenia" rather than "a schizophrenic") they are more likely to seek and receive the treatment they need because they have been primed to feel less shame.

The same principles hold true for the language we use with ourselves. As we've discussed, the language you use to describe various circumstances can determine how optimistic or pessimistic you are. People who describe negative or suboptimal events as pervasive, permanent, and personal tend to be more pessimistic than those who describe those same events as situational, temporary, and beyond their control. After being late to an important meeting due to unusually bad traffic, the pessimistic person will throw up their hands and say, "Ugh! What a terrible day! It's *always* something, isn't it? Of course there would be an accident on the one day I can't afford to be late to work. I have the worst luck!" A more optimistic person, on the other hand, may still experience frustration and disappointment but shrug the event off as a normal everyday case of unfortunate luck. "Wow. It really sucks that I was late today. Next time I have a meeting like this, I'll make sure to check traffic and leave a little early just in case."

My four-year-old is currently in a stage where he uses words like *never* and *always* a lot. I know this is developmentally appropriate for kids his age, since they are still learning how to make sense of the world and manage their emotions, but I also know that kids often mimic what they see and hear. I try to be extremely particular about how I use these all-or-nothing phrases, since I know how suggestive they can be, but hearing him say these things helps me realize that maybe my husband and I are using them more than we think we are and need to be more conscientious. At the same time, whenever Dio uses these phrases, I try to use them as teachable moments, directing him to look at the situation in a different, more optimistic way.

I've also started asking my older kids to point out when I do or say things I'm trying to stop, and they take the job *very* seriously. For example, just the other day, I was struggling to open a jar while trying to make dinner for all three kids while Alex was out of town for work. I could not get the damn thing open, and in a burst of frustration, I said, "Ugh! I can't do this! I am never going to figure this out!" I didn't realize anyone was listening until I heard Dio call to me from across the room: "I think you can do it, mama. Just try again three more times. You'll get it." Isn't it amazing how kids can be a mirror and teach us things without even realizing it?

You'd be surprised what even a subtle shift in language can do to improve your mood and outlook. In early 2020, at the start of the shutdowns and quarantine spurred by the Covid-19 pandemic, I found myself grumbling incessantly about how I was "stuck at home." *This sucks!* I thought at least three dozen times a day. *When will this be over?* As a result, I started thinking of all the things I would rather be doing—going for a walk in my neighborhood, meeting friends for tea, taking Jag to the beach, having date night with my husband, and so forth. With no end to the pandemic in sight, I grew increasingly depressed and despairing at the thought of being trapped in my house for the indefinite future.

Then one day I decided to take a page out of my own optimist's handbook and flip the script on its head. Instead of complaining that I was stuck at home, I started taking comfort in the fact that I was safe at home. This one-word change made a huge difference. It didn't change the circumstances at all—we were still very much forced to stay at home—but it changed my perspective, which then changed my thoughts, emotions, and behaviors. Instead of dwelling on all the things I felt like I was missing out on, I began expressing gratitude that I had a home to quarantine in, that I had a job that I could (mostly) do remotely, that my family was healthy and had good healthcare, and that we would eventually get through this together.

As you go throughout your day, I challenge you to pay attention to the language you use with yourself and others. Pay attention to the ways you internalize and exacerbate negativity while downplaying positive events, news, and interactions. Try reframing how you describe those situations to yourself using more optimistic language. How does it make you feel? Here are some examples:

Shifting Perspectives: Pessimism to Optimism

"They're so much better than me."
➙ *"I'm on my own unique path, and that's enough."*

"I can't handle the pressure."
➙ *"Pressure helps me rise and perform at my best."*

"I don't know what to do; it's too uncertain."
➙ *"Uncertainty is an opportunity to explore and grow."*

"The future seems hopeless."
➙ *"The future holds endless possibilities."*

"I can't handle rejection."
➙ *"Rejection is redirection to something better."*

"This problem is too big."
➙ *"I can break this problem into smaller steps."*

"I made a mistake."
➙ *"Mistakes help me grow."*

"They probably don't like me."
➙ *"I can connect authentically."*

"This is taking forever."
➜ *"I can make steady progress."*

"I'm not good enough."
➜ *"I have unique strengths."*

"Nothing ever goes my way."
➜ *"Opportunities are in every situation."*

"I always fail at this."
➜ *"Every failure is a chance to learn."*

CHAPTER 8

"Trust Your Gut"

Reconnect with Your Intuition to Improve Decision-Making

Your intuition isn't lost; the world has just become too loud. Trust that beneath the noise is a knowing that never left you.

When I first noticed the red mark above Dio's eye, I assumed it was a scratch. Like many siblings, Dio and Jag are always wrestling with each other, so it was perfectly reasonable for me to think they'd gotten a little rough one afternoon and Dio had bumped his head on something. But when the mark got bigger after a few days, I decided to make an appointment with our pediatrician.

"It looks like an infection," she told us, as she wrote Dio a prescription for antibiotics. I'm no doctor, but everything I knew about the body told me that this was something else. Dio wasn't in any pain, there was nothing oozing out of his eye, and he wasn't running a fever, all of which are symptoms of an infection. She told me that we should notice an improvement within forty-eight hours, but when I didn't notice any improvement at all within twenty-four hours, I was right back at her office. She gave us a different antibiotic, but when that one didn't work, it confirmed my suspicions: If he had an infection, shouldn't antibiotics take care of it? At a loss, our pediatrician referred us to an ophthalmologist, who said the mark looked like an abscess and that oral antibiotics don't usually work on those. She suggested we try an intramuscular antibiotic and observe it for another day. The next morning, when we still didn't notice an improvement, we took Dio to the ER.

The ER doctor laid out a few options—more antibiotics (this time intravenous) and surgery so they could determine if it was in fact an abscess and then drain it—but I hesitated. I wasn't thrilled at the idea of dosing my toddler with even more drugs and putting him under the knife for what might turn out to be no reason. "Shouldn't we know what it is before we try more interventions that might not work?" I asked. "Can't we run more tests just to be sure?"

It may sound like my hypochondria was getting the better of me, but ironically, I actually thought we had nothing to worry about. I wanted to get more tests because I thought they would confirm the red mark (and now swelling) was nothing serious and we wouldn't have to put Dio through any more unnecessary procedures. We just needed to stop guessing and figure out what was actually going on.

"We could do a CT scan," the ER doctor explained. "But I would strongly advise against it. Dio is still really small. I worry that a heavy dose of radiation would be riskier for him than any of the other treatments we could try right now. The choice is ultimately yours, of course, but I have two kids of my own, and, if I were you, I would not choose a CT scan in this scenario."

I could feel a nervous energy swirling in my gut as I let all this sink in. I am a woman of science. With few exceptions, I trust doctors, and I'm certainly not presumptuous enough to think I know more about medicine than they do. I didn't have any alternative explanations or solid reasons to ignore the doctor's advice. And yet something inside me was telling me to go ahead and get the CT scan.

"Babe, I think we should listen to the doctor," my husband, Alex, said. "He knows what he's talking about, *and* he's a dad. He wouldn't lead us astray."

"I know," I said. "But something in my gut is telling me that we need to be sure. I can't explain it, but I just know we're not supposed to ignore it, and that rushing into having some doctor we just met cut open his eye without truly knowing why doesn't feel right." I decided to call our pediatrician to get her opinion. She agreed that a CT scan made sense, and so, validated, I told Alex and we agreed to move forward.

To protect Dio's privacy, I don't want to get into the details of what happened next, but let's just say that we were *all* wrong. It wasn't an infection. It wasn't an abscess. And unfortunately it wasn't nothing. Still, the scan showed us what we needed to see in order to get Dio the right treatment—and quickly. If I hadn't listened to my gut telling me to get the CT scan, who knows how much time we might have wasted—and how many surgeries Dio would have had to endure—before we got to the bottom of the diagnosis?

I'm sure at least a few of the doctors I encountered throughout this process thought I was just another anxious, overprotective mom, but I know myself, and I knew there was something else at work. Am I prone to hypochondria? Sure, I've been honest about that throughout this book. But over the years, as I've become more self-aware, I've developed a pretty solid gauge to determine if I'm merely being hypersensitive or if I'm actually onto something. Even if I feel anxious, I can usually talk myself out of doing anything drastic—drawing on my experience and judgment to quiet, if not totally silence, my racing thoughts. That's not what happened here. Some part of me *knew* the doctors were missing something, even though I couldn't explain why.

This is the power of intuition—that little voice in the back of our head or that nagging feeling in the pit of our stomach that seems to arise out of nowhere to give us important information we may not otherwise perceive. Through my work and firsthand personal experiences, I have come to appreciate that intuition is one of the most powerful tools we have at our disposal—and one of the most misunderstood. Many of us have been taught to doubt our intuition based on the assumption that it is unreliable and irrational, rooted more in feelings than in facts. But this could not be further from the truth. Research shows us that our intuition is an essential and sophisticated process that can help us make decisions, keep us safe, and lead us toward our goals.

When we learn how to trust our intuition, we learn how to trust ourselves. We become more attuned to our feelings, values, and desires, and we develop the ability to navigate the world with purpose, authenticity, and curiosity. We become more optimistic and resilient because we know that no matter what life throws our way, we can use our intuitive knowledge to figure out how to respond in a way that works best for us.

In order to tap into the full power of our intuition, we first need to understand what it is (and what it isn't) and when it can help us the most. Once we can appreciate the role that intuition plays in our lives, we can develop it to be most effective. Like optimism, intuition acts like a muscle, growing stronger and more reliable the more you use it. The better you get at working this muscle, the easier it is to use when you need it most.

Think Fast: The Science of Intuition

Everyone has intuition, and whether we're aware of it or not, it is always working. It's working when we meet someone new and get the feeling that we should get to know them better or avoid them at all costs. It's working when we try to make complicated decisions, like whether to accept a new job in another city or to move in with our significant other. It's working in mundane everyday decisions, like whether to take the long way or the short way home; or in potentially life-threatening situations, like whether to leave an interaction that is making us feel unsafe.

Unfortunately, we live in a world that often interferes with our intuition. Intuition works only when we listen to it, and it is exceptionally difficult to listen to anything—let alone a subtle alert deep within our consciousness—when we are always distracted. From the moment we wake up in the morning until the point we go to bed at night (and sometimes even while we sleep), someone or something is vying for our attention. I was born in the early 1980s, and for the first half of my life, boredom was a pretty regular part of my day. If I was standing in line at the mall or waiting for my mom to pick me up from somewhere, I couldn't just call a friend or turn on my favorite podcast. Instead I was forced to be alone with my thoughts and pay attention to my surroundings. Now, thanks to social media, the twenty-four-hour news cycle, emails, text messages, group chats, streaming services, and a seemingly infinite number of apps and sources of entertainment, I can be stimulated 24/7. These days, I actually have to stop myself from texting the second I pull up at a stoplight or scrolling through Instagram while waiting for a friend at a restaurant. In fact, the only time I'm *not* attached to my phone is in the shower (though I definitely know people who take their phone into the shower with them!). At all other times, I have to actively force myself to disconnect. I don't expect this reality is going to change anytime soon, but trust me, we were not meant to live this way!

If it wasn't bad enough that we're so easily and often distracted, we're also usually stressed. While our earliest ancestors had to worry about getting attacked by hungry predators, the events that triggered their stress response were usually nearby and immediate. Sure, daily life is much less dangerous in the twenty-first century (at least for most of us in developed countries), but we are also much more aware of all the threats—immediate and projected, real and imagined, around the corner and halfway around the globe—that exist in our world. We basically spend our days in a constant state of fight or flight, our minds constantly racing and our cortisol spiking at every new text message, notification, or alert. To put it not so subtly, our sympathetic nervous systems are raging! Under these conditions, it is nearly impossible to have a moment's peace. How can we learn to listen to the voice inside our head when it's constantly drowned out?

It doesn't help that society teaches us to trust logic, reason, and data more than gut feelings. Think about it. Have you ever talked yourself out of trusting your gut because you told yourself you were being irrational, ridiculous, or silly? Have you ever dismissed that little voice or nagging feeling because you couldn't think of a single logical reason to listen to it? Even though most people have experienced the power of intuition, we've come to believe that it is inferior to our rational, analytical minds. Hunches and gut feelings may occasionally be right, we're told, but without hard data and reasoning to support them, they're not worth all that much.

True, rational thought is critical for good decision-making. It's also what distinguishes us from every other living creature on the planet. Our ability to collect facts, learn from the past, analyze patterns, and draw conclusions means we are not beholden to instinct and habit alone. We can look at the situation before us, ask questions, examine old beliefs and assumptions, and use all the information we have at our disposal to decide what to do next. But when we dismiss intuition as irrational, unreliable, or inferior to this more deliberate type of thinking, we overlook the critical role it plays in lives.

One of the reasons we often downplay the importance of our intuition is that we misunderstand what it's trying to do. We confuse it with our primitive lizard brain—the part of us that operates on instinct and emotion alone. Because intuition often manifests as a gut feeling—similar to how we feel emotions physically within our bodies—and because it operates at the subconscious level—meaning we can't usually figure out *why* it's telling us to do the thing it's telling us to do—we tend to dismiss it as less trustworthy than our rational, conscious mind. But intuition is *not* just primal instinct, nor is it driven by emotion. It is a complex cognitive process that works in tandem with our rational, conscious mind to help us interpret loads of information quickly, efficiently, and, hopefully, accurately.

Thanks in large part to the work of the Nobel Prize–winning behavioral economist and cognition expert Daniel Kahneman, scientists now understand that humans engage in two very different but equally important types of thinking. The first type, which Kahneman calls System 1 thinking, happens automatically, immediately, and subconsciously. It is informed by all the information we have amassed over our lives (whether that information is accurate or not) and helps us quickly process large amounts of complex information so we can make decisions more efficiently. System 1 helps us recognize an acquaintance from behind while walking down the street, memorize our route to the grocery store, and assess whether the new restaurant downtown fits the vibe check for date night.

The second type of thinking, known as System 2, is slower, conscious, and more analytical and effortful. System 2 is what we think of when we describe our rational minds, cognitive thinking, or reason. We engage in System 2 thinking when we work out a math problem, analyze a spreadsheet, prepare a speech or presentation, or compare the specifications of various car models before deciding which one to buy. While System 2 may seem more evolved, deliberate, and error-proof, the fact is, we almost always engage in both types of thinking whenever faced with a decision, and both are equally important for us to thrive. Without the efficiency of System 1, we would constantly have to analyze every situation as if it were completely novel—even if it's something we've encountered hundreds of times before. Without the discipline of System 2, we'd never pause to consider any new information we receive; we'd jump to conclusions based on first impressions, ingrained biases, and old information that might not be accurate.

Biases, habits, rules of thumb (what psychologists call heuristics), and other types of mental shortcuts are all examples of System 1 thinking. But intuition is unique because, in addition to being subconscious, complex, and quick, it is also informed by all the information, wisdom, experience, and beliefs we have acquired throughout our lives. While we are all born with a certain amount of intuition, our intuitive powers naturally expand as we get older and learn more about how the world works. In fact, research shows that as we age and our conscious cognitive faculties (System 2) start to decline, we rely on our intuition even more to make good decisions. Even though we may not be able to control when and how our spidey senses start to tingle whenever we have a choice to make, we *can* develop our intuition over time so that it becomes more robust and accurate when we need it. We do this by staying attuned to the world around us, assessing the outcomes of our decisions and actions, and giving ourselves the space to really *listen* to what our subconscious is trying to tell us.

When Intuition Works

While System 1 and System 2 thinking are both necessary, research shows that intuition, when used in certain contexts, can actually result in better decision-making than reason. Studies show that while more deliberate consideration is useful when the factors involved are relatively limited or straightforward, intuition is crucial when processing large amounts of complex data from which it may be more difficult to draw confident conclusions. In fact, several studies demonstrate that when people use intuition to parse complex—perhaps even conflicting—factors, they make better decisions and are more confident in and satisfied by those decisions than those who rely on critical thinking and analysis. For example, if you're at the grocery store trying to figure out what kind of bread to buy, you'll probably make the best decision by comparing the ingredients, nutritional information, and price of a few varieties. You'll probably also consider which type of bread you like best, how familiar you are with the brand, and what you're using the bread for. Maybe a crustier bread is better for eating with soup or a saucy pasta, but something softer is better for your toddler's PB&J. There's no need to bring intuition into the mix here because the information you need is clear and readily available. Plus, the downsides of making a bad choice are pretty minimal.

On the other hand, if you're weighing something more complex, like which house to put an offer on, you'll probably want to factor in the practical aspects of the decision alongside more ephemeral things. Sure, you'll want to consider things like the cost of the mortgage, the amount of the down payment, property taxes, necessary renovations, the safety and livability of the neighborhood, the quality of the school district, and a bunch of other characteristics that you can easily quantify and compare; you don't want to rely solely on blind faith for such a huge decision. But you also might just get the sense that one place *feels* more like home than the others. Maybe you automatically envision yourself living in the area for the long term or get a good vibe from the neighbors—all with little to no evidence as to why. If the facts alone don't lead to an obvious choice or you sense some unseen force pulling you in one direction or another, you'll likely be happier with your ultimate choice if you at least try and figure out what that force is trying to tell you.

In some cases, rationality can actually get in the way of sound decision-making. Research shows that while conscientious analysis works best in stable, predictable environments, intuitive thinking results in better outcomes in unstable or unpredictable ones. For example, in one survey, researchers found that intuitive decision-making among managers corresponded with strong financial performance in highly competitive and speculative industries, like computing, but was negatively associated with financial performance in more stable, established industries like banking and utilities. Another study from the business world showed that while all managers rely on their intuition to a certain extent, it tends to become more important at higher levels of an organization where decisions become more strategic and less straightforward. When faced with unprecedented or tumultuous circumstances—when you're not confident the usual rules apply or the traditional way of doing things will get you where you want to go—you can benefit from looking inward for guidance on the correct path to take.

What's more, despite the popular belief that it is irrational or unreliable, intuition is far from the domain of the unskilled and uneducated. In fact, multiple studies show that experts rely on intuition within their domain of expertise more than those who are less experienced. As a result, they tend to make sounder, more confident decisions. For example, chess grandmasters can spot better, more strategic moves more quickly than less experienced players. Likewise, fire ground commanders—highly experienced firefighters responsible for figuring out the best way to combat an active fire—can usually determine the best strategy within an extremely short period of time and without having to weigh multiple options. Because these experts have spent so many years studying and amassing experience within their specific field, they have accumulated a ton of information about how decisions within that field usually play out. As a result, they are extremely adept at recognizing patterns and scenarios and drawing on their existing knowledge to decide what to do next.

The relationship between expertise and intuition explains why we may feel strong, inexplicable gut feelings in certain circumstances but not in others. For example, you may feel confident arguing against your colleagues at work, even if they all agree on a specific issue, because some unconscious part of you is signaling that they're wrong. Or you may decide to end a date early because the other person is giving you the creeps—and your subconscious is reminding you of times in the past when you've ignored that feeling and regretted it. But if you feel out of your depth on a particular topic, you may feel less inclined to push back, understanding that even if you have questions or doubts, your intuition might be leading you astray. This is essentially what happened before Dio was diagnosed. I knew my intuition was telling me something, but since I'm not a medical expert, I wasn't 100 percent confident it was right. This is why I ultimately sought a second opinion before making a final decision. While my intuition was off about exactly what was going on (remember, I thought the scan would confirm that nothing was wrong), it was right that what the doctors were telling me wasn't hitting the mark, either.

In these moments of fear, anxiety, and uncertainty, I have found that the only thing that helps is to turn toward my intuition. Whenever I feel overwhelmed, I close my eyes, find some stillness, and create a space to go within.

How to Tune Into Your Intuition

When you are faced with a choice—like uprooting your family and your life after a once-in-a-generation natural disaster in order to relocate to a safer neighborhood—your intuition will send you a signal that you can choose to heed or ignore. Here are a few guidelines to keep in mind, no matter the scenario.

Listen to Your Body

Just as your stomach rumbles when you're hungry or you may feel tension in your neck or shoulders when you're stressed out, your intuition often manifests itself as a physical sensation within your body when it is trying to get your attention. You may feel the hair on the back of your neck stand up, an unsettled feeling in the pit of your stomach (hence the term *gut feelings*), or some other sensation that arises in these moments. I know my intuition is at work whenever I feel a knot in my stomach, my heart starts racing, and my breath becomes shallow. I also sometimes get a tingly feeling at the base of my neck that tells me I need to take a pause. When this happens, I usually retreat to a familiar quiet place where I can be alone with my thoughts for a few minutes, like my car or, if possible, the shower.

If you're distracted, anxious, stressed, or experiencing other stimuli at the same time, you may not notice these feelings—or choose to ignore them if you do. But this is your intuition's way of getting you to notice it, so if you want to start listening to it, you need to figure out when it's trying to talk to you in the first place. When faced with an important decision, take a moment to pay attention to any peculiar sensations that arise within your body. How does this compare to the way certain emotions manifest in your body? Do you feel similar to the way you do when you're afraid? Anxious? Angry? Based on your previous experience with this feeling, what information is your subconscious trying to share?

Assess Your Experience

As we've discussed, intuition works best in areas where you have a lot of experience or wisdom. Therefore, even when you feel like your intuition is trying to lead you down a certain path, pause to consider whether you know enough about this specific domain for your gut to be reliable. If you're not an expert, you may be confusing intuition with bias, doubt, insecurity, trauma, or some other unconscious process that arises from old, incomplete, or incorrect information. This is why it's important to weigh both facts *and* feelings when making a decision.

Keep in mind that listening to your intuition doesn't mean automatically doing what it says. Sometimes, especially in situations where you feel out of your depth, this is an indication that you should ask for more information or seek help from someone with more expertise. This is what I did in the aftermath of the fires: I sought out as much expert information and perspective as I could find and tried to educate myself as much as possible. Then and only then was I able to trust that what my intuition was telling me was correct.

To be clear, you don't need a PhD to consider yourself an expert on a subject. In fact, one of the areas in which I have found intuition to be extremely helpful—for myself and others—is parenting. No parent in their right mind considers themselves an expert on raising children, and the amount of (often conflicting, sometimes downright wrong) information and advice that parents receive about child rearing can make even the most intelligent, capable, and self-assured individuals feel as though they have no idea what they're doing. Even people who work with children for a living—such as pediatricians, child-development specialists, therapists, or other highly educated experts and professionals—often admit to a lack of confidence when it comes to raising their own kids. Given the responsibility inherent in raising a child and the number of complex elements that can threaten a child's safety or development—not to mention the fact that every child is unique—it's no wonder parents feel overwhelmed by the choices they need to make every day. The reality is, there is no one right way to raise a child, and even though you may not be an expert on child rearing in the academic sense of the word, you are—or will eventually become—the foremost expert on your child and their specific needs and preferences.

Monitor Your Mood

Several studies show that intuition is strongest when we are in a good mood and weakest when we're in a bad one. In one study, participants who were induced to feel anxiety demonstrated less ability to rely on their intuition to make decisions than those who were in a positive or neutral state. When we feel strong unpleasant emotions, our attention focuses on whatever is triggering them. So next time you're faced with a complex problem or choice while you're in a bad mood, take some time to work through your emotions before moving forward. Not only will doing so prevent you from acting on impulse, but it will also hopefully give you the time and space to discern what your intuition is trying to say.

Pause (If You Can)

If your intuition and your rational mind are in conflict—or if you're not sure exactly what your intuition is trying to tell you—take a time-out before you make a final decision. Unlike emotions, which can shift from moment to moment, your intuition about a particular situation tends to linger as long as the facts of the situation stay the same. If you don't have to make a decision *right at this minute,* take a step back and see how you feel after a few hours or even days. Use the time to gather more information and consider whether some other force may be at work that you're confusing for intuition.

Whenever I get the little ping in the back of my neck that signals my intuition is trying to get my attention, I try to question myself a little bit before figuring out what to do next. Am I rushing this decision unnecessarily? Could I be confusing a cognitive bias or an unrecognized emotion for intuitive wisdom? Am I perhaps being too pessimistic—or even optimistic—about the situation? Maybe your alarm bells are jangling because someone is pressuring you, and your subconscious is warning you of their potentially selfish intentions. Or maybe you just feel overwhelmed and need more information or another opinion from a trustworthy source. Most of us aren't like action heroes, trying to figure out which wire to cut before the countdown ends and the bomb explodes; if you have the luxury of waiting, take advantage of it.

Reflect

When scientists conduct an experiment, they have to accept the results they get—even if these are unexpected or disappointing. The same is true for intuition. Even when your intuition gives you bad advice—or you misinterpret it and make a bad decision—you have an opportunity to learn something from the experience. How did your intuition factor into the choice you made? Did you interpret it correctly or was something else getting in the way? Now that you know the result of your decision, what did it teach you that you can apply the next time you face a similar situation? Taking the time to reflect on your decisions not only helps you sharpen your intuition but also gives you the opportunity to practice optimism by reinforcing the wisdom you've gained and the resilience you've built as a consequence.

The Intuition Habit: Prime Your Brain to Develop Your Inner Voice

As I said earlier, intuition, like optimism, is a muscle, which means you need to strengthen and condition it before you can get the most out of it. In addition to the steps above, which are designed to help you discern your intuition during critical decision-making moments, the steps below can help you develop the self-awareness necessary to nurture your intuitive senses. Think of these like training exercises that you can and should practice regularly.

Create Space to Be Alone with Your Thoughts

If you've ever spent time around a small child, you know that sooner or later they will start to complain: "I'm *bored*!" The human mind is always at work, so it's no wonder we constantly crave stimulation—something to focus our energy and attention. That's also why we often feel uncomfortable when left alone with our thoughts, especially if we're prone to anxiety spirals or are dealing with a particularly challenging or upsetting issue. And thanks to modern technology, we can choose to always be stimulated if we want to. But when we never make the effort to look inward, we cut ourselves off from the knowledge and self-awareness that allows us to proactively create lives of meaning, purpose, and joy. As I like to say, there is no time wasted in getting to know yourself. Sometimes we just have to be diligent about making that time a priority.

Luckily, you don't need to throw away your smartphone or unplug from the world in order to do this. In fact, if you pay attention, you will notice moments throughout the day where you can reclaim this space in easy but profound ways. Do you listen to podcasts while walking your dog or folding laundry? What might happen if you opted for silence during those times instead? Once upon a time, not so very long ago, if someone was commuting, they were completely unreachable. So what if you tossed your phone in the back seat or turned it off until you reached your destination? Maybe you'll miss a call or a message, but chances are the world won't end if you return it later. In the meantime, observe your surroundings, check in with yourself, or just let your mind wander—these habits can increase your ability to notice and interpret your intuitive senses when they arise.

One of my favorite places to tune into my intuition is the shower. Yes, yes, I know I've mentioned the shower before, but there's a reason for it! It's quiet; I'm usually alone; I'm relaxed and comfortable; I can engage all my senses; and since washing myself doesn't require a lot of concentration, I can let my mind wander freely. I used to listen to music while I showered, but now I relish the time I have alone with nothing to focus on but my thoughts or immediate surroundings. Sometimes I concentrate on a problem that needs solving or an upcoming project or conversation, or I let myself brainstorm new ideas for my business. Other times, I'll try to tune into my body, paying attention to the feel of my fingers shampooing my hair, the smell of my body wash, or the sound of the water, which always puts me in a tranquil state. Or I might just let my thoughts go wherever they please—and am often surprised by where they end up.

Ever since I started this practice, I'm amazed by how many breakthroughs I've had—all because I quieted the noise around me to let the voice inside me speak. For example, I was recently stuck for weeks on how to structure a workshop that a prominent global corporation had asked me to lead. Then one day, mid-shampoo, it came to me. The ideas just started flowing without my really trying at all. They actually came so quickly that I had to jump out of the shower soaking wet and record a voice note so I wouldn't forget.

Quiet Your Mind

If you're one of those people who can wake up first thing in the morning, cross your legs in lotus pose, and meditate for an hour and a half, then I salute (and am envious of) you. Unfortunately my mind is extremely active—and more than a little prone to anxiety—so I don't see this type of serenity in my future. I often compare my mind to a purse or a tote bag: every so often I clean it out and try to organize it—only to fill it back up with more things until all of a sudden it's cluttered again. The same is true of my mind: The second I try to empty it of one thought, another comes swooping in to fill the void. Fortunately, you don't need to have the mind of a monk in order to benefit from a regular meditation practice. As long as you are consistent and intentional, even a few short moments of Zen throughout the day can help you quiet the noise inside your head long enough to get in touch with your deepest self.

Commit to whatever length and frequency works for you, but if you're new to meditation or have grown frustrated with it in the past, I recommend starting with one to three minutes, three times a day. Choose whatever activity you prefer. I personally enjoy doing a short guided visual meditation, as we discussed in chapter 6, or the Adult I Spy exercise I described in chapter 3—basically anything intentional and active that allows me to refocus my thoughts instead of trying to banish them. For some other directed meditations, see the box below.

Three Meditation Exercises for Beginners

1. 4-7-8 Breathing
Breathe in for 4 counts, hold your breath for 7 counts, and release your breath for 8 counts. Repeat three times. This breathing pattern helps to reduce anxiety, relax the sympathetic nervous system, and regulate breath. It also helps to reduce emotional impulses so you can spend some time with and tune into your intuition.

2. Full Body Scan
Find a comfortable position, either sitting or lying down. Focus your attention on each part of your body, starting from either your head or your toes and working your way down or up, respectively. As you move through each part of your body, notice what, if any, sensations you are feeling and try to relax any tension. Paying attention to your

body this way helps quiet your thoughts and redirect your focus. It also helps you listen for signals your body may be sending that something is wrong or requires your attention.

3. Meditate Through Music

Pick a song—any song you like. Take the time to really *listen* to the full song. Pay attention to the beat, the instruments employed, and any changes in tempo or key. What are the lyrics saying? How does the song make you feel? Do you notice something you haven't noticed before? What do you notice?

Take Small Intuitive Risks

I have a terrible sense of direction. It's so bad that my family actually jokes that "If Deepika says we should go left, we should probably go right." The thing is, they're usually correct, but because I was born with a broken internal compass, I find navigation a useful way to practice my intuition.

A sense of direction is of course not the same as intuition, but it is a form of knowledge that we can develop—and that our modern world has largely disconnected us from. Ever since I was a teenager, I've outsourced my sense of direction. When I first started driving on my own, I'd print out directions from some early 2000s websites (raise your hand if you remember MapQuest!) and consult them periodically as I tried to figure out how to get to my best friend's house or the mall. Even though I had lived in the Los Angeles area all my life, I never felt confident making my way around town without step-by-step instructions, and now that I have a smartphone and a car with GPS, I basically never have to. However, as a result, I've also never had to pay attention to all the environmental cues—landmarks, the names and order of streets, the characteristics of each neighborhood, etc.—that could help orient me. I never acquired the knowledge that could have improved my sense of direction.

So now, whenever I'm taking an unfamiliar route and have a little time to spare, I try and figure out how to get where I'm going without relying on technology. To be honest, I'm still usually wrong, but every time I try, I notice something that will help me make a better decision next time. I feel less lost in my own city.

Doing this also helps sharpen my intuition because it forces me to rely on my own judgment and wisdom to make decisions. To be clear, I *do not* suggest going on vibes alone for big decisions or in situations where you're pressed for time or where the outcome could be dangerous. Rather, look out for moments where you can take small, low-stakes chances to follow your gut and then observe what happens next. Maybe you can put a small bet down on a football game based solely on who your gut is telling you will win (regardless of how much you know about the sport). Buy a book you've never heard of without reading reviews, or surprise your best friend with tickets to a concert you know nothing about. Do you feel compelled to talk to the person sitting across from you at the coffee shop? Or call up that person you met at the networking event because something tells you that maybe you could do business together?

A colleague of mine once told me a story about how she first met the person who would become her best friend on the subway in New York City. One morning, in the middle of rush hour, she noticed a woman about her age standing on the platform and reading a book by one of her favorite authors. "Something immediately struck me about this woman," she told me. "I can't explain it, but I just had the overwhelming urge to talk to her." At first, though, she hesitated. No one wants to be bothered by a stranger on their morning commute, and what if the woman got the wrong idea, assumed my colleague was hitting on her, and got uncomfortable? Her rational mind was trying to talk her out of it, but her gut was telling her to go for it. Still, she was self-conscious and didn't say anything, even though she kept seeing the woman on the same train platform for the next few days. Finally, after about a week, she worked up the courage to strike up a conversation. "I knew I'd kick myself if I didn't say something," she explained. "And what did I have to lose?" Flash-forward fifteen years later, and they're now extremely close and have even made additional new friends through one another. Clearly, my colleague's intuition was telling her that she and this stranger had something in common—and they did.

Stay Curious About Yourself

Because intuition is informed by our unique experience while being rooted deep within our subconscious, chances are it knows you better than you know yourself. How many times have you ignored your intuition only to realize it was telling you something you already knew—but maybe didn't want to admit—all along? The person you were dating may have looked great on paper, but your intuition knew they weren't the one for you. That job with the fancy title and fat paycheck sounded like a dream, but part of you always knew it wasn't the right choice for your goals and personality. Your intuition told you that you needed a night at home to yourself, but instead you accepted the invitation out of a sense of obligation and now you've spent time and money doing something that provided no value and maybe even drained you.

This happens when our System 1 and System 2 processes are disconnected from one another and our rational, conscious mind disregards our intuitive, subconscious one. The best way to resolve this conflict is to get clear on your most important values, needs, and desires so that you can better interpret what your intuition has to say. The ikigai exercise from chapter 5 is a great start, but don't stop there. Start a journal; ask yourself questions during your quiet, mindful moments; take stock of what brings you joy and what doesn't; talk to those close to you about your dreams and priorities. Whatever method you choose, stay curious and let your inner voice guide you to a more authentic, intuitive life.

CHAPTER 9

"We Never Fight!"

How Optimists Embrace Conflict to Cultivate Strong Relationships

The strength of a relationship isn't measured by how rarely you argue, but by the grace you extend to each other when you do.

When Alex and I got engaged, I (like most brides-to-be) couldn't wait to share the good news with everyone I knew. I told every friend and relative I could get a hold of and was met with the usual mix of "Congratulations!" and "I'm so excited for you!" Then came the questions. "What's he like?" they asked. "How do you feel?" "How did he propose?" "Have you set a date yet?"

Then I called my great-uncle. "That is wonderful news, Deepika," he told me. "Tell me about him."

"Oh, he's just so wonderful!" I exclaimed, grinning so widely my face actually hurt a little bit. "He is so kind, intelligent, funny, creative. He plays the guitar and was a college baseball player. We have the same favorite author, and he is always invested in working on himself and being better. He's such a good listener and is so caring and nurturing."

"That is all lovely," my great-uncle replied. "I am very happy for you. But now, tell me, how does he do under pressure or when things don't go well or his way? How does he act when you are in an argument or in a fight?"

This may seem like an odd—perhaps even a rude—question to ask someone who just got engaged. Who wants to think about fighting with your partner when you're head over heels in love?! Talk about a buzzkill! But as someone who has studied the science of relationships and worked with dozens of couples to help them overcome challenges together, I knew my great-uncle was trying to make an important point. Conflict is inevitable in every relationship. The difference between happy, long-lasting ones—whether they're with a romantic partner, a family member, or a friend—and those marked by dysfunction is not whether or how often the people within them fight; it's *how* they fight. Do they choose to bicker and get defensive? Do they try to avoid conflict altogether? Or do they approach disagreements with a sense of shared purpose, optimism, and respect?

How Conflict Strengthens Relationships

Human beings are wired for connection. We are, after all, social creatures. We literally could not survive, let alone thrive, without one another. Not only do we rely on other people to keep us safe and share resources, but we also need them emotionally. Anyone who has experienced the joy and satisfaction of a close personal relationship (or the pain and loneliness that comes when we lack these connections) knows this all too well. When we bond with someone in a way that makes us feel safe and supported and with whom we can be our authentic selves, our mood improves and our bodies relax. We are better able to cope with stress and are naturally more optimistic about our lives because we know we have the resources necessary to overcome whatever challenges life throws our way.

Science bears this out. Research shows that our relationships not only make us feel good but are essential to our mental and physical health. People who have multiple high-quality relationships live longer, are more satisfied with their lives, and are less likely to suffer from depression, anxiety, heart attacks, high blood pressure, strokes, and other ailments that negatively impact our well-being. A landmark study out of Harvard University that followed nearly three hundred former students (and later their families) over the course of nearly eighty years found that the quality of one's relationships was the number one factor that determined whether they were happy in old age. Another study found that close relationships are more directly associated with long-term well-being than money, fame, IQ, genetics, or social class.

Our relationships are so important, and yet research shows that Americans are currently in the middle of a loneliness epidemic. According to one survey, only 39 percent of Americans say they feel very connected to other people, and roughly half of American adults say they have experienced loneliness or isolation in recent years (even before the shutdowns and quarantine mandates caused by the Covid-19 pandemic in 2020). Commenting on these findings, Vivek Murthy, the former surgeon general of the United States wrote, "Social connection is a fundamental human need, as essential to survival as food, water, and shelter. Throughout history, our ability to rely on one another has been crucial to survival. Now, even in modern times, we human beings are biologically wired for social connection. Our brains have adapted to expect proximity to others." In other words, our relationships are as vital to us as breathing.

A key theme that emerges from all this research around human relationships is that it's not just the *number* of relationships we have that matters; it's the *quality* of those relationships. Quality connection arises when we can be our true selves around someone else without fear of reprisal, judgment, or rejection. We create space for that connection by being vulnerable with one another. Whenever we tell a story, disclose a secret, express an emotion, reveal a desire, or just generally share a fact about ourselves that not everyone gets a chance to hear, we are making ourselves vulnerable. And whenever another person responds to this gesture with love, acceptance, understanding, or praise, we build a sense of intimacy and trust with them that strengthens our connection. The more we do this—and the more we are rewarded for it emotionally—the better our relationships become.

Of course vulnerability also involves risks. As much as the act of opening ourselves up to someone offers an opportunity for connection, it also presents the possibility of rejection, pain, humiliation, judgment, and abandonment—all the things our socially wired brains are afraid of. This is why conflict is so uncomfortable: We know, even before an argument or disagreement starts, that whatever we're about to say or do might upset the other person. And because we're so afraid of how they might respond, our fight, flight, or freeze response often kicks in. We react defensively and selfishly, we shut down, or we may try to avoid the interaction altogether and pretend that nothing is wrong—all to preserve our sense of self and fight for our needs.

You probably know from experience that approaching conflict from a point of defensiveness usually just makes things worse. You say things you don't mean, start to resent the other person, withdraw your affection, insult or reject them, and generally just build up walls around yourself that discourage vulnerability and erode connection. After a certain amount of time, it's hard to tear down those walls, let alone repair the bond you once had.

Avoiding conflict is not better. I don't know how many couples I've worked with who tell me, "Oh! We have the perfect relationship! We never fight." Sure, everyone wants a peaceful household and a harmonious union, but fighting and conflict are not the same. Even if you don't fight or argue per se, if you spend enough time with someone—whether a romantic partner, a family member, a friend, or an acquaintance—you will eventually butt heads, fundamentally disagree about some issue or another, hurt each other's feelings, or just generally do something that pisses them off. Pretending otherwise is naive and sets you up for a massive disappointment when, inevitably, something upsetting happens and you don't know how to address it constructively. The ability to acknowledge and accept conflict is not a sign of weakness; it is a sign of real optimism, a demonstration of your belief that your relationships can withstand challenges and that people who love and care about you will respect your needs and emotions.

This is what my uncle was trying to get at by asking how Alex and I fight. When you learn how to fight optimistically, you improve your chances to build stable, quality relationships. As with any challenge, optimists see interpersonal conflict as something that can be overcome and managed, not as an intrinsic threat to their identity, safety, or the relationship itself. They also understand that even though conflict is uncomfortable, it provides an opportunity to deepen the relationship. If they and their partner can work together to come up with a solution, and if they can accept and appreciate each other's vulnerability, they will likely become even closer as a result. When people approach conflict with curiosity, empathy, and an eye toward resolution, instead of responding out of fear, anger, or defensiveness, they develop a deeper sense of trust and intimacy. They learn how to better communicate their needs, feelings, and desires to one another, and in turn gain a deeper understanding of what the other person needs from them in order for the relationship to thrive.

This is one of the reasons optimists have more fulfilling and stable relationships than people with more neutral or pessimistic outlooks. They know, as my uncle put it, how to fight. Studies show that when optimists engage in a disagreement with an intimate partner, they use more cooperative problem-solving tactics because they naturally perceive their partners as supportive and willing to work with them to arrive at a solution. In turn, their partners also behave more cooperatively because they, too, feel more confident and secure working through the conflict together. They can sense their partner's optimism about the situation and respond in kind. Another interesting point? It doesn't matter how supportive the optimist's partner actually *is*; as long as they trust that their partner has their back, they are more likely to act in a way that promotes productive problem-solving and leads to a satisfying resolution for everyone. As a result, both optimists and their partners report greater overall satisfaction within their relationships and are less likely to break up than partners who don't fight optimistically.

Fortunately, you don't have to be the most optimistic person in the world in order to fight like one. As long as you approach conflict with a sense of shared purpose and trust, you can weather even the most difficult conversations and issues that arise in your relationships. As a result, you will learn how to advocate for your own needs, desires, and values while simultaneously deepening your connections and enjoying all the amazing benefits that will come as a result.

Fight Like an Optimist

Below are some guidelines that help promote optimism during conflict. When I work with two people who are in a relationship with each other (whether it's romantic, platonic, familial, or professional), I like to guide them through each of these steps together, but you don't need a professional counselor or therapist in order to reap the benefits of these exercises. Also, an important point: Don't wait until you're in a fight to do this. Think of it like preparing for a hurricane. You don't board up the windows, hoard bottled water, and buy a backup generator after the storm hits landfall; you do so in advance so you're protected if and when you need to be. The same is true for the storms that happen in relationships. You want to figure out the best way to resolve conflict when you're happy and at peace with each other, not when emotions are high or something has upset the status quo.

If it helps, write down the agreements and commitments you make with each other so you can ensure you're on the same page, commit them to memory, and refer back to them when necessary. When you approach conflict in this way, you're essentially building a contract that outlines how you promise to fight with each other—how you literally agree to disagree.

1. *Reframe conflict as an opportunity.* Optimists understand that conflict is inevitable, but instead of looking at it as a sign of dysfunction or a threat to their sense of self, they see it as an opportunity to strengthen their relationships through collaborative problem-solving and mutual vulnerability. They also see it as a chance to advocate for themselves and build their personal resilience, regardless of the ultimate outcome. This latter consideration is key, because even if you have the best intentions, you can't control how someone else responds. You may be the most patient and effective communicator on the planet, but not everyone has the same tools at their disposal to meet you where you are. Optimism can help you resolve conflict, but it also gives you the confidence to know that you'll be fine if things don't work out exactly like you planned.

Next time you find yourself in a contentious situation, try looking at it through the lens of opportunity and hope instead of fear. A subtle shift in perspective from "What if this ruins our relationship?" to "We can get through this together" can have a profound impact on what you do next.

2. *Remember to respect.* When you're angry, afraid, stressed out, or upset, it's easy to resort to shameful behaviors you would otherwise never tolerate. When you get caught up in emotions, you may lash out or say something you don't mean—just because you're hurting and don't know how to process all the thoughts and feelings rushing through your head. If you feel your emotional temperature rising or find yourself fighting the urge to say or do something you know you'll regret, one of the best—and easiest—things to do is to simply remind yourself who you're talking to. Take a moment to look at the person across from you and say to yourself, "This is someone I love. I don't want to hurt them." This will direct your attention away from all the angry, emotionally charged thoughts pinging around your head and toward finding a possible solution. All of a sudden, your goal shifts from trying to get your point across and defending yourself toward trying to resolve the situation in a way that works for everyone (and without escalating the conflict by saying and doing things you don't mean).

Once you've done this, it will immediately become easier to communicate in a respectful, less emotionally charged way. Language has power. Choosing words and phrases that convey your needs while acknowledging the needs of the other person will defuse any tension and signal to your partner that you care about them and are ready to fix the situation.

Remember the 3 Ps of pessimism? While optimists frame challenges as temporary and surmountable, pessimists see them as permanent, pervasive, and personal. So if you want to fight like an optimist, avoid words and phrases that convey any contentious aspects of the situation in this way. An accusation like "You never help me out around the house!" or "You're so self-involved!" will immediately put someone on the defensive, making it even less likely that they'll hear what you're trying to say or that you'll come to a resolution. On the other hand, sharing that "sometimes I feel overwhelmed by everything that has to get done, and it angers me when you go to play pickleball with your friends instead of asking if I need help" allows them to see your perspective without accusing them of doing anything intentionally hurtful or malicious. They don't need to get defensive because you're not accusing them of anything. Another strategy is to use *we* statements (for example, "Can we discuss a way to avoid this in the future?" or "We both have so much going on, and we both need time to relax. Let's figure out how we can help each other out"). These promote collaboration and a feeling that you're in this together instead of at odds.

3. *Give grace*. When people feel threatened, they get defensive. And when people get defensive, they fight back. They say horrible things to one another, sling false accusations (that they usually know are false), raise their voices, slam doors, or do other things they might eventually (if not immediately) regret. While emotions don't excuse bad behavior, they usually explain it—and everyone deserves a little grace. If your relationship is built on mutual love and respect and you are committed to preserving it, you need to be able to forgive each other and move past these moments. If someone says or does something hurtful, but you know deep down that they're only acting on emotion, remind yourself that it's not personal and try to move on. This is of course a whole heck of a lot easier said than done, but you'll be surprised how freeing it can be to let this negative energy go instead of holding on to it so tightly it hurts.

To be clear, giving grace is not the same as accepting a pattern of disrespect or abuse. Nor does it mean that you don't deserve an apology. It's more an exercise in extending compassion and grounding yourself so you don't lose sight of what you're trying to accomplish. If you can't forgive the people you love, anger and resentment will fester and the relationship will break down.

4. *Identify and respect triggers*. I am very long-winded. I tend to repeat myself or overexplain things—especially if I'm anxious or emotional—and this drives Alex crazy. If I repeat myself after he's already acknowledged that he understands what I'm trying to say, he feels like I don't trust him or am accusing him of not listening—or that I'm not listening to him—and then he gets upset. When we first got together, these opposing communication styles often got in the way of us resolving whatever initial conflict we were trying to solve. Fortunately, over time, we've both come to understand what the other person needs during these times and have both gotten better at respecting and acknowledging each other's triggers: I need reassurance that he's heard me, and he needs me to trust that he has.

We all have things that trigger us, especially when our emotions are already high. Maybe a caregiver you had as a kid used certain language or tactics that now remind you of feeling embarrassed, criticized, or hurt. Maybe you were scarred by a previous relationship in which you learned to equate conflict with abandonment or abuse. Or maybe you come from a cultural background in which certain behaviors (like raising one's voice) were unacceptable, but your loved one grew up in a household where those things were totally normal—perhaps even modeled or encouraged. While it's not fair—to yourself or anyone else—to be beholden to these triggers or to use them as excuses for bad behavior, it's also not fair to ignore or dismiss them. Pay attention to what sparks your stress response and try to communicate this to those closest to you. Encourage them to do the same. Simply pausing to acknowledge you are triggered can help lower the temperature of a situation and refocus everyone's energy on working toward a solution.

One of the biggest potential triggers I've seen in relationships involves communication style. Some people are adept at acknowledging and articulating conflict in the moment, while others prefer to take a step back and compose their thoughts—perhaps even writing them out and sharing them with the other person before discussing it face-to-face. While different communication styles aren't inherently triggering, they can cause a lot of strife—not to mention a breakdown in communication.

5. *Choose a safe word.* No, not *that* kind of safe word. Yes, I'm sure you know the term *safe word* in the context of sex, and there's a good reason. When partners agree to engage in BDSM or other activities that can potentially cause pain, discomfort, or even psychological harm, it's critical that they agree in advance about what is and isn't allowed. To make sure that no one crosses a line, they also come up with a safe word that any party can say if they want the action to stop. This allows everyone to have fun, relax, and experiment while ensuring that no one feels unsafe or pressured to do something they don't want to do.

Now hear me out: Safety is also critical when it comes to everyday interpersonal conflict. In order to work through a challenge together, both parties have to feel safe expressing their needs, desires, and emotions without fear of retribution or harm. By working through all the steps I've outlined above, you've essentially created a pact for how to do just that. But even if you've agreed on how you're going to disagree, it can be easy to forget those guidelines when tensions are high. Your safe word is a shortcut to remind you of the commitment you've made to each other—a lighthouse guiding you back to shore in the middle of the storm.

Pick a word that you wouldn't usually use in conversation—maybe *mashed potato* or *lampshade* or *giraffe*. If you sense conflict arising or if an argument is starting to get heated, say the word, take a deep breath, and allow yourself and the other person a moment to remember your agreement. You may technically be saying *mashed potato,* but what you're really saying is "I remember what is at stake here. I love and respect you, and I want to find a resolution to this problem. Even though I am upset and frustrated, I will not go below the belt. We will get through this together."

Not only does the safe word remind you of your commitment to resolve conflict, but it also refocuses your attention on what you're *actually* trying to accomplish. One moment you may be seething because your friend canceled plans at the last minute, but once you've interrupted that train of thought, you'll understand that what you actually want to say is that you're feeling lonely or going through a difficult time and you need your friend to understand how important their presence and support is during this time.

To be clear, while a safe word is designed to protect both parties from harm, it does not protect anyone from consequences. You can't confess to your spouse that you've been cheating on them for six months, shout "Bermuda!" and expect immediate forgiveness. If, however, the conversation that follows starts to get ugly and you're committed to doing whatever you can to save your marriage, you can say it and hopefully help avoid making a bad situation worse.

I've also found safe words to be extremely helpful with children. My seven-year-old, Jag has always been really open and honest with me about what he's feeling or thinking—even if he's experiencing something new, confusing, or difficult. This is one of the things I love most about our relationship; he knows he can be vulnerable with me no matter what. At the same time, I understand that, as he gets older, that relationship might change. Peer pressure, hormones, and all of the other stressors that occur as kids grow up could challenge the easy intimacy we currently have. I want my kids to be able to tell me anything, so, as a preemptive measure, I recently decided he and I should have our very own safe word. I said to him, "Babe, there are going to be times when you might feel anxious or uncomfortable to tell me about something you did or a feeling you're having. And that's okay. And yes, sometimes there will be consequences, but I want you to know that no matter what, I will always love you. You are safe to tell me *anything*. Even if it's something you're not proud of." Then I suggested he and I come up with a safe word he could use whenever he wants to tell me something he's worried might make me upset. Now whenever he says our secret sacred safe word, I know that he's nervous and that I should be extra careful with my emotions and the way I talk to him in the next few minutes. It's a great practice because it reminds us both what we need from each other in that moment.

Keys to Your Heart: Scientific Secrets to Create Quality Relationships

One of the beautiful things about learning how to fight optimistically is that it helps deepen the quality of your relationships. When we create emotional safety within a relationship, we give ourselves permission to be vulnerable and express our true, authentic selves. This is how committed partnership forms. When we know we don't have to hide certain parts of ourselves to gain acceptance, when we feel loved and respected for who we *really* are, we develop a sense of security that allows us to move through the world with greater confidence and joy. This is the key to true well-being, and it is why our relationships are so critical.

Fortunately you don't have to wait for a disagreement to arise or start an argument in order to fortify this connection. Any time you spend with another person is an opportunity to increase emotional intimacy. Here's how.

Prioritize True Connection

Given how connected we are to one another in the virtual world (I would argue we're a bit *too* connected), it's easy to take for granted how much quality time we spend with the people closest to us. Strong relationships require intentional, meaningful, and—this is key—in-person interaction in order to thrive. Research shows that it takes ninety hours of time together to consider someone a friend—and two hundred hours to consider someone a close friend. People who hang out with friends multiple times a week are more likely to be satisfied with their lives than those who do so only once a week or a few times a month. People who meet less frequently are also less satisfied with the quality of their relationships and, by extension, less satisfied with their lives overall. Face-to-face interaction helps facilitate conversation because it allows us to better respond to verbal, visual, and social cues. By contrast, the lag time that occurs with digital communication makes it difficult for our brains to interpret information and stay engaged, which is vital for building connection. This helps explain why face-to-face communication is more closely associated with individual well-being than electronic communication, like social media. Another bonus to hanging out IRL? In-person gatherings create opportunities for physical touch. A warm hug, a literal shoulder to cry on, a hand to hold, an affectionate kiss on the cheek (or elsewhere . . .)—all of these boost our mood and increase intimacy.

One study out of the University of Kansas showed that just one high-quality interaction per day with a friend can increase happiness, and the more of these interactions you have, the better off you are. While face-to-face communication is more strongly associated with positive results, phone calls and electronic communication can also boost mood when used to facilitate quality conversation. Fortunately, in this case, quality doesn't necessarily mean deep or emotional or existential. Researchers classified seven types of conversations, all of which increased individuals' daily well-being and reduced stress: catching up, enjoying meaningful talk, joking around, showing care, listening, valuing others and their opinions, and offering sincere compliments. In other words, you don't need to force connection in order to foster it.

Even though it's important to prioritize your closest relationships, science shows that you can experience meaningful connection with just about anyone. While we usually think of our chats with the barista at our local coffee shop or the stranger in the elevator or the parent whose name we can never quite remember at school drop-off as merely polite and superficial, people who interact with others throughout the day—even those they don't know well—experience more happiness than those who don't. In some cases, these random encounters can prove surprisingly meaningful, allowing people to connect over shared experiences and engendering positive emotions and a sense of community among all parties involved. We all have memories of that time a stranger complimented our outfit or told us a joke that still makes us laugh. It feels good to connect with people, even if just for a moment and even if we never see them again.

The best connection happens in real life. While social media sites and other online platforms can be great for staying in touch with people you don't see very often or interacting with like-minded or special interest groups you might not otherwise have access to, it's difficult to *really* know someone unless you spend time with them in person. That's not to say that virtual connection is bad or irrelevant; just that we should prioritize real-time and real-life interactions as much as possible if we want to build and sustain our strongest relationships.* What's more, research

---

* I learned just how important this type of online connection can be after Dio was diagnosed. I didn't know anyone else who had been through exactly what we were going through, so I turned to the internet to connect with other parents whose children had

shows that using our phones frequently while hanging out with others actually impairs our connections by increasing distractions, reducing the quality of conversation, and generally lowering our overall enjoyment of in-person interactions. In a world where we spend on average six hours a day online and roughly a third of American adults say they are "almost always" online, this should be a wake-up call to put down the phone, look someone in the eye, and talk to them the way humans were designed to do.

Celebrate Each Other's Wins

One of the hallmarks of a quality relationship is that each party feels supported by the other when they are going through a hard time. This is why our relationships are so vital to our well-being: They literally provide the resources (emotional, mental, and physical) to help us cope with whatever life throws at us. When someone we care about is going through hard times, we demonstrate our love by showing up for them, and as a result, everyone—and the relationship itself—benefits.

But research shows that while it's important to show up for your loved ones in a crisis, it's equally, if not more, critical to acknowledge and celebrate their joyful moments as well. Back in the 1980s, researchers identified "sharing good news" as one of the most important rules of friendship, and multiple studies have demonstrated that human beings frequently seek out others—particularly those with whom they are close—to share positive events. Scientists call this process *capitalization* and have found that the simple act of sharing happy news with someone else actually increases and extends the positive feelings one has about the event. People who disclose good news experience a boost in positive emotions, well-being, and self-esteem and report more satisfaction, intimacy,

---

received the same diagnosis. To be honest, it was mostly not helpful, and many of the stories I read left me feeling even more anxious, not less. However, I was able to get in touch with another mother who was going through something similar, and having her to talk to, learn from, and lean on helped make this truly horrific experience just a little more bearable. She lives on the East Coast, so we've never met in person, but we are bonded just the same.

commitment, trust, and stability within their relationships. No wonder we so often want to call our best friend, our partner, or our parents when something good happens to us.

Critically, the way others respond to our good news impacts our feelings about it. You probably know how disappointing it can be when you race to tell another person about something exciting and they respond negatively or halfheartedly. We share information because we crave connection and validation—and when we don't get it, our relationships suffer. Fortunately, the opposite is also true. When people respond actively and enthusiastically to someone else's good news (for example, by asking encouraging questions or expressing pride or joy), the impact of the event becomes even stronger and lasts even longer. In fact, according to some studies, the way you respond to a loved one's good news may have an even greater impact on the relationship than how you show up during times of stress. When asked how they felt about various interactions with their partners, participants in one study were more likely to report feeling supported when their partner responded enthusiastically to good news than they did when their partner offered support in response to stress or bad news.

While it is, of course, important to celebrate big events like landing a dream job, publishing a book, or getting married, you don't need to wait for huge life milestones in order to break out the sparklers and champagne. Is your friend going on their first date after six months of mourning a terrible breakup? Help them pick out an outfit and send an encouraging text before the big night. Did your partner resolve a difficult issue that had been causing them anxiety at work? A simple "I'm so proud of you" and a big hug can do wonders for their confidence and self-esteem—and help you feel closer because it shows you've been paying attention. Did your kid ace a test they'd been studying for all week? Why not use it as an excuse to make their favorite dish for dinner so the whole family can mark the occasion? Even something as mundane as having a great meal or trying a new activity can be an opportunity to capitalize on—and it really is so easy (and fulfilling) to show the people you love just how much you care.

I met one of my closest friends in my mid-thirties. (I know—shocking—given how hard it can be to make new friends as an adult.) It happened organically and ended up being one of those rare connections in which I also love her husband and she loves mine. It's a friendship that quickly became like a family, and I don't take it for granted at all. One of the hallmarks of our relationship is that I cannot wait to celebrate her (or her husband's) wins. When she self-published a children's book, I was giddy with excitement for her—full to the brim with pride, almost like it was my own accomplishment. When her husband won an award for entrepreneur of the year, I wanted to scream the news from the rooftops. (To be honest, I actually might have.) And both of them have done the same for me and Alex. Small wins or big ones, it is truly incredible to feel celebrated and authentic happiness from and for a friend. Yes, these friends have been there for us in our dark times, but it's this reciprocal joy and support that has truly transformed the way I understand—and how much I appreciate—genuine friendship.

Nurture with Optimism

When our loved ones are going through a difficult time, we naturally want to do whatever we can to help. Too often, however, our initial response is to try and fix the situation or attempt to make them feel better instead of supporting them in ways that actually work. This is understandable; it pains us to see the people we love in pain, so we want to alleviate that discomfort as quickly as possible. Unfortunately the impulse does not come from a place of connection; it's a result of toxic positivity.

As we discussed in chapter 3, toxic positivity is a consequence of our misguided desire to avoid negative emotions—the distressing, messy, uncomfortable ways we feel when we are going through something stressful or challenging. Just as we must allow ourselves to lean into these feelings if we want to live authentically, we must also give our loved ones the space to do this for themselves. When we allow others the opportunity to be vulnerable, to express the full range of their emotions, and to show up as their true selves, we make it possible for them to tap into their innate resilience so they can engage with the situation realistically but optimistically.

It may seem like a cliché, but one of the best things you can do for someone who is experiencing a hard time is just to listen. In my work, I have come to realize after all these years that most people who seek out help—even professional help—are mostly looking for a safe nonjudgmental place to share and process their feelings, not for a solution to any particular problem. In fact, multiple studies have found that simply talking about one's problems and sharing feelings about a situation can reduce physical and emotional distress. Meanwhile, the mere presence of a supportive person during a period of stress can help prevent cardiac reactivity, like a spike in blood pressure or a racing pulse, and words of encouragement from a loved one can reduce cortisol levels, all of which make it easier to cope.

When trying to offer words of encouragement, however, be sure to opt for the language of optimism over that of toxic positivity. Instead of urging someone to "look on the bright side," reminding them that "things could be worse," or resorting to platitudes like "everything happens for a reason," give them the chance to express whatever it is they're feeling while making it clear that their emotions are natural and valid. Give them the time to sit in their tough emotions and really feel everything that comes up—grief, sorrow, anger, heartache, worry—while at the same time creating a small space for hope in a way that honors their needs. Listen to what they're asking of you, if anything, and don't rush in to fill the awkward silences, break the tension, or try to get them to stop crying if you sense they just need to let something out.

If, however, you sense they're craving perspective or solace, lean into the language of optimism. For example: "I see what a tough time you are going through, and I can understand why you feel the way you do. It is okay to cry or to feel angry—I would, too. And I am glad you feel safe expressing those emotions with me." Or "I understand that right now you aren't sure how or when you will ever get through this, and that's okay. I know you can do hard things because I have been here as a witness to see you do them before." If you want to offer further support, be sure to do so in a way that takes into account what the other person actually needs—not what you think they need or what feels good for you to provide. Studies show that providing a type of support that does not honor the recipient's needs can actually backfire, harming the relationship more than helping it. When someone is going through a tough time, it's important that they feel understood, so when we speak or behave in ways that don't validate their true needs, we can inadvertently make them feel worse, not better.

It sounds counterintuitive, but one surprisingly effective tactic is to ask for help from someone who is going through a difficult time. Usually, when we see our loved ones struggling, we avoid asking them for help because we don't want to burden them, but research shows that might be the very thing they need the most. Helping others is a well-known antidote to depression and can make us feel more hopeful and optimistic about our lives because it gives us the opportunity to step outside of ourselves and redirect our attention to something else.

In one study, participants with moderate to severe depression, anxiety, or stress were divided into three groups and instructed to do one of three therapeutic interventions several times a week for a few weeks: scheduling social activities, carrying out cognitive reappraisal,* or performing random acts of kindness for strangers. By the end of the study, only the random acts of kindness group reported feeling less depressed. The reason? Helping others allowed them to feel a stronger sense of social connection and focus on others instead of themselves. Another advantage of this strategy is that it doesn't *look like* you're offering support when you're asking for support—but research shows that you are. When people knowingly accept assistance from others, they often end up feeling incompetent, helpless, or indebted to the person who offered the help in the first place. Their emotional burden isn't alleviated; instead, it now feels heavier, potentially leading to resentment or discomfort within the rela-

---

* In cognitive behavioral therapy, cognitive reappraisal occurs when a patient consciously shifts their thoughts about a situation or trigger in a way that changes their feelings, and by extension their behaviors, about that situation.

tionship. By contrast, invisible support—defined as an act that provides material or emotional assistance but that the recipient does not recognize as support—helps the recipient feel loved and cared for without any of the downsides. When you ask someone for assistance—maybe by helping you plan a mutual friend's birthday party or volunteering at your local animal shelter—you counteract this effect, giving your loved one the opportunity to feel needed instead of needy and boosting their self-esteem without their even realizing it.

Model the Energy You Want Others to Match

Try as we might, we all know it's impossible to change someone else, but that doesn't mean you can't influence how other people interact with you. If you're trying to strengthen a relationship or repair a broken one, the first step is to shift your behavior so that it matches the behavior you'd like to see from the other person. To borrow a maxim from (and with apologies to) Gandhi: Be the change you wish to see in your relationship.

Happiness is literally contagious. In a widely cited study published in 2014, researchers followed 4,739 participants over the course of twenty years and found that when someone experiences happiness, the people physically closest to them are more likely to become happier themselves. This was especially true of spouses, siblings who lived within one mile of each other, and next-door neighbors. The same study also found that happiness could spread up to three degrees—to friends of friends or neighbors of neighbors. If ever there was proof that the energy we put out into the world reverberates, this is it.

It's not just happiness that works this way. Our emotions and behaviors can influence the emotions and behaviors of others in several ways. For example, do you want to get to know someone better, but they seem hesitant to share a lot about themselves? Studies show that disclosing personal information about yourself increases the likelihood that other people will respond in kind. People who hang out with people who exercise are more likely to exercise, and as we mentioned earlier, people who behave optimistically and cooperatively in relationships are more likely to elicit cooperative behaviors from their partners. Struggling to communicate with someone? Change the way you communicate and see how they respond. If you focus on what you're doing and what you want to achieve, nine times out of ten, the other person will pick up on your energy and respond to it.

This strategy works especially well for relationships that are important to you but that you can't choose: family members, neighbors, co-workers, roommates, etc. You may not have chosen these particular individuals to be part of your life—in fact you may even find them difficult or unpleasant to be around—but the way you decide to interact with them can have a profound impact on the quality of that relationship and, as a result, the quality of your life. Is someone cold and standoffish? Make a point of smiling, saying hi, and asking how they're doing when you encounter them. Does a family member always find *something* to complain about whenever you're together? A well-placed compliment can disarm even the most negative Nancys. Even if you don't suddenly become best friends with your grumpy uncle or toxic boss, you can still elevate your mood and perspective, making it easier to direct positive energy to places where it's most important. And if the other person doesn't match your energy and continues to be miserable, well then, perhaps it's time to end the relationship or at least to create some distance.

Protect Your Peace

Picture this: You wake up one morning feeling refreshed and excited to take on the day. (Okay, maybe this is easier for some to picture than others, but bear with me.) You get ready for work, hop in your car or on the train, pop on your favorite get-up-and-go tune (for me, it's usually anything on a nineties grunge playlist, but lately, thanks to my *Star Wars*–obsessed son, it's been "The Imperial March" from *The Empire Strikes Back*—which is surprisingly invigorating first thing in the morning). You arrive at the office (or in our remote-work era, maybe your local coffee shop) and immediately encounter someone (maybe you know them, maybe you don't) who is *not* matching your vibe. The person seems stressed out and rushed and keeps sighing heavily—clearly hoping someone will ask what's going on. You're feeling friendly, so you ask, "Rough day?" not realizing you've opened the floodgates.

"Ugh, you have no idea!" they reply. "I slept through my alarm and was already late for my morning meeting, but then I spilled coffee all over myself, so I had to change, and I just realized I left my wallet at home. Could the day get any worse?"

Now, consider what you would do in this situation. Humans are naturally empathic and social creatures, so most of us would probably feel bad for this person. "Oh, man, that sucks!" you might offer. "Something like that happened to me last week! I was rushing out the door when all of a sudden . . ." Before you know it, you're thinking about how stressed out you were at some random moment in the past, and your enthusiasm from this morning is quickly replaced by anxiety as you remember all the things you have to get done today.

We've all had an experience like this; we feel just fine—maybe even excellent—and then encounter someone whose bad mood brings us down. This is completely normal. After all, one of the ways we connect with and relate to other people is to bond over shared experiences. But if we're not mindful, that same sensitivity can interfere with our optimism practice, ultimately impacting our own well-being and the health of our relationships. This is why, in order to preserve our peace, we need to set boundaries.

In psychology, boundaries refer to the limits and guidelines we set, both for ourselves and others, in order to protect our emotional energy, our mental and physical health, and our sense of self. You can set boundaries that apply only to yourself (e.g. "I will put my phone away at least one hour before bedtime" or "I will drink alcohol only once a week") but also to the way you interact with others. When it comes to interpersonal relationships, boundaries are especially important (and often essential) in challenging relationships that we're not willing or able to walk away from. For instance, if your parent or sibling is dealing with a substance-abuse problem and shows no signs of wanting to get sober, you may establish a boundary that you won't spend time with them if they are drunk or high. Or perhaps you might choose not to disclose information about your private life with someone who is judgmental or gossipy, or to abstain from certain activities—like games or sports—with a friend who is, in your opinion, overly competitive. Remember that boundaries are not punishments; they're practices that allow us to stay grounded in our values while maintaining relationships.

In other words, boundaries can help preserve relationships you don't want to lose while simultaneously protecting your inner peace, integrity, and self-respect. They are not designed to control other people's behavior, nor are they a carte blanche to get out of things you simply don't want to do. Thanks to the rise of so-called therapy speak on social media, the term *boundaries* has gained widespread acceptance, but it's frequently misunderstood, even weaponized in popular culture. From what I've seen (in real life and online), many people have come to use the term *boundaries* as a way to try to dictate someone else's behavior, to get out of doing things they simply don't want to do, or in some cases, to end a relationship without warning or explanation. While someone who truly cares about you should not force you to do something upsetting, dangerous, or triggering, any relationship that is worth keeping is worth sacrificing a little bit of your time and energy for. You may not want to go to your significant other's annual holiday party because you find it stuffy and boring and would rather be home in your sweatpants watching *Love Island*, but the damage you will cause to your relationship by staying home will likely far outweigh the nuisance of having to spend a couple of hours making small talk with Gary from accounting and munching on hors d'oeuvres. Healthy relationships will at times require compromising, enduring discomfort, and showing up even when you'd rather not. Boundaries protect your well-being, but they work best when they coexist with empathy, flexibility, and mutual respect.

That said, not every relationship is worth your time, and if you find yourself having to set lots of boundaries in order to enjoy, or even just tolerate, hanging out with someone, then it might be time to let go. We all know that toxic, abusive, volatile, or unsupportive relationships are detrimental to one's mental and physical health, but even ambivalent relationships—ones in which you feel both positive and negative feelings about another person—can be equally harmful. Research shows that both negative relationships *and* ambivalent ones can cause health issues, such as high blood pressure and poor immune response. In addition, if you have regular negative experiences with someone, it can lead you to engage in unhealthy or at least unproductive behaviors. If you find that a relationship is no longer serving you, consider whether you need to walk away.

If it's not possible or desirable to end a relationship completely, then figure out what boundaries you need to set in order to maintain it in a way that is healthy and bearable for you. This requires a lot of self-awareness, considerable dedication, and a commitment to hold yourself to those boundaries, which can be extremely difficult if the relationship is charged with a lot of history and emotion. As you move through the process, it will likely feel uncomfortable, especially in relationships with a lot of history, passion, obligation, or love. It's often within that discomfort that we find our deepest growth. Remind yourself that you are not being selfish for wanting to feel safe, seen, and supported, and you are not being too much for setting out to protect your peace.

Real optimism doesn't ask you to tolerate pain or harm. It asks you to believe in the possibility of something better. Sometimes the most hopeful thing you can do is draw a line, set a boundary. Hold it with grace and trust that your well-being is worth the effort it takes to protect it.

CHAPTER 10

Optimism Is an Inside Job

The Science of Self-Care

Self-care isn't selfish; it's survival.

When Jag first started sleeping through the night, he would wake up every morning at seven a.m. after spending a glorious twelve hours in his crib. The second I heard his sweet little voice calling for me, I would jump out of bed and run into the nursery. I didn't take a moment to pee, brush my teeth, or even drink a sip of water. The pressure of being a new mom made me act like nothing else—not even going to the bathroom—was nearly as important as my newborn's needs. I mean, he was a helpless infant who had just spent twelve hours all alone without food, milk, or a diaper change. Surely he needed my attention more than I needed to relieve myself?

By contrast, when it was my husband's turn to get up with Jag, he would wake up slowly, go to the bathroom, brush his teeth, wash his face, and sometimes even stretch for a few minutes before calmly heading into the nursery. I'll admit that the first few times I watched this happen, I resented him a little bit (okay, *a lot* a bit). Why didn't he rush into Jag's room like I did? Why was he so relaxed in the morning even though I was so frazzled? Couldn't he hear our precious child crying in the next room?! The poor thing had been alone for twelve whole hours. How could he make him wait even one second longer?!

Spoiler alert: Jag was fine. In fact, he seemed no better or worse off regardless of which parent was in charge—and how quickly they arrived at his crib. Meanwhile, guess who got a bladder infection from holding their pee in every morning? That's right. I did. *I did!*

This may sound ridiculous coming from a mental health expert, but this was an eye-opening experience for me. Once I was able to squash the anxiety (and envy) I was directing toward Alex for going at his own pace in the morning, I realized he was onto something. Our son was safe. Nothing bad happened in the five minutes it took Alex to pee, brush his teeth, and stretch—and nothing bad would happen if I did the same. From that moment on, I resolved to start my mornings off differently, taking a page from Alex's book and using those first few minutes of the morning to wake myself up, wash my face, and yes, go to the bathroom. Sure, my kid may have been alone for a little longer, but he was fine—and I was a much better mama in the morning because of it.

I didn't have a lot of time for self-care during this period of my life. My routines and habits had been thrown into chaos the second Jag was born. But this little ritual—however mundane, however short—became an essential part of my day. Not only did it allow me to tend to my basic physical needs, but it also became my way of acknowledging that these needs were just as important as my son's (or anyone else's). And if I was going to be a good mother, I *had* to prioritize them because no one else was going to see to it that I didn't get a bladder infection. Those few minutes I spent in the bathroom didn't look like anything you'd see on a wellness influencer's Instagram reel or in a glossy women's magazine, but they established the groundwork for the way I now tend to my mental health.

Whenever I see something that promises "top ten self-care tips for a healthier you!" or "the self-care routine that will change your life," I usually have two thoughts. First, "This is great! I'm so glad people are talking about this, because self-care really is essential to our well-being." And it is. As I like to say, self-care isn't selfish, it's *survival*. Human beings were not meant to work and stress all the time. In order to function, let alone thrive, we *need* to take time away from things that drain our energy in order to do things that replenish it.

The second thought? "Why do all these tips and routines look so complicated? And who has time for them?" Case in point: Over the years, I have received a ton of requests from media outlets who wanted to interview me about my morning self-care routine. When I asked for more ideas on what they might be looking for (because I had the distinct sense that "I go to the bathroom and brush my teeth" was not the aspirational content their readers craved), they gave me several examples—every single one of which sounded like it would take at least half an hour, if not longer, to perform. *Who* are *these people?* I thought. I am a working mother of three. I am happy if I get thirty seconds to myself in the morning, let alone thirty minutes, and I know very few people who could dedicate thirty whole minutes to anything first thing in the morning except managing some basic personal grooming, downing a quick breakfast, and (if applicable) getting the kids out the door. I'm all for morning routines (science shows that the way you spend your mornings often sets the tone for the rest of your day), but to read articles like this, you'd think you are doing yourself a disservice if you don't wake up at five a.m., stretch, meditate, and perform a twelve-step skin-care regimen every day before breakfast. Oh! And of course these articles always assume that you've had seven to eight hours of uninterrupted sleep prior to that predawn wake-up time. If you're someone who can pull this off—and it makes you feel good—bless you! And keep it up! Most of the individual suggestions in these articles are actually pretty good (or at least not bad), and I'll be the first person to advocate for anything that helps you get excited and energized to start your day. The issue I have with this type of content is that it presents self-care in a way that for most people feels completely unattainable.

Yes, self-care is absolutely critical to our mental and physical health; there is a ton of science to back this up. But so much of the popular advice around it is packaged and presented in a way that makes it feel like some aspirational, indulgent, and often time-consuming thing; not a necessity but a privilege reserved for those with way too much time (and often money) to spare. They also often leave us feeling like we're not getting self-care *right* if we can't seem to get out of bed at five a.m. or meditate in silence for twenty minutes—or if we don't have the budget to afford whatever product or service this celebrity or that expert swears by.

Fortunately, science shows us that you don't need a lot of time, money, energy—or any other resource—to practice genuine, effective self-care. In fact, sometimes simply giving yourself a chance to pee first thing in the morning even if your newborn is crying *is* self-care. Sometimes RSVP'ing no to an invitation is self-care. Sometimes doing nothing at all is self-care. And when you start to look at self-care this way—as the simple act of honoring your mental, emotional, and spiritual needs so you can show up more fully in the world instead of some specific activity or routine you read about on social media—then you become more optimistic about your ability to make room for the things that bring you pleasure, joy, rest, and inspiration.

Self-Care Isn't Selfish, It's Survival

Even though the term *self-care* has gone mainstream in the past few years, the idea of dedicating time and energy to our personal, emotional, mental, physical, and spiritual needs has been around for as long as humans have walked the earth.[*] We have always known—intuitively, even if not always scientifically—that our minds and bodies need moments of peace, relaxation, comfort, and joy in order to survive, let alone thrive.

Unfortunately, in our modern society, we tend to prioritize work over rest, even if we don't want or intend to. We praise people for their work ethic and admire those who seem to defy the laws of physics in order to get stuff done. Right next to the posts and articles about intricate self-care routines, we see advice and stories about how to be more productive or how to "enhance" or "optimize" our performance in some way. Even if you don't subscribe to the "rise and grind, sleep is for the weak, hustle at all costs"

---

[*] Way back in the fifth century BC, the Greek philosopher Socrates became what some consider the founder of the original self-care movement after cautioning people against "devoting all your care to increasing your wealth, reputation, and honors, while not caring for or even considering your reason, truth, and constant improvement of your soul." Today, many credit the civil rights activist and feminist Audre Lorde for advancing our more modern notions of self-care when she wrote: "Caring for myself is not self-indulgence. It is self-preservation, and that is an act of political warfare."

mentality that some people do, chances are you have, on some level, internalized the belief that it's better to be busy than idle or that if you spend too much time simply enjoying your life, people will think you're lazy. Think about it. How often have you skipped lunch because you felt overwhelmed with work or other responsibilities? Powered through a day at school or the office when you were sick? Unloaded the dishwasher instead of curling up with a good book and a mug of your favorite tea? Tried to multitask by checking email, shopping online, or paying bills while watching a movie with your partner? Trust me, you're not alone. Surveys show that 62 percent of Americans who are entitled to paid time off through their jobs don't use all of it, and, of those surveyed, 5.5 percent didn't use any PTO *at all*. This is despite the fact that 44 percent of Americans report feeling burned out at work, while 51 percent describe themselves as feeling used up by the end of a long day.

So often we focus on what we think we need to do instead of spending time on what feels good—but this does not serve us. For most of our history, humans' default physiological state was rest. While our adrenaline and cortisol might spike when we experienced an immediate threat, stressful moments were relatively rare and short lived. The rest of the time, our bodies had plenty of time to recover from the temporary shocks to our system. But a recent study out of the University of California at San Francisco shows that is no longer the case; today our default state is stress. That's right: our bodies have literally started behaving as though we are constantly under attack —not because we're in any real mortal danger (for most people living in the twenty-first century, the world is actually safer than it's ever been) but because we *feel* like we are. Yes, of course, there is still a whole lot of danger in the world: gun violence, natural disasters, global pandemics, humanitarian crises, the existential threats of nuclear war, climate change, the rise of AI, etc. All of these create genuine cause for concern, but in previous generations, we were not constantly reminded of all the horrible things going on in the world. Today, every phone notification or news headline is a potential trigger—not to mention that we still have to deal with everyday stressors like work deadlines, family emergencies, financial concerns, health scares, and on and on. With all these things to worry and think about, our anticipatory brains keep flooding our bodies with adrenaline and cortisol, which create stress. As a result, research shows, we are growing increasingly prone to disease and disability and are aging more rapidly at the cellular level.

You cannot remove all stress from your life, but you can absolutely give your mind and body more opportunities to recover from it. Not only will this make you feel better, but it will also make you more effective at whatever it is you choose to do and allow you to enjoy those pursuits more. Studies show that the top performers in their fields are those who allow ample time for rest when they are not engaged in deep, focused work. For example, after studying how certain individuals achieve the highest levels of expertise in their careers, researcher K. Anders Ericsson found that the most accomplished people across various disciplines (including music, writing, and sports) practice roughly four hours a day on average and usually don't work for more than an hour at a time without rest. Other research has shown that most people benefit from roughly four hours a day of downtime, though the exact amount varies from person to person, and that taking a short rest every ninety minutes (much like we naturally feel the most rested when we sleep in ninety-minute cycles) can help improve concentration and focus.

Fortunately, all it requires to practice effective self-care is a little bit of self-awareness and a commitment to set aside at least a little bit of time each day for it. You need to remind yourself that rest is not a reward for completing a task or working yourself to the point of exhaustion; it is a vital component for optimal health. Yes, some things need to get done right now, but many things don't. It's up to you to create the space necessary to tend to your mental and physical health.

Self-Care Can Be Simple

Although it can be rejuvenating to book a silent yoga retreat or escape to the mountains for a weekend, you don't need any special tools or a picture-perfect setting to practice effective self-care. In fact, science shows that some of the best things you can do to bring your brain and body back into balance require nothing more than you yourself and a few things you probably have lying around the house. Here are some of my favorite ways to attain a quick mental boost.

Express Gratitude

In the past few years, the idea of showing gratitude or counting your blessings has become something of a trend—and there's a good reason for that. Numerous studies show that taking time to reflect upon the things you are thankful for can provide seemingly endless benefits, including boosting your mood, improving your sleep and cardiovascular health, lowering your risk of depression, reducing stress, and increasing longevity. Making gratitude a habit, by, for instance, keeping a daily gratitude journal has also been shown to rewire the brain; those who regularly express their gratitude come to expect and anticipate that feeling and are thus more likely to seek it out in the future. In other words, being grateful naturally makes you even more grateful over time.

My favorite way to show gratitude is to state out loud who and what I'm thankful for, usually during a meditation or visual imagery. Whenever the opportunity presents itself, I also like to share my gratitude directly with the people I'm most thankful for. But studies show that the way you express gratitude usually matters less than the act of simply focusing on the things you're thankful for. And while it's certainly important to remember big blessings (your health, your family, the roof over your head), it's often just as (if not more) powerful to consider the little mundane things that make your life full. Sharing a belly laugh with a friend; enjoying a warm, sunny day; relishing a delicious meal—these are things you can enjoy at pretty much any time, and taking a moment to acknowledge them can be a great way to prime your brain for optimism. Doing so also keeps your gratitude practice fresh, genuine, and creative because you'll never run out of things to be grateful for or start to take your blessings for granted. Expressing genuine gratitude for life's little pleasures broadens your perspective and strengthens the optimism muscle, so that over time you can learn to see the meaning and beauty in basically any situation.

One aspect of gratitude that we often overlook is self-gratitude. When was the last time you took a second to appreciate all the work, energy, and thought you put into meeting your goals, fulfilling your responsibilities, or even just making it through the day? But doing so is one of the simplest and most powerful ways to boost your mood and self-esteem. One way to do this is by creating what I call a *ta-da list*. Unlike a to-do list, which reminds you of all the things you need to get done, a ta-da list is an inventory of all that you've accomplished on a given day. Your ta-da list can include all the things you crossed off your to-do list, but it can also take note of unexpected or less tangible things. For instance, maybe you kept your cool while your kid threw a tantrum on the way to school or set a boundary with your boss about taking on work outside of your job description. Or maybe you just followed through on something you said you were going to do, like eating more vegetables or not scrolling through your phone right before bed. By reminding yourself of all the things you do to make your life better, you can draw strength for the future and build a more optimistic outlook.

Practice Mindfulness

The term *mindfulness* can refer to many activities, but I like to describe it as simply living in the moment. "Only this actual moment is life," wrote the beloved Zen Buddhist monk, teacher, and philosopher Thich Nhat Hanh in his book *The Miracle of Mindfulness*. "Don't be attached to the future. Don't worry about things you have to do. Don't think about getting up or taking off to do anything. Don't think about departing."

Mindfulness has been shown to improve our mental and physical health in many ways, including by reducing symptoms of anxiety and depression, lowering blood pressure, improving sleep, and helping people deal with chronic pain. The key to incorporating mindfulness into your life is to do so in a purposeful and intentional way that works for you. For example, in my personal and professional experience, most people struggle with traditional forms of meditation, which essentially ask you to empty your mind of all thoughts and sit in stillness for a specific length of time. While devotees of meditation swear by the impact it has on their health and well-being, the fact is, our brains are designed to *always be working*. Even if we're not preoccupied with something right in front of us, we are constantly anticipating things that could happen, reevaluating events that have happened recently, or trying to solve problems for the future.

With so much going on in the world, not to mention the daily demands of our personal lives, it's no wonder you may feel uncomfortable—and probably more than a little frustrated—trying to quiet your mind for several minutes. Trust me, I can relate. You might think that a South Asian American professional psychologist who was born and raised in Southern California and whose name sounds *extremely similar to* one of the most famous metaphysical gurus on the planet would be all about meditation. Well, I'm not. Sorry to disappoint you, but I can barely sit still for fifteen seconds, let alone an hour.*

Of course, if you're not like me and find it relatively easy and fulfilling to empty your mind of all thoughts and sit still in silence for an indefinite period, then of course keep doing it! If you *are* like me, then I suggest trying a more self-directed, focused meditation practice that forces you to redirect your attention instead of suspending it. While traditional meditation compels you to turn your attention toward the present moment by emptying your mind of all thoughts, mindfulness meditation asks you to simply redirect your focus to what is going on in and around you so that you can quiet anxiety and reset your attention toward what is most important. I've already introduced a few of my favorite mindfulness practices throughout the book, such as the Adult I Spy game or focused breath exercises in chapter 3, but here are a few others.

Savoring joy: Research shows that the act of savoring positive feelings and experiences can help strengthen and prolong their benefits. The next

---

* I'm also terrible at yoga. I know! Even though I know that yoga is extremely beneficial to both mental and physical health, it's just not my sport. Something about having to lie still on a mat for an indefinite period of time or hold a complicated pose for thirty seconds makes me antsy. I wish it weren't the case, but alas . . .

time you feel a surge of happiness—whether it's from something major like a reunion with an old friend or something more mundane like the wave of contentment you might experience at the first signs of springtime—take a few seconds to sit with that feeling and really savor it. According to psychologist and author Dr. Rick Hanson, even though our brains are primed to focus on negative events in order to keep us safe, turning toward the good things in life and taking the time to savor them is how we achieve well-being. When you feel a moment of joy, "stay with the experience for a breath or longer," he suggests, recommending that you savor for at least twelve seconds, which is how long it takes neurons to form new connections with one another. "Try to feel it in your body . . . Focus on what feels good about it." Need a quick mental health boost? Refer back to your joy list, pick an activity from it, and try to engage in it mindfully and with an eye toward relishing every second of positivity it provides.

Engaging your senses: Paying attention to what you taste, see, smell, feel, and hear is a great, simple, and quick way to get in touch with your body and your surroundings and mindfully return to the present. One of my favorite ways to do this is through mindful eating. You have to eat every day—often several times a day—but when was the last time you really *savored* your food? Not just noticed that it tasted sweet or maybe a tad too salty, but really savored it? What does it feel like in your mouth? Smell like? What distinct flavors do you notice? How does it make you feel? You can also do this exercise in my favorite place—the shower!—or pretty much at any time when you are using all your senses at once.

Paying attention to simple routines: One of the easiest ways to practice mindfulness is to focus your full attention on a basic activity you perform every day. Brewing your morning coffee or tea? Driving your normal route to work? Brushing your teeth? Notice how you move through every step of the process—really focus on what you're doing and how you're doing it. When you're done, observe how you feel. This can be especially useful if you're feeling stressed or anxious about something in the past or future because it forces you to return to the present moment. It also helps you get in the habit of paying attention to what's going on around you when it's most important. Consider how often your mind wanders when having a conversation with someone or reading a book. Wouldn't you like to stay engaged with these activities?

Spend Time in Nature

I was born and raised in Los Angeles and have lived here my entire life. As much as I love the hustle and creative energy of my city, one of the absolute best things about living here is its proximity to nature. Want to go to the beach? I can literally walk to it from my house, and if I want something more secluded, it's a short drive up the coast to Malibu. If I have the time, I can take a scenic drive along the stunning Pacific Coast Highway or plan a day trip to the vineyards of Santa Barbara or to Joshua Tree National Park. Not to mention, the city itself is full of beautiful parks and stunning views—all of which help buffer the sometimes overwhelming stress and stimulation of city life.

So much of our modern life disconnects us from the natural world, but research shows that human beings are literally programmed to desire the outdoors. For example, when asked to draw their favorite places, children overwhelmingly depict outdoor spaces like local parks or playgrounds. Later in life, when asked to recall favorite places from their childhood, adults will typically name the same types of places, thus indicating that they associate the outdoors and green spaces with positive memories. Scientists have a name for this phenomenon: biophilia, a term used to describe our innate drive to connect with the natural world and the negative consequences of becoming detached from it.

We crave nature because it's good for us. Studies show that spending time in nature regulates our sympathetic nervous system, which is triggered by stress and controls things like our blood pressure, blood sugar, and heart rate. People who spend time in nature report less anxiety and depression and improved mood and perform better on memory and cognitive tasks than those who spend most of their time indoors or in fully urbanized areas. Many studies also show that spending time in nature may have cumulative and long-term effects, lowering the risk of chronic illness and mortality and lessening the symptoms of chronic pain, PTSD, and even ADHD. Children who live in close proximity to nature experience fewer ill effects from stressful events (for example, moving, being bullied at school, or experiencing peer pressure) than those who don't, and children living in urban areas exhibit better motor skills and attention and less stress when they have regular access to natural settings. The benefits that spending time in nature confer to our mental health are so numerous and profound that some doctors have started prescribing it as a mental health intervention, with some reports indicating that it can be just as, if not more, effective as medication or therapy.

While secluded areas like forests, national parks, or remote beaches convey exceptional benefits due to their ability to inspire awe (more on this below), you don't need to retreat to the woods or a faraway island in order to experience the positive impact of nature. Sit in your backyard or on your front stoop and soak up the sun while listening to the birds chirp nearby. Have a picnic or read a book in a nearby park. Stroll along your local waterfront and listen to the water lapping against the shore. One of my favorite natural spaces is a small private garden just two blocks away from my house. I literally crave seeing it because it brings me awe, inspiration, and serenity—and it's so close by. If you find it hard to work nature into your routines, try bringing the outdoors indoors by filling your home with houseplants, adorning your walls with photos of landscapes, or buying a small tabletop fountain to simulate the sound of a babbling brook. Get creative and—better yet—invite others to accompany you on your excursions, since sharing experiences augments their impact.

Experience Awe

Awe is the feeling we get when we witness something that ignites our sense of wonder and broadens our perspective. It's the feeling we get when we marvel at a vibrant sunset, behold the night sky full of stars, or observe an exceptional act of athleticism or artistry. It's the feeling we get when we contemplate the miracle of existence, the meaning of life, and our place in the universe.

Scientists have a name for the effect that awe has on us: the small self.

When we experience something truly awe-inspiring, our perspective shifts so that suddenly our own concerns and desires feel insignificant—or at least not all that unique—and we start to appreciate the world around us in a new way. We feel, to put it simply, small. Astronauts, for example, frequently experience the overview effect, a specific version of the small-self phenomenon that occurs when they view Earth from space for the first time. Researchers who have studied the overview effect have found that many astronauts report feeling more connected with the world and its people than they did prior to their first spaceflight. "I was hit with the realization that this delicate layer of atmosphere is all that protects every living thing on Earth from perishing in the harshness of space," wrote NASA astronaut Ron Garan on his experience with the overview effect.

When we experience awe, our nervous system calms, slowing our heart rate, deepening our breathing, and aiding digestion. We release oxytocin, the "love hormone" that makes us feel connected to others, and dopamine, which helps us feel a sense of reward. Awe disrupts the default mode network (DMN), which is involved in advance planning and developing self-awareness, and thus temporarily quiets anxiety and negative self-talk. When we experience awe, we become more curious, open-minded, generous, humble, and in harmony with the world.

While we tend to associate awe with singular or once-in-a-lifetime moments, we can also feel it in more personal or seemingly ordinary events, like watching your child learn to read a new word or seeing one stranger perform a random act of kindness for another. And while awe can sometimes take us by surprise, we can also train ourselves to experience it by purposefully attuning ourselves to it. When we do this, we find that awe is a lot more accessible than we realize. For example, in one study, researchers divided participants into two groups, each of which was instructed to walk in nature for at least fifteen minutes a day for eight weeks and take pictures along the way. One group was given additional instruction to look out for opportunities to experience awe. In the end, those who took these "awe walks" reported a greater increase in joy and other positive emotions, a decrease in stress, and a stronger sense of connection with others. They also ended up taking fewer pictures of themselves the more time they spent in nature, thus indicating a shift in perspective toward the small self.

Nature is one of the most reliable sources of awe, thus making it a great way to double up the impact of your self-care practice. Next time you're outside—whether you're enjoying some quiet time in your backyard or beholding the vastness of the Grand Canyon—try to tap into your innate sense of wonder and pay attention to what happens. Take a deep breath, engage all your senses, and pause for a moment to really sit with everything you notice. The more you practice doing this, the easier and more automatic it becomes.

Move Your Body

I'm happy to say that, while I still make sure to pee first thing every day, my morning routine has grown a little more exciting than it was when I first became a mom. I am not a very physical or athletic person, but one thing I've always loved is moving my body to music. Whether it's celebrating with my family at a huge Indian wedding or dancing to my favorite nineties grunge or some mid-aughts pop-punk right before I get in the shower, I love the feeling of matching the rhythm of my body to a beat. To be honest, I don't really need an excuse or special place to dance; if there is music on, I sort of just intuitively and naturally move. I think this may be genetic. My dad, who was the CEO of a public company for most of my life and probably the most talented entrepreneur and business mind I know, has not met a table he didn't dance on. His mom, my *dadiji*, definitely had this gene in her as well.

No matter the situation, dancing immediately lowers my stress level and improves my mood. So a few years ago—not long after I started prioritizing my self-care in the mornings—I started a little ritual that I call Wake Up and Dance. It's pretty straightforward: Every morning, right after I get out of bed, I put on a favorite song and dance around my room. Most days I only have time to dance to one song, or my kids open the door thirty seconds in (which is fine because they usually join in), but I've found that simply setting aside this time every day, no matter where I am or how I feel when I wake up, gets my blood flowing, pumps up my energy, and sets an optimistic tone for the rest of my day. Plus, it allows me to enjoy my favorite artists and absorb all the mental benefits that come from meaningfully engaging with art. It's a perfect way to prioritize self-care in a way that works for me.

We all know that exercise is essential for good health, but if, like me, you're not naturally athletic or experienced (or motivated or disciplined to do it, lol) or haven't found a sport or workout that really clicks for you, then you know it can be extremely difficult to make it a habit. If you want to prioritize physical activity, you need to start by finding something you *actually like* and that works with your schedule. That's why my Wake Up and Dance routine works for me. And while it certainly doesn't look like much of a traditional workout, ample research shows that dancing can be an extremely effective form of mental and physical fitness, even if you've never taken a lesson.

Dancing is one of the oldest and most universal forms of exercise, cultural and self-expression, and communal bonding among humans, and recent research suggests it is incredibly powerful at improving one's mental and physical health. In one wide-ranging meta-analytic study, Australian researchers found that individuals who participated in a structured dance program for at least eight weeks saw benefits ranging from improved memory, less depression, more motivation, and improved cardiovascular and musculoskeletal function and that the impacts were equivalent to or greater than those experienced by individuals who engaged in other types of physical activity. The same results were found regardless of the dance genre or whether the dancing was performed individually or with others. Another study out of UCLA found 98 percent of individuals who practiced conscious dance, an unchoreographed form of dance designed to help people ease their minds, release stress, and become more connected to their bodies, reported improved mood and reduced stress and anxiety. This was also true of individuals who suffered from chronic conditions like PTSD, substance abuse, or chronic pain, most of whom said the dancing helped them cope with their condition.

I love dancing as a tool for self-care because it requires absolutely no skill, money, or equipment and you can do it anywhere and in basically any context. Of course, if dancing isn't your favorite thing, there are plenty of other simple ways to move your body that meet the criteria for great self-care: yoga or simple stretching, taking a walk, tai chi, roller skating, riding a bike, Hula-Hooping, jumping rope, playing badminton or pickleball or your favorite group sport, or just throwing a Frisbee around at the beach—all of these are ways to stay active that don't feel like a regular workout.

"Steal Time" for Self-Care Through Micro-Moments

While you can experience immediate benefits from practicing any of the above-mentioned activities, the impact will compound if you do them consistently over a long period of time. This is where a lot of people trip up. Because there are only so many hours in a day and our to-do lists never seem to get shorter, we feel like we can't dedicate ample time to a sustainable self-care practice. We say we want to exercise three to four times a week, but if we don't have ninety minutes to get ready, warm up, commute to and from the gym, work out, and then freshen up, we figure there's no point. Or we resolve to spend more time outdoors but can't seem to squeeze in the time between meetings, errands, childcare, and everything else on our to-do list. Also, sometimes, we just get bored.

But here's a fun secret: You don't need hours of uninterrupted free time in order to reap the benefits of self-care. Even just a few minutes a day—or spread throughout the day—can go a long way in resetting your mind and body and lowering your stress level. Research shows that as little as ten to fifteen minutes of a self-care activity can be enough. For example, one study showed that while the ideal length for a midday nap (an excellent tool for self-care!) is between ten and thirty minutes, people who slept for only ten minutes received the same benefits but experienced less post-nap grogginess and recovered more quickly after waking. Meanwhile, researchers who study the effect of nature on our bodies have found that as little as five minutes a day spent outdoors can help regulate our sympathetic nervous system and buffer the negative impact of stress.

Other studies suggest that shorter, more frequent breaks may convey similar but potentially longer-lasting benefits than longer, less frequent ones. For example, while longer vacations of at least four or five days can be great for our health and well-being, studies show their impact usually wears off after only a few weeks. By contrast, shorter, more frequent breaks—like regular days off during the week or a standard four-day workweek—help to increase well-being, concentration, and productivity over time. Of course, depending on your situation, a shorter workweek might not be possible, but I just want to emphasize that you don't need to spend months (or thousands of dollars) planning the trip of a lifetime in order to be able to afford rest. While you wait to fulfill your dream of hiking the Inca trail or lazing on the beaches of Hawaii for a week, see if you can bring the experience closer. Try a nature or historical walk in your neighborhood or plan a picnic near the closest body of water. (Research shows that spending time near water conveys tons of health benefits.) The trick is to make the most of the time you have by actively creating space for self-care.

If you can't figure out how to consistently set aside time, try stealing it instead. I credit Alex, my husband, for helping me come up with this concept, because he is great at stealing time wherever he can find it. He works from home, which makes this easier, but he also has a high-pressure corporate job that requires him to attend lots of meetings and travel several weeks a year. With a schedule like this, he finds it hard to plan breaks throughout the day, but whenever a call is canceled at the last minute or something else comes up that leaves him with an unexpected free chunk of time, he uses it to maximum advantage. Most of us (myself included) usually use these periods just to do more work, check off yet another task on our to-do list, or scroll mindlessly through social media. Alex, on the other hand, will go for a quick run or lift weights in our basement, using the time to refocus his energy, do something that brings him pleasure, and tend to his health. I have not yet mastered his ability to do this, but I admire it so much and am working on it.

One way to practice stealing time is through what I call micro-moments. Micro-moments are small spaces of free time we all find ourselves with throughout the day. The ten minutes you have to spare when you show up at your destination early; the gap between meetings when the first one ends a little sooner than expected; the time between your friend sending a text to say they're running five minutes late to dinner and when they show up—these are all micro-moments. They're too short to fit in any big project or errand, but they are perfect opportunities for a mental and physical reset.

For example, one day when Jag was still a baby, I was walking home with him from the grocery store when I spotted a nail salon with a sign in the window that said "$1/minute massages." I *love* physical touch and always feel incredible after a great massage,* but when I first became a mom, I stopped practicing pretty much all forms of regular self-care because I didn't think I had time for it anymore. Gone were the days where I could set aside time for an hour-long massage and three Pilates sessions each week or daily sessions of visual imagery first thing in the morning. And because my usual preferred routines were no longer realistic, I just gave up completely. By the time I arrived in front of that nail salon, I was miserable—low on sleep, completely depleted, and craving even just a few moments for myself. And then I had an epiphany. I walked into the parlor—Jag, stroller, and groceries in tow—and asked if I could have a five-minute neck and back massage. The woman at the front desk looked at me a little funny, but she led me over to an empty massage chair, where I rolled Jag's stroller up beside me and planted my face in the pillow. Five dollars and five minutes later, I walked out of that parlor feeling like a new woman. I couldn't believe how much more energy I had. I was less irritable and more solution-focused, and I certainly felt more empowered

---

* I am hardly unique in this. Plenty of research shows that human beings need physical contact. Regular touch—whether through a massage, a hug from a friend, or a cuddle with your partner—aids childhood development, communication, interpersonal relationships, and immunity. In fact massage promotes the growth of the body's natural killer cells, which help fight off the cells that cause disease, including chronic diseases like HIV and breast cancer.

and relaxed. Sure, it wasn't as luxurious as what I used to do, but I made that stolen micro-moment count and realized that not only did I *need* self-care, but it was entirely within my power—and only my power—to practice it. After that, I started treating myself to five-minute massages as a regular part of my weekly routine, and let me tell you, it made *all* the difference.

Ritualize Your Routine

I can list study after study about scientifically proven mental health interventions and share story after story about my favorite self-care practices, but at the end of the day, the best things you can do to improve your well-being are those that work *for you*. It's called *self*-care for a reason.

If you start to feel any sort of pressure to do a specific thing, or if you don't feel rejuvenated after engaging in a particular activity, well then, it's not really self-care, is it? It's so easy for activities that are supposed to bring us joy and comfort to turn into some all-encompassing self-improvement project or a series of tasks we feel like we *should* do. How often have you felt guilty or lazy for skipping a workout or abandoning a New Year's resolution that was supposed to change your life for the better? It is of course useful—and a key component of optimism—to set goals, anticipate your future needs and well-being, and try to strive for the best life possible. And while many of these goals (for example, exercising regularly, going to bed earlier, cooking a nutritious meal) are excellent forms of self-care, they can quickly backfire if we start to beat ourselves up about not doing them in a particular or supposedly correct way.

Real optimism requires a deep sense of self-compassion and awareness. That's why I put this chapter close to the end of the book: If you've read this far, you've already spent a lot of time thinking about your needs, values, and goals for your life, what's important to you and what isn't. As you brainstorm ways to prioritize and practice self-care, I urge you to remember the big picture of your life and who you want to be. I love dancing in the mornings, taking a hot shower every day, savoring a hot cup of tea in the afternoon, hosting nineties movie nights with my closest friends, going on short daily walks, and getting the occasional massage. These things feed my soul and bring me immense pleasure. But maybe, for you, they don't. For example, so many of my friends swear by acupuncture, and I have always wanted this to be a method of self-care that works for me. Unfortunately, I have a huge phobia of needles, and even though I have tried acupuncture several times, I can never seem to get out of my head enough for the process to be effective. While other people can lie serenely on the table, my mind starts racing: *There are dozens of needles sticking into my skin! What if I move or roll over involuntarily and the needles lodge inside me even deeper?!* I start to feel stuck, claustrophobic, and anxious about not being able to move and, well, the fact that there are *dozens of needles sticking into my skin!* So no, acupuncture is not relaxing for me.

In short, any advice you read about optimal self-care—even the stuff in this book!—should be taken as inspiration, not instruction. Even the scientific literature supports this. For example, one of the studies I cited earlier about the benefits of spending time in nature found that the optimal time to spend outdoors is between twenty and ninety minutes at a time, but, knowing that this is not possible for everyone to do every day, researchers added that shorter but more frequent periods of time may work just as well—if not better—for some people simply because it is more doable. Similarly, one study on gratitude found that writing longer gratitude essays or letters has more long-term benefits than writing lists, but if you can't commit to writing several pages at a time, you may be better off writing lists once a day or several times a week, just because you'll be more likely to stick with the practice that day. As long as you approach the exercise mindfully, you will still reap the benefits. The only wrong way to do self-care is to not do it at all.

One strategy that I've found works well is to approach your self-care routine as a ritual. Unlike tasks (that is to say, activities we have to do or items we tick off a checklist) or habits (actions we perform routinely but automatically), rituals are defined by their spiritual, emotional, or symbolic significance as well as the purposeful and exact way in which they are performed. Rituals are a universal and unique component of human life. Every culture that has ever existed has had rituals to help mark the passing of time, significant occasions, and rites of passage, and many other types of groups—from governments to families, religious institutions to for-profit corporations—use rituals as a way to bring people together and indicate a sense of belonging.

But we as individuals can also create rituals on our own. You might even do this already by, say, doing something special on your birthday or performing the same routine every night before bed. You may not consider these rituals, but they are—and many of the things we do for self-care can be ritualized in a way that makes them even more powerful. For example, you can look at your morning skin-care regimen as a way to prevent skin damage or signs of aging, but you can also look at it as a ritual to get ready for a new day, nourish your skin, and engage your senses. Or your nighttime routine of washing your face, turning off your phone, climbing into bed, and writing in your gratitude journal could become a ritual to indicate that it's time for your body to rest and reflect on the blessings of the day. Maybe you've been thinking of your three p.m. latte as nothing more than a post-lunch caffeine boost, but what if it's also a much-needed break from work to get outside, socialize with others (even if it's just the other people in line), and prepare for the latter half of your day?

Multiple experiments suggest that performing basic actions in a ritualistic way can help regulate negative emotion and anxiety because, by doing so, we give these actions meaning and significance. For example, several studies have found that when people engage in rituals prior to performing a typically stress-inducing task, they experience less performance anxiety and perform better than those who did not engage in a ritualistic practice beforehand. Rituals also help us feel a sense of control and autonomy over our lives—a key component in fostering optimism, since we tend to be more hopeful about the future when we feel like we are at least partially responsible for directing its outcome. For example, researchers found that when participants who had experienced a major loss performed behaviors labeled as rituals, they felt a greater sense of personal control compared to those who performed the same behaviors as random actions. In other words, the simple act of calling something a ritual may be enough to give it the power to shape your life in a positive way.

One of the best rituals I can recommend to improve your health and well-being is to ritualize your breaks throughout the day. As mentioned above, studies show that we are most productive when we work in ninety-minute cycles. Much like the circadian rhythm of the sleep cycle, ultradian rhythms occur in regular intervals throughout the day. Each cycle includes a roughly ninety-minute period of high brain frequency, followed by a shorter, roughly twenty-minute period of low brain frequency. During times of high frequency, we feel alert, energetic, and productive, but after a while, we start to feel tired, unfocused, maybe a little hazy. We all know what this feels like: One moment you're super engaged in whatever work you're doing, brimming with creative ideas and productivity; then all of a sudden, you feel like you desperately need a nap, a cup of coffee, or a splash of cold water in the face. Often, in our always-on culture, we try to work through this period, trying to stay productive even when our bodies are clearly signaling that we need a break. This is entirely by design. Our body does need rest, and research shows that when we lean into that post-productivity slump and actually take a break, we bounce back more quickly and effectively. Far from being a waste of time or a sign of laziness, regular and frequent periods of rest help us recover and get back in the game sooner.

My advice to you is to create a ritual around these rhythms so that you intentionally pause throughout your day. Set a timer, and when you reach that ninety-minute mark or feel your brain slowing down, take a step away from what you're doing and reset your brain. This could entail actual physical rest—like a power nap—but it just needs to be something different from whatever it was you were previously doing. If you were sitting at your computer, go for a walk outside or do a few jumping jacks to get your body moving. If you were exerting yourself physically, pause to hydrate and relax your muscles. If you were doing something mentally taxing, try doing something with your hands—knitting or doodling or making a cup of tea. It doesn't matter what you do as long as you honor your body's and brain's need to rest.

Exercise: Create Your Perfect Self-Care Ritual

1. *Think of the things you do that bring you joy and relaxation.* Write them down. (Hint: this is a great way to refer back to—or expand on!—your joy list.)

2. *For each item on the list, write down how often you do it.* Daily? Weekly? Hardly ever? Keep in mind that some of these things won't be possible to do every day or every week (like spending time with loved ones who live far away or going on a weeklong vacation to some far-flung destination), but others should be fairly easy to accomplish on a regular basis if you prioritize them (having dinner with a friend, practicing music, going for a walk, etc.).

3. *Pick three activities from this list that you wish you could do more often.* Think about how you could incorporate them into your daily or weekly routines. Feel like you don't have the time? Consider ways you could steal time or practice them through micro-moments. For example, maybe you want to exercise more, but it's difficult for you to make it to an hour-long class three times a week. Could you do a fifteen-minute calming yoga session in the morning or before bed instead? (There are tons of free apps and online videos to guide you!) Could you use that dead time between meetings for a quick stretch? Even though I am not an avid exerciser, I've started doing fifteen squats in my closet while I figure out what I'm going to wear every day. I also balance on one foot while I brush my teeth to help with flexibility and strength. I know—how lucky for Alex that he gets to see these little rituals throughout my day!

4. *Commit to prioritizing these three things this week and see how it feels.* Don't stress if it doesn't look perfect or turn out the way you envisioned; this exercise is about seeing what works for you and making self-care a habit. The more you commit to your self-care routine, the easier it becomes to sustain it, because you start to realize the pleasure and benefits of putting yourself and your needs first.

CHAPTER 11

The 33-Day Optimism Challenge

Ritualize optimism into your most powerful habit.

Whew! That was *a lot* of information. Now that you've reached the final chapter of this book, I hope you have a better appreciation for what real optimism is and how it can work in your life. I also hope you understand that optimism is not a zero-sum game. You don't have to identify as an optimist—you don't even have to be all that optimistic in general—in order to create a practice that can foster and sustain an optimistic outlook. Optimism, as I've said many times before, is a muscle; we are all born with the capacity for it, but we need to exercise it regularly in order to make it as strong as we want it to be. I've given you a lot of advice throughout this book, some of which you may have already started using. But in order to leave you in the right frame of mind as we say goodbye to one another (for now), I wanted to close with a special call to action that I designed specifically with you in mind.

I call this the 33-Day Optimism Challenge. Why thirty-three days? Excellent question. If you've ever tried to start a new habit, you've probably heard—in a magazine or a self-help book or maybe on social media—that it takes twenty-one days to create a habit. This magic number—twenty-one days exactly—has been floating around the self-help world for years. I almost feel like I was born knowing this fact, that's how pervasive it is. Unfortunately, it's a total myth. The idea that it takes only three weeks to form a habit was entirely made up by, of all people, a plastic surgeon named Maxwell Maltz, who observed that it took about twenty-one days for his patients to get used to their new appearance and then decided to write a whole book called *Psycho-Cybernetics* about how he thought this happened. While a lot of the ideas Maltz proposed in the book—including visualization and self-affirmation—have turned out to be scientifically sound (when practiced correctly), his whole theory of three weeks was basically based on vibes. Maltz did not perform a single scientific experiment—because he *wasn't* a research scientist—and yet the theory has persisted for decades. Why? For one reason, it *sounds* good. "Change your life in just twenty-one days!" is catchy! Perfect for our busy, frenetic culture where we're all looking for a tangible, reliable, and achievable fix. (Though if you've ever tried to start a new habit, you know it's actually pretty difficult to sustain something new for twenty-one straight days.)

Unfortunately, simply by virtue of it sounding good, this idea may have persisted much longer than it should have. There's a well-known psychological phenomenon that explains how this may have happened. It's called the *illusory truth effect,* and it basically describes how bogus information can become accepted as fact simply because it gets repeated a lot. Chances are, you have experienced this: You heard something once that may or may not have been true but then didn't bother to verify it because it didn't seem important. Then a little while later you hear the same thing from a different source and assume, *Well, if this person heard it, too, then it must be true.* The more this falsehood spreads, the more people believe it. At some point, it becomes so widely accepted that even if solid evidence exists that proves it's not true, we probably don't hear about it unless we actively seek it out. That's basically what happened with the twenty-one-day myth.

In reality, studies show it usually takes much longer to form a habit—and the exact amount of time usually depends on the particular person and the habit they're trying to form. In one study, researchers found that it took participants anywhere from eighteen to 254 days to create a new habit, with the average being roughly sixty-six. I chose thirty-three days for my optimism challenge because the most important part of habit creation is getting started—and the first half of any endeavor is usually the most difficult. You can't get to sixty-six or 600 days until you put in the first one; and the more days you put in, the more you get used to whatever it is you're trying to do and the more you can start to see results. Thirty-three days is also just a little over a month, and we're used to challenges taking about a month: think dry January or Movember or the Whole 30 Diet. And yeah, okay, frankly it sounds pretty catchy, but unlike Maxwell Maltz, I am in no way proclaiming that this is a scientifically proven way to create a habit. All I'm saying is that if you can do this and then you decide to keep doing it, well, that's how habits start. If you can do something for thirty-three days, you can probably do it for another thirty-three if you stay motivated.

The best part about this challenge is, it's hard not to stay motivated once you start to prioritize your mental wellness. As we've learned, the more you do something, the more your brain changes to accommodate the new information and patterns it's learned and the easier it becomes. As you start to open yourself up to new ways of thinking and behaving and perceiving the world, you'll start thinking and behaving and perceiving this way automatically and be even more motivated to continue to do so in the future. The benefits inspire you to continue the behavior, so you receive even more benefits. Before too long—though I can't promise it will happen in a certain number of days—you will have made optimism a habit.

I designed every single one of these interventions based on the principles and research you've learned in this book, and while most of the results are cumulative, in many cases you will see results *immediately* after performing the specific exercise just one time. The other unique thing about this challenge is that it involves a new activity every day. You'll never be bored. While I hope you will end up making at least some of these regular habits, I wanted to create variety so you could figure out what feels best for you. Again, this is not all-or-nothing. Every little thing you do to strengthen your optimism muscle will help you change your outlook, which will change your behaviors and eventually change your life.

The 33-Day Optimism Challenge

Day 1: Think of a goal you wish to accomplish. It can be anything: writing a book, changing careers, finding a life partner, exercising more, eating healthier—whatever you can dream of. Now name one small step you can take toward that goal *today* and commit to doing it. For instance, if you want to write a book, maybe you spend a few minutes researching the publishing process. If you want to change careers, update your résumé. If you want to exercise more, sign up for a local class or carve out time for a quick workout. Even the biggest journeys are achieved only through a series of very small steps, so figure out what's important and what feels good. Breaking down your goals this way makes them feel much more manageable and realistic and therefore shifts your perspective to be more optimistic. Now, can you stick to doing one small step toward this goal every day or every week? How much closer would you be to your goal in a year? Two years? If you stuck to your commitment.

Day 2: Start a gratitude practice. Reflect on at least three things you are grateful for today. You can write them down, record them in a voice memo, or simply meditate on them—whatever feels right for you. Anything counts! From belly-laughing at a friend's joke to receiving a long-awaited promotion at work; being able to sleep in an extra hour or getting good news from your doctor. It doesn't matter what you choose to give thanks for; all that matters is that you take a few minutes to sit in gratitude for all the blessings in your life. We are so used to living in fight, flight, or freeze mode that even this small shift in perspective can have a profound impact on our mood, well-being, and optimism muscle. Try to do this every day—preferably before you go to bed so you can reflect on the day and decompress before going to sleep.

Day 3: Write a gratitude letter. Even if you're already in the habit of practicing gratitude, it's easy to take for granted that the people you care for know how you feel about them. Think of someone who has had a positive impact on your life and take a few minutes to express gratitude to them. You can write an old-fashioned letter (people love getting letters or cards because it feels more special—and is rarer—than a text or an email). Or better yet, pick up the phone and call them! Not only is this a great exercise in gratitude, it's also a great way to connect with people on a deeply personal and human level and strengthen the relationships that are critical to our emotional well-being.

Day 4: Take a moment to remember a time when you *really* wanted something that you now have today. It could be something tangible—like attaining a certain career or lifestyle or becoming a parent—or something more personal—like a sense of self-confidence or sound judgment. Reflect on how badly you used to wish for this thing and take a moment to appreciate all the effort you made to manifest and realize it. You made this happen for yourself. How incredible is that? An often-overlooked form of gratitude is self-gratitude, but we can draw an immense amount of resilience and strength from appreciating how much we have accomplished—even if those achievements are invisible to others.

Day 5: Instead of making a to-do list, make a ta-da list. Jot down all the things you have already accomplished today, and keep adding to it as the day goes on. To-do lists are great for staying organized and on-task, but we rarely take the time to celebrate all our wins throughout the day, especially the ones that aren't directly related to our productivity. That's what the ta-da list is for. Best part? You can include pretty much anything on a ta-da list, even if it's something you usually take for granted or that you wouldn't usually think of as an accomplishment. Did you get out of bed even though you were sleepy? Ta-da! Did you brush your teeth? Ta-da! Did you spend quality time with a loved one? Ta-da! When you get in the habit of making ta-da lists—even if it's not every day—you'll be amazed at how much you start to appreciate—instead of always criticizing or getting down on—yourself. Consider this part of your self-gratitude practice.

Day 6: **Think of an issue in the world or in your community that you care deeply about.** Maybe you're worried about climate change or a conflict halfway around the world. Or maybe you're worried about people speeding through a local intersection and wish someone would install a traffic light—or a neighborhood park that has fallen into disrepair due to budget cuts. Chances are there are probably a lot of things you care about like this, but pick one that has been on your mind the most lately. Now think of one small action you could take today to help get involved. We often feel powerless to change our communities—let alone make an impact on the world—but each and every one of us has the power to make a difference. Even if it seems too small to matter, it *does* matter, and no change ever happened because people thought, *There's nothing I can do*. Activism does not exist without optimism. Change can happen only if you believe change is possible. So call your city council member. Read an article or listen to a podcast to educate yourself on the subject. Sign up to attend a meeting about the issue or donate money to an organization that is doing good work in that area. One of my favorite things to do is to read about how other people have made or are currently making change around a particular problem; it's so inspiring! How does it feel to take a proactive step toward a larger goal? Now, can you do the same thing tomorrow? Or maybe you want to try something else? What impact might you have if you committed to doing something—*anything*—around this issue once a week or for a few minutes a day?

Day 7: **Connect with your community.** When people hear this, they often think this means activism, organizing, running for a local office, or making a big commitment to volunteer for a nonprofit—all of which may sound intimidating if you've never done something like this before. Of course if those things inspire you, *do them,* even if you need to start off small by attending an info session or helping out with a specific action or event. But *community* means a lot of things, and chances are there are ways you can become more connected to the communities of which you are already a part. Shop at locally owned businesses and get to know the owners. If you don't already know your neighbors, introduce yourself and make a point of saying hi. Have a favorite hobby? Start or join a craft circle or a book club or teach your skill to other community members. Do you have school-age children? Join the PTA or volunteer for parents' night. Our society tends to prioritize and praise individualism and tight-knit families and groups, but when you get to know the people who live and work within your community—even if that's the only thing you think you have in common—you create a social support network that people (including you) can rely on if things get tough. This is the essence of community resilience and will dramatically shift your outlook on what is possible in your life.

Day 8: Practice mindful breathing. Try the Focused Breath exercise from chapter 3 or the 4-7-8 Breathing Method from chapter 8. Notice the effect it has on your body. Do you feel less tense and anxious? Do you notice a change in how you felt before? Mindful breathing—in which you redirect your attention to your breath and the sensations in your body and away from whatever other thoughts are racing through your head—is hugely beneficial for regulating emotions and reducing the impact of stress because it calms the sympathetic nervous system, which controls our stress response. You can try this any time throughout the day, but definitely give it a go if you can feel yourself getting upset about something. The more you practice this breathing technique, the easier it will be to employ it when your emotions run high.

Day 9: Engage your senses. Take a moment—or several moments—during the day to stimulate at least one, if not all, of your senses. Light some incense or peel the zest off a juicy piece of citrus. Now inhale and breathe in the beautiful aromas that come alive from it. While taking a shower or bath, relax into the sensation of the hot water and the sound of it against your body. When eating, pay attention to the way the food feels and tastes in your mouth. Try to discern the various flavors—and don't worry if you can't identify something. The point is not to get it right; the point of this kind of sensory-based mindfulness is to turn your attention inward and toward the present as a way to interrupt and soothe your always-anticipating future-oriented brain.

Day 10: **Pick a song—any song.** It could be one you know by heart or one you've never heard before. Listen to it, *really* listen to it, all the way through. How does it make you feel? If the song is familiar, do you notice something you haven't noticed before? What are the lyrics about? Human beings are wired to love music; from birth, our brains learn to anticipate rhythms and phrases, and many studies show that we respond to music in unique and profound ways. This practice is an excellent way to connect with the artistry and creativity of music while also soothing your mind for a few minutes. No matter how busy and stressed you are, chances are you can set aside three to five minutes to listen to a song.

Day 11: **Play a game of Adult I Spy.** This is especially useful as a way to regulate intense and uncomfortable emotions, but you can also practice it as a mindfulness tool any time you need a little reset. For thirty seconds—or longer if you want to—stop what you're doing and focus on your immediate surroundings. What do you see, hear, feel, or smell? Identify these things by name without judging or telling a story about them. *I see a picture frame. I feel the breeze on my skin. I hear the sound of traffic.* And so forth.

Day 12: **Lean into your emotions.** Do this when you have a few minutes of uninterrupted time to yourself. Take a deep breath and reflect on what emotions you are feeling *right now*. If you're not sure, pay attention to any sensations in your body that might serve as clues. For example, a tightness in your shoulders, an ache around your heart, or a bubbling sensation in your belly may indicate stress, sadness, anger—or some other emotion that only you will be able to intuit. If you're feeling excited or joyful, you may also feel a racing heart or a surge of energy. Can you put a name to that emotion? What is causing you to feel that way? How does it feel to acknowledge that feeling? What might happen if you leaned into that feeling and let yourself feel it to its full potential—even if just for a minute? The goal here is to get comfortable feeling *whatever* you are feeling and to experience it with curiosity and compassion and without judgment. Contrary to popular belief, optimism is not the absence of difficult emotions; it's about honoring your authentic feelings, showing yourself compassion, and learning to draw on your personal resilience to learn from and move through whatever life throws your way. You don't need to do anything about this emotion, and if you find yourself trying to talk yourself out of feeling that way, stop. If you're struggling with an emotionally challenging situation, this exercise might help you find a solution to it, but it may also be enough to just listen to your emotions and let them tell you what they are trying to say.

Day 13: Schedule worry time. Take a look at your schedule for the day and set aside five minutes to worry. Use this time to worry about anything and everything that is bothering you or making you feel anxious. If it's helpful, make a list of the things you're worried about, and if something comes up between now and your scheduled worry time, add it to the list. The trick here is that outside of those scheduled five minutes of worry time, you can't worry about anything else for the rest of the day. This takes practice—especially if you're an anxious person like me. If you find yourself struggling to stick to just one five-minute worry session a day, schedule two or three throughout the day and see how that feels. The goal here is to be mindful of the mental energy you're devoting to anxiety. This doesn't mean you can't *think* about troubling things throughout the day, just that you can't give into your anxiety about them. I find worry time a great way to gain perspective.

Use it to figure out what you can actually *do* something about and what you're worrying about for no real reason. If you get in the habit of limiting the latter to worry time, you'll soon find it's a lot easier to let things go if you just decide not to worry about them. Isn't it amazing what you can do when you can focus your energy on what really matters?

Day 14: **Reflect on your resilience:** Think of a time when you went through something emotionally challenging: A breakup? Loss of a job? A huge life change? Death of a loved one? Take a few minutes to think about how you responded in those times. What emotions did you feel? How did you assess the situation at the time, and how do you assess it now? What did you learn from the experience? How did you grow? One of the best ways to develop resilience—a key component to optimism—is to remember that you have already overcome so much in your life. You may not know how you're going to get through whatever challenge you're currently facing—or whatever may lie ahead—but you know you will get through it because you've already proven you can.

Day 15: **Think about a challenge you're currently facing:** a difficult conversation you've been dreading; conflict with a friend or partner; a large, unexpected expense—whatever it is. Now disrupt whatever narrative you have going on in your head about the situation and ask yourself, "What might I learn from this experience? How will this help me grow?" If it helps, try to visualize yourself having gotten through the situation in a way you consider ideal. How did you behave to get to this place? How did you feel while you were doing it? What can you do to help achieve the outcome you want? This exercise helps us shift our perspective so that, instead of focusing on all our anxieties and what might go *wrong*, we turn our attention to what could go right and what we might get out of the experience—even if it doesn't turn out exactly the way we plan or hope. Learning to reframe problems as challenges we can overcome rather than threats to our well-being is one of the hallmarks of becoming more optimistic.

Day 16: Shift your language. Pessimists tend to view unpleasant events as pervasive, permanent, and personal. Optimists, meanwhile, view them as isolated, temporary, and impersonal; bad things are inevitable, but they do not define who we are or how we live our lives. One of the primary ways our tendency toward optimism or pessimism shows up is through our language. Whereas pessimists describe challenges using all-or-nothing language ("I'm awkward at parties and don't know how to make friends" or "I'm a terrible negotiator, which is why I'm not cut out for that senior position"), optimists are much less catastrophic. As you go about your day, pay attention to the language you use when you're frustrated. Do you take setbacks in stride or do you let them threaten your self-image? If you catch yourself using the language of pessimism, try to pause and consider how you can shift it so that it's more optimistic while remaining realistic.

Day 17: **Intentionally seek good news.** So many unbelievably horrible things are happening around us—and thanks to the internet, social media, and the never-ending news cycle, we are aware of most of them. While it's good to be aware of various problems going on in the world so you can stay informed and engaged, it's also useful to remind yourself that, despite everything, there is *so* much good to be found in humanity. The brain likes to believe what it already believes, and because it is future oriented, it tends to prioritize threatening information in an effort to protect us from harm. If we believe the world is a horrible place, we will naturally prioritize information that confirms this bias. But if we actively seek out new information, we can start to gradually shift our perspective. Take a few minutes today to proactively seek out a piece of good news that you didn't otherwise know about. A simple Google search for "good news today" will turn up a whole bunch of websites dedicated to aggregating the most optimistic, heartwarming, awe-inspiring, and inspirational headlines from around the globe. For instance, I just learned that scientists recently identified a type of charcoal that can extract the cancer-causing chemical chromium from industrial waste and convert it into an important bionutrient. How cool is that?

Day 18: Admire your strengths. So much of the self-improvement work we do each day involves trying to fix our weaknesses or get better at something we think we're not good at. But science shows that when we spend time leaning into our strengths instead of trying to fix our perceived weaknesses, we end up being more productive and fulfilled. For today's challenge, I want you to spend some time focusing on those things you already do well. What skills do you have? What do people consistently ask for your help on? What do you receive praise for? What are you confident in? Write down anything that comes to mind. It could be a hard skill like digital marketing or coding software, or a soft skill like anticipating other people's needs or communicating with empathy. It can be something you get paid for or something you do for fun. Now, as you go through the rest of your day, see if you can spot opportunities to lean into these strengths. Or if you find yourself questioning your ability to do something because of a certain skill or trait you lack, consider how you could leverage a current strength to get it done. Look at how amazing you already are!

Day 19: Create affirmations using the 7/10 rule. List out at least ten things that you like about yourself. You could pull some of these from the strengths list you made in the last exercise or you could add new ones like "I feel things deeply" or "I like my sense of humor." Once you have your list, go through each one and assign it a value on a scale of 1 to 10, based on how strongly you believe it to be true. If you believe something to be at least a 7 out of 10, try to reframe it as an affirmation. For instance: "I am an empathic person who is in touch with their emotions" or "People enjoy my company because I make them laugh." An affirmation can be any positive statement about yourself. As long as you believe it to be at least mostly true, your brain will start to seek evidence to back it up. Try reciting each of your affirmations first thing in the morning and before you go to bed at night.

Day 20: Practice a random act of kindness. Do something nice for someone today. Leave a cute note of gratitude or an uplifting doodle for your server (this is a favorite of mine). Compliment a stranger's outfit. Offer to help someone carry groceries to their car or a suitcase up a flight of stairs. One of my favorite things to do is to let other drivers merge in front of me when I see they have their signal on. If you've ever driven in LA traffic, you know that this is *not* standard practice for most Angelenos, who usually just speed up or pretend they don't see the other person. But, for me, it feels good, and it's no skin off my back anyway. Maybe it adds a couple of seconds to my drive, but that's it. A small price to pay to make someone else's day a little easier. Happiness is literally contagious. The small positive interactions we have with people—even strangers—have enormous power to improve our lives and theirs. Humans crave connection and validation. What can you do today to make that happen?

Day 21: Affirm a loved one. We often take for granted that the people we love know we love them, but when was the last time you told them something specific about what you love about them? When was the last time you told your partner you were proud of them? Or your parent how much you admired their resilience? Or thanked your best friend for the positive impact they've had on your life? Affirming someone you care about not only helps boost their sense of self but also helps you create connection with the people you care about most. Imagine how your relationships might transform if you did this intentionally and more often.

Day 22: Call someone you care about. Research shows that even one short, positive conversation per day with a friend can boost your mood and help you feel more optimistic about the world. Pick up the phone and call—*actually call*—someone you haven't spoken to in a while. Maybe you'll end up catching up for two hours, or maybe you'll have only enough time to let them know you were thinking about them. Either way, you've connected with someone you care about *and* you've made them feel special.

Day 23: Take a small, intuitive risk. Science shows that intuition is more than just a hunch or a gut feeling—it's a highly sophisticated neural process that allows us to make sound decisions, even in the midst of conflicting or incomplete information. Unfortunately, modern technology has made it possible to outsource so many of our everyday decisions. This is great for efficiency, but it's not great for getting in touch with your intuition and innate skills. At some point today, when faced with a low-stakes decision like what to have for lunch or what color shirt to wear, let your intuition guide you to the right choice. Don't try to rationalize the decision—just do what your gut tells you to do. How does it feel? Were you happy with the decision or not? What would you do differently? If you feel overwhelmed by a choice you have to make, try tapping into your intuition to see where it leads. The more you do this, the easier—and more intuitive—it becomes.

Day 24: List your top three values. When we understand and acknowledge the things that are most important to us in life, it becomes easier to make decisions, and we tend to be more satisfied with those decisions. Values are basically a guide to making choices because they serve as lenses through which we can assess our decisions. Examples of values include empathy, critical thinking, humility, family, financial stability, curiosity, open-mindedness, justice, and a whole bunch of others. Basically, if it's something you believe is critical for you to achieve your best possible self and live a life you can be proud of, then you can consider it a value.

Day 25: Move your body. Take five minutes out of your day to move your body in a way that feels pleasurable and relaxing to you. Do a few quick yoga poses. Stretch. Put on your favorite song and dance around the room. Jog around the block. Do some jumping jacks to get your heart rate up. Whatever it is, just shake it out! This exercise doesn't have to be particularly intense or exhausting and you certainly don't need to do it *well* or correctly. This is just about focusing your attention on movement and your physical body so you can relieve some stress and distract yourself for a few minutes. As long as you're doing something that actually *feels good* and satisfying, you can't go wrong.

Day 26: Take an awe walk. Set aside at least ten to fifteen minutes today to go outside, walk around, and tune into your sense of awe. If you have the luxury of going somewhere secluded or where you haven't been before, that's great! But you'll be amazed at what you notice when you show up to the world with an active sense of curiosity and wonder. The child learning how to ride a bike; the neighbors laughing on their front step; squirrels chasing one another through the trees; flowers budding on an early spring day; the way the sun reflects off a tree—we so often take these things for granted, but if we pay attention, we realize they're evidence of all of the beauty and mystery of life. Awe helps us appreciate everything we already have and all that's possible because it shifts our perspective to what is most important. As a result, research shows, the experience of awe can have a profound positive impact on our mental outlook. It's an incredible tool to foster optimism, and it's available to you *right now*.

Day 27: Make a joy list. Write down all the things big and small that bring you joy—anything you can think of. Exploring a new, far-off city or staying in to watch a favorite movie. Hosting a lavish dinner party or meeting a dear friend for coffee. Working on a novel—or just reading one. Listening to a favorite song, hugging your child, taking a bath, chewing a piece of cinnamon gum (maybe that's just me?), driving with your window down, smiling at a stranger, etc. These days one of my absolute favorite simple joys is to sneak in a quick thirty-minute game of mahjong with a small group of friends whenever we have time to spare during the day. You can write the list in a notebook or journal, but I prefer keeping it in the notes app on my phone. It's one of the few ways in which I find technology to be a help, not a hindrance, to mental health because it allows me to access my joy list no matter where I am. Once you've written down a bunch of things, look at it and pick one thing—just one thing—you can do today to bring a little joy to your life.

Every time you think of something else that brings you joy, add it to the list, and whenever you're feeling a little down or like you need a little pick-me-up, choose something from the list to do. For the bigger things that require more time, money, or planning, try to figure out ways to include these in your life at regular intervals in a way that works for you. Prioritize joy.

Day 28: Unplug. Set aside at least one period of time today where you will completely unplug from your phone or the internet. If you're spending time with someone, turn your phone on silent and put it away for the duration of the meeting so you're not tempted to look at it. Reading a book at home alone? Put your phone in another room so you're not distracted and can focus on the storytelling in front of you. Try avoiding your phone for at least an hour before bed to help promote relaxation and reflection. Technology is an essential part of modern life, and because it is always available, we have let it creep into spaces where it really doesn't belong. Get in the habit of unplugging at least a few times a day, and observe how much less anxious and more present you feel. Better yet? Make this a ritual by choosing a specific time of day and a specific period of time—like thirty minutes before and after dinner every evening or for an hour first thing in the morning—so it becomes part of your regular routine and takes on a more sacred meaning.

Day 29: Be bored. Do you tend to fill your downtime with distractions? Do you check your phone at the traffic light or listen to music while walking down the street? Is a podcast always on when you're doing dishes or taking a shower? Your challenge for today is to force yourself to be bored for at least a few minutes. When we're constantly distracted, we disconnect from our emotions and intuition and overload our brains so that it's difficult to focus. Sit with yourself and your thoughts and see what happens. Take in your surroundings and tune into the present moment. What do you notice? How do you feel?

Day 30: Spend time in nature. There is a whole body of research that shows how spending time in nature can help reduce depression and anxiety, boost mood, and improve key markers of physical health, so take five minutes today to get outside. If you have the luxury of going to the beach or taking a short hike in the woods, that's great! But if that's not possible, try to find a green or blue space in your neighborhood (a park, a greenbelt, a river or canal, etc.). Take a walk around or find a place to sit quietly for a while. You can even just sit on your porch or stand on a patio and watch the surrounding trees blow in the wind, search for a ladybug or a butterfly, or go for a five-minute walk around your block. My grandfather, who is ninety-eight, can't go on long walks anymore, so in order to get his daily nature fix, he makes a point of sitting on the balcony of his condo for a few minutes several times a day. Notice how your mood changes. Do you feel calmer and more relaxed? Is your breathing slower? Do you have more energy? Can you figure out a way to make nature a routine part of your day?

Day 31: Steal time through micro-moments. As you go through your day, look out for micro-moments—small pockets of time between bigger, more demanding activities—and use them to steal time for self-care. Got five minutes between meetings or before you have to pick the kids up from school? Read a few pages of a book. Call a friend. Dance around your room. Make a cup of tea. Self-care is extremely important to our mental and physical health—we need to rest and recharge in order to survive—so do something, anything, just for yourself, right here and right now.

Day 32: Practice the art of visualization. Think of a goal you currently have that feels intimidating or overwhelming. It could be something short term and specific like an upcoming job interview or something more complex and long term like starting a business. Now set aside a few minutes to create a sensory-based visualization about achieving this goal. Because our brains respond to our imaginations in much the same way they respond to reality, visualization is an excellent way to convince your brain that something is possible and thus prepare yourself to behave the way necessary to make your dreams a reality. See the instructions in chapter 6 for more detailed instructions on how to go about this. Try repeating the exercise at least once a day for two weeks (for shorter-term goals) or once a week for a month (for longer-term ones).

Day 33: Set aside at least twenty minutes in your day to visualize your best possible self. Find a quiet, comfortable spot and imagine what you want your life to look like five years from now. Pick a particular time and place for this visualization so you can add as much detail to it as possible. What do you look like? What are you surrounded by? Who are you with? What are you working on? What have you accomplished? For a full guide to this exercise, refer to the step-by-step instructions in chapter 6. Once you're finished, consider how close you are to becoming your best possible self. What are you doing in your life right now to help you achieve your goals? What is getting in your way? What needs to change? If this feels like a big undertaking, don't worry. Try practicing it once or twice a week until it sharpens into something that feels equal parts possible and aspirational to you. The more you visualize your best possible self, the more realistic it will start to feel and the more motivated you will become to do the things necessary to achieve it. Once you believe the future you want is possible, it's almost impossible not to do the things you'd need to do to make it a reality.

Acknowledgments

To my family and friends—you know who you are—thank you for being the soft place, the hype squad, the mirror, and the grounding force. To Alex, my person through every season, there is no one I'd rather walk through the dark with or dance in the light beside. Thank you for holding it all with me. Always.

To my agent, Mollie, thank you for championing this book into existence with your steady fire and belief. To the brilliant team at Simon Element, especially Lauren, Doris, and Richard, thank you for loving and bringing this book into real life, and to my girl Brooke, who met me deep in the beautiful trenches—thank you for your partnership, grace, and grit.

To every teacher, mentor, and past supervisor who gave me room to stretch, question, create, and leap—thank you for letting me be bold and stay soft, and for showing me the ropes.

To my clients and past patients—you have taught me more about resilience, humanity, and real optimism than I could ever put into words. Thank you for letting me witness your stories, your struggles, and your strength. You continue to inspire me every single day.

To the wins, the stumbles, and every single hard thing—thank you for shaping me. I'm still becoming, and that's the point.

And then there's the undercurrent: This book was written to a backdrop of Radiohead, Mazzy Star, the Flaming Lips, Nirvana, and LCD Soundsystem. Scrawled in the margins of motherhood. Fueled by wonder, stubborn hope, and a frankly unreasonable number of Arnold Palmers over crushed ice. So thank you to good music and good beverages.

If you're reading this, I hope you find something here that reminds you that you can keep going. Especially when it's hard.

Notes

Introduction

5   *people with a greater sense of optimism*: M. F. Schier, C. S. Carver, and M. W. Bridges, "Distinguishing Optimism from Neuroticism (and Trait Anxiety, Self-Mastery, and Self-Esteem): A Reevaluation of the Life Orientation Test," *Journal of Personality and Social Psychology* 67 (1994): 1063–78, https://doi.org/10.1037/0022-3514.67.6.1063.

5   *increases personal resilience*: Charles S. Carver et al., "How Coping Mediates the Effect of Optimism on Distress: A Study of Women with Early Stage Breast Cancer," *Journal of Personality and Social Psychology* 65, no. 2 (1993): 375–90, https://doi.org/10.1037/0022-3514.65.2.375.

5   *promotes and improves relationships*: Charles S. Carver, Lisa A. Kus, and Michael F. Scheier, "Effects of Good Versus Bad Mood and Optimistic Versus Pessimistic Outlook on Social Acceptance and Rejection," *Journal of Social and Clinical Psychology* 13, no. 2 (1994): 138–51, https://doi.org/10.1521/jscp.1994.13.2.138; Michael A. Cohn et al., "Happiness Unpacked: Positive Emotions Increase Life Satisfaction by Building Resilience," *Emotion* 9, no. 3 (2009): 361–68, https://doi.org/10.1037/a0015952.

5   *individuals who scored high in optimism lived*: Lewina Lee et al., "Optimism Is Associated with Exceptional Longevity in 2 Epidemiologic Cohorts of Men and Women," *Proceedings of the National Academy of Sciences* 116, no. 37 (2019): 18357–62, https://doi.org/10.1073/pnas.1900712116.

5   *better cardiovascular health*: Alan Rozanski et al., "Association of Optimism with Cardiovascular Events and All-Cause Mortality: A Systematic Review and Meta-Analysis," *JAMA Network Open* 2, no. 9 (2019), https://jamanetwork.com/journals/jamanetworkopen/fullarticle/2752100; Michael F. Scheier et al., "Optimism and Rehospitalization After Coronary Artery Bypass Graft Surgery," *Archives of Internal Medicine* 159, no. 8 (1999): 829–35, doi: 10.1001/archinte.159.8.829.

6   *because of all these associations*: Kimberly K. Assad, M. Brent Donnellan, and Rand D. Conger, "Optimism: An Enduring Resource for Romantic Relationships," *Journal of Personality and Social Psychology* 93, no. 3 (2007): 285–97, https://doi.org/10.1037/0022-3514.93.2.285; Charles S. Carver and Michael F. Scheier, "Origins and Functions of Positive and Negative Affect: A Control-Process View," *Psychological Review* 97, no. 1 (1990): 19–35. For a summary of several studies that link optimism with favorable life outcomes, see Charles S. Carver, Michael F. Scheier, and Suzanne C. Segerstrom, "Optimism," *Clinical Psychology Review* 30, no. 7 (2010): 879–89, https://doi.org/10.1016/j.cpr.2010.01.006; Ciro Conversano et al., "Optimism and Its Impact on Mental and Physical Well-Being," *Clinical Practice & Epidemiology in Mental Health* 6 (2010): 25–29, https://www.ncbi.nlm.nih.gov/pmc/articles/PMC2894461/pdf/CPEMH-6-25.pdf.

8   *the brain is terrible at distinguishing*: Marianne Cumella Reddan, Tor Dessart Wager, and Daniela Schiller, "Attenuating Neural Threat Expression with Imagination," *Neuron* 100, no. 4 (2018): P994–1005, https://doi.org/10.1016/j.neuron.2018.10.047.

Chapter 1: "Stay Positive!"

17   *a way of thinking that assumes*: Michael F. Scheier and Charles S. Carver, "Optimism, Coping, and Health: Assessment and Implications of Generalized Outcome Expectancies," *Health Psychology* 4, no. 3 (1985): 219–47, https://doi.org/10.1037/0278-6133.4.3.219.

18   *people tend to be relatively optimistic*: Max Roser and Hannah Ritchie, "Optimism and Pessimism: Why Are So Many People Pessimistic About the Future? And What Can This Tell Us About Tackling the World's Largest Problems?" Our World in Data, July 27, 2018, https://ourworldindata.org/optimism-and-pessimism.

20   *only about 25 percent*: R. Plonim et al., "Optimism, Pessimism, and Mental Health: A Twin/Adoption Analysis," *Personality and Individual Differences* 13 (1992): 921–30. Several studies have attempted to determine how much an individual's outlook depends on genetic factors. While some studies have found a higher correlation between genetics and outlook (see Mavioğlu, Boomsma, Bartels, 2015, https://doi.org/10.1007/s00787-015-0680-x), most have found the range to be roughly 25 to 30 percent.

20   *determined by environmental factors*: Timothy C. Bates, "The Glass Is Half Full *and* Half Empty: A Population-Representative Twin Study Testing if Optimism and Pessimism Are Distinct Systems," *Journal of Positive Psychology* 10, no. 6 (2015): 533–42, https://doi.org/10.1080/17439760.2015.1015155.

20   *They simply gave up*: Charlotte Nickerson, "Learned Helplessness," Simply Psychology, May 2, 2024, https://www.simplypsychology.org/learned-helplessness.html.

21   *when presented with the same information*: Catherine Moore, "Learned Optimism: Is Martin Seligman's Glass Half Full?" Positive Psychology.com, December 30, 2019, https://positivepsychology.com/learned-optimism; Christopher Peterson, "The Future of Optimism," *American Psychologist* 55, no. 1 (2000): 44–55, https://doi.org/10.1037/0003-066X.55.1.44.

22   *known as* defensive pessimism: Julie K. Norem and Nancy Cantor, "Defensive Pessimism: Harnessing Anxiety as Motivation," *Journal of Personality and Social Psychology* 51, no. 6 (1986): 1208–17, https://doi.org/10.1037/0022-3514.51.6.1208.

23   *some evolutionary biologists argue*: Lionel Tiger, *Optimism: The Biology of Hope* (New York: Simon & Schuster, 1979), accessed via Internet Archive, https://archive.org/details/optimismbiologyo00tige.

23   *In one 2015 study*: Jerry Boucher and Charles E. Osgood, "The Pollyanna Hypothesis," *Journal of Verbal Learning and Verbal Behavior* 8, no. 1 (1969): 1–8, abstract https://www.sciencedirect.com/science/article/abs/pii/S0022537169800022; Peter Sheridan Dodds et al., "Human Language Reveals a Universal Positivity Bias," *PNAS* 112, no. 8 (February 24, 2015): 2389–2394, www.pnas.org/cgi/doi/10.1073/pnas.1411678112.

23   *researchers asked soon-to-be-married couples*: Charles S. Carver, Michael F. Scheier, and Suzanne C. Segerstrom, "Optimism," *Clinical Psychology Review* 30, no. 7 (2010): 879–89, https://doi.org/10.1016/j.cpr.2010.01.006.

26   *cancer patients who ranked high on an optimism scale*: Tamar Icekson, Marieke Roskes, and Simone Moran, "Effects of Optimism on Creativity Under Approach and

Avoidance Motivation," *Frontiers in Human Neuroscience* 8 (2014): 105, https://doi.org/10.3389/fnhum.2014.00105; Carver, Scheier, Segerstrom, "Optimism"; Charles Carver et al., "How Coping Mediates the Effect of Optimism on Distress: A Study of Women With Early Stage Breast Cancer," *Journal of Personality and Social Psychology* 65, no. 2 (1993): 375–90, https://doi.org/10.1037/0022-3514.65.2.375; Lisa G. Aspinwall, Linda Richter, and Richard R. Hoffman III, "Understanding How Optimism Works: An Examination of Optimists' Adaptive Moderation of Belief and Behavior," in E. C. Chang, ed., *Optimism & Pessimism: Implications for Theory, Research, and Practice* (American Psychological Association, 2001), 217–38.

27 *tended to give up*: Lisa G. Aspinwall and Linda Richter, "Optimism and Self-Mastery Predict More Rapid Disengagement from Unsolvable Tasks in the Presence of Alternatives," *Motivation and Emotion* 23, no. 3 (1999): 221–45, https://doi.org/10.1023/A:1021367331817.

Chapter 2: "It's All in Your Head"

35 *When we want to change*: Theo Tsaousides, "What Makes Change Difficult?" Psychology Today, October 16, 2020, https://www.psychologytoday.com/us/blog/smashing-the-brainblocks/202010/what-makes-change-difficult.

37 *studies show that the mechanisms*: David Hecht, "The Neural Basis of Optimism and Pessimism," *Experimental Neurobiology* 22, no. 3 (2013): 173–99, https://doi.org/10.5607/en.2013.22.3.173.

37 *a meta-analysis of several studies*: Fatima Erthal et al., "Unveiling the Neural Underpinnings of Optimism: A Systematic Review," *Cognitive, Affective, & Behavioral Neuroscience* 21 (2021): 895–916, https://doi.org/10.3758/s13415-021-00931-8.

38 *the body produces insulin*: Wolfgang Langhans, Alan G. Watts, and Alan C. Spector, "The Elusive Cephalic Phase Insulin Response: Triggers, Mechanisms, and Functions," *Physiological Reviews* 103, no. 2 (2023): 1423–85, https://doi.org/10.1152/physrev.00025.2022.

38 *When conversing with people*: Stephen C. Levinson, "Turn-Taking in Human Communication—Origins and Implications for Language Processing," *Trends in Cognitive Sciences* 20, no. 1 (2016): 6–14, https://doi.org/10.1016/j.tics.2015.10.010, https://pure.mpg.de/rest/items/item_2193297_10/component/file_2240007/content.

38 *One study showed how individuals*: Niels C. Hansen et al., "Predictive Uncertainty Underlies Auditory Boundary Perception," *Psychological Science* 32, no. 9 (2021): 1416–25, https://doi.org/10.1177/0956797621997349.

38 *one of the researchers on this study*: Richard Sima, "Does Music Make You Move? Here's Why Our Brain Loves to Groove," *Washington Post*, July 4, 2024, https://www.washingtonpost.com/wellness/2024/07/04/music-groove-complexity-rhythm/.

39 *if you're looking for a lost object*: University of Glasgow, "What Our Eyes Can't See, the Brain Fills In," University News, April 5, 2011, https://www.gla.ac.uk/news/archiveofnews/2011/april/headline_194655_en.html.

39 *the DMN is composed*: Michele W. Berger, "What Happens in the Brain When We Imagine the Future?" Penn Today, May 17, 2021, https://penntoday.upenn.edu/news/Penn-neuroscience-research-what-happens-in-brain-future-imagining.

39 *our brains need to process information*: Karl Friston, "The Free-Energy Principle: A Unified Brain Theory?" *Nature Reviews: Neuroscience* 11 (2010): 127–38, https://doi.org/10.1038/nrn2787.

41 *In the face of imaginary threats*: Howard E. LeWine (reviewer), "Understanding the Stress Response: Chronic Activation of This Survival Mechanism Impairs Health," Harvard Health Publishing, April 3, 2024, https://www.health.harvard.edu/staying-healthy/understanding-the-stress-response.

41 *It has been well documented that Olympians*: Owaves, "The Olympian's Eye: Visualization Techniques," July 20, 2016, https://owaves.com/olympians-eye-visualization-techniques/; Christopher Clarey, "Olympians Use Imagery as Mental Training," *New York Times*, February 22, 2014, https://www.nytimes.com/2014/02/23/sports/olympics/olympians-use-imagery-as-mental-training.html.

41 *people who engaged in virtual workouts*: A. J. Adams, "Seeing Is Believing: The Power of Visualization," Psychology Today, December 3, 2009, https://www.psychologytoday.com/us/blog/flourish/200912/seeing-is-believing-the-power-visualization.

42 *"[I tell my athletes to] strive for excellence"*: Deepika Chopra, "How to Practice Effectively for Just About Anything: Overcoming Performance Anxiety with Dr. Don Greene," October 2020, in *Looking Up with Dr. Deepika Chopra*, produced by Dear Media, podcast, MP3 audio, 49:32, https://open.spotify.com/episode/7zv1daIfbi9DIfNJrsJXsG?si=c92775baad8d4e18.

42 *the act of purposefully imagining*: Craig Anderson, "Imagination and Expectation: The Effect of Imagining Behavioral Scripts on Personal Intentions," *Journal of Personality and Social Psychology* 45, no. 2 (1983): 293–305, https://www.craiganderson.org/wp-content/uploads/caa/abstracts/1979-1984/83A.1.PDF.

44 *researchers asked participants to read examples*: Craig A. Anderson, Mark R. Lepper, and Lee Ross, "Perseverance of Social Theories: The Role of Explanation in the Persistence of Discredited Information," *Journal of Personality and Social Psychology* 39, no. 6 (1980): 1037–49, https://doi.org/10.1037/h0077720.

47 *Meanwhile, emotions like aggression*: Goran Šimić et al., "Understanding Emotions: Origins and Roles of the Amygdala," *Biomolecules* 11, no. 832 (2021): 1–58, https://doi.org/10.3390/biom11060823.

47 *"Stress is what happens in your body"*: Deepika Chopra, "How to Make Stress Your Friend with Kelly McGonigal," July 2020, in *Looking Up with Dr. Deepika Chopra*, produced by Dear Media, podcast, MP3 audio, 39:20, https://open.spotify.com/episode/6kuwgcGqYFVI8ea8mJET2I?si=daac44c9e2714693.

48 *try to suppress an unwanted thought*: Daniel M. Wegner, "You Can't Always Think What You Want: Problems in the Suppression of Unwanted Thoughts," *Advances in Experimental Social Psychology* 25 (1992): 193–225; Daniel M. Wegner and James W. Pennebaker, "Changing Our Minds: An Introduction to Mental Control," in Daniel M. Wegner and James W. Pennebaker, eds., *Handbook of Mental Control* (Englewood Cliffs, NJ: Prentice-Hall, 1993), 1–12.

50 *the brain continues to learn*: A. Houillon et al., "The Effect of Novelty on Reinforcement Learning," *Progress in Brain Research* 202 (2013): 415–39, https://doi.org/10.1016/B978-0-444-62604-2.00021-6.

50 *the brains of Covid-19 patients*: Sara Youngblood Gregory, "The Power of Neuroplasticity: How Your Brain Adapts and Grows As You Age," Mayo Clinic Press, April 12, 2024, https://mcpress.mayoclinic.org/healthy-aging/the-power-of-neuroplasticity-how-your-brain-adapts-and-grows-as-you-age/.

50 *Deaf people develop certain types*: Gregory D. Scott et al., "Enhanced Peripheral Visual Processing in Congenitally Deaf Humans Is Supported by Multiple Brain Regions, Including Primary Auditory Cortex," *Frontiers in Human Neuroscience* 8 (2014): 177, https://doi.org/10.3389/fnhum.2014.00177.

50 *some people who lose their vision*: Lore Thaler, Stephen R. Arnott, and Melvyn A. Goodale, "Neural Correlates of Natural Human Echolocation in Early and Late Blind Echolocation Experts," *PLoS One* 6, no. 5 (2011), https://doi.org/10.1371/journal.pone.0020162.

Chapter 3: "Good Vibes Only"

58 *Meanwhile, emotional dysregulation*: Giulia Ballarotto et al., "Does Mindfulness Mediate the Relationship Between Emotion Regulation and Pro-Environmental Behaviors Differently Based on Gender?" *Mindfulness* 15 (2024): 1958–71, https://link.springer.com/article/10.1007/s12671-024-02405-7; Goran Šimić et al., "Understanding Emotions: Origins and Roles of the Amygdala," *Biomolecules* 11, no. 6 (2021): 823, https://doi.org/10.3390/biom11060823.

59 *As Martin Seligman*: Martin E. P. Seligman, *Learned Optimism: How to Change Your Mind and Your Life* (New York: Vintage, 2006).

61 *people who attempt to tamp down*: James J. Gross and Oliver P. John, "Individual Differences in Two Emotion Regulation Processes: Implications for Affect, Relationships, and Well-Being," *Journal of Personality and Social Psychology* 85, no. 2 (2003): 348–62, https://doi.org/10.1037/0022-3514.85.2.348.

61 *People who practice toxic positivity*: Gross and John, "Individual Differences in Two Emotion Regulation Processes"; Scott O. Lilienfeld and Hal Arkowitz, "Can Positive Thinking Be Negative?" *Scientific American*, May 2011, https://www.scientificamerican.com/article/can-positive-thinking-be-negative/; Lau Ung Mui and Jamayah Saili, "Toxic Positivity and Its Role Among Young Adult Workers," *Journal of Cognitive Sciences and Human Development* 10, no 1 (2024): 50–71, https://doi.org/10.33736/jcshd.6437.2024.

61 *are prone to burnout*: Anishka Jain et al., "Relationship Between Dominating Personalities and Toxic Positivity: Mediating Roles of Intrapersonal and Interpersonal Control," *Journal of the Indian Academy of Applied Psychology* 50, no. 1 (2024): 186–95.

61 *a more difficult time forming connections*: Tori Rodriguez, "Negative Emotions Are Key to Well-Being," *Scientific American*, May 2013, https://www.scientificamerican.com/article/negative-emotions-key-well-being/.

61 *they may struggle*: Gross and John, "Individual Differences in Two Emotion Regulation Processes."

62 *traditional wisdom held that*: David Brooks, "You're Only as Smart as Your Emotions," *New York Times*, August 15, 2024; Lisa Feldman Barrett, "The Theory of Constructed Emotion: An Active Inference Account of Interoception and Categorization," *Social Cognitive and Affective Neuroscience* 12, no. 1 (2017): 1–23, https://doi.org/10.1093/scan/nsw154.

63 *They help us learn*: Chai M. Tyng et al., "The Influences of Emotion on Learning and Memory," *Frontiers in Psychology* 8 (2017): 1454, https://doi.org/10.3389/fpsyg.2017.01454.

63 *Our most basic emotions*: Šimić et al., "Understanding Emotions." If you're familiar with the *Inside Out* franchise from Pixar, you will recognize five of these six emotions as the main characters.

63 *difficult emotions also play*: Šimić et al., "Understanding Emotions."

65 *People who grow up in nurturing*: Ian de Terte, Julia Becker, and Christine Stephens, "An Integrated Model for Understanding and Developing Resilience in the Face

of Adverse Events," *Journal of Pacific Rim Psychology* 3, no. 1 (2009): 20–26, https://doi.org/10.1375/prp.3.1.20.

65   *It can vary dramatically*: Gundugurti P. Rao et al., "Developing Resilience and Harnessing Emotional Intelligence," *Indian Journal of Psychiatry* 66, suppl. 2 (2024): S255–61, https://doi.org/10.4103/indianjpsychiatry.indianjpsychiatry_601_23.

65   *Crucially, though, resilience*: de Terte, Becker, and Stephens, "An Integrated Model for Understanding and Developing Resilience."

66   *putting a name to your emotions*: Amelia Aldao, "Why Labeling Emotions Matters: An At-Home Experiment on Emotion Labeling," Psychology Today, August 4, 2014, https://www.psychologytoday.com/us/blog/sweet-emotion/201408/why-labeling-emotions-matters; Vera Vine and Amelia Aldao, "Impaired Emotional Clarity and Psychopathology: A Transdiagnostic Deficit with Symptom-Specific Pathways Through Emotion Regulation," *Journal of Social and Clinical Psychology* 33, no. 4 (2014): 319–42, doi:10.1521/jscp.2014.33.4.319.

66   *Several studies show that writing*: Susan A. David, *Emotional Agility: Get Unstuck, Embrace Change, and Thrive in Work and Life* (New York: Avery, 2016); Kim Mills, "Expressive Writing Can Help Your Mental Health, with James Pennebaker, PhD," in *Speaking of Psychology*, produced by American Psychological Association, 43:59, https://www.apa.org/news/podcasts/speaking-of-psychology/expressive-writing.

66   *the style of writing matters less*: Rodriguez, "Negative Emotions Are Key to Well-Being."

67   *Expressing your emotions to another person*: Eric Barker, "10 Ways to Boost Your Emotional Resilience, Backed by Research," *Time*, April 26, 2016, https://time.com/4306492/boost-emotional-resilience/.

68   *It's also okay—and completely normal*: Jonathan M. Adler and Hal E. Hershfield, "Mixed Emotional Experience Is Associated with and Precedes Improvements in Psychological Well-Being," *PLoS One* 7, no. 4 (2012), https://doi.org/10.1371/journal.pone.0035633.

69   *the act of identifying the positive*: Michele M. Tugade and Barbara L. Fredrickson, "Resilient Individuals Use Positive Emotions to Bounce Back from Negative Emotional Experiences," *Journal of Personal and Social Psychology* 86, no. 2 (2004): 320–33, https://doi.org/10.1037/0022-3514.86.2.320.

70   *positive emotions broaden our repertoire*: Barbara L. Fredrickson, "The Role of Positive Emotions in Positive Psychology: The Broaden-and-Build Theory of Positive Emotions," *American Psychologist* 56, no. 3 (2001): 218–26, https://doi.org/10.1037/0003-066x.56.3.218.

75   *may seem kind of silly*: Paul Farrand et al., "Use and Engagement With Low-Intensity Cognitive Behavioral Therapy Techniques Used Within an App to Support Worry Management: Content Analysis of Log Data," *JMIR Mhealth and Uhealth* 12 (2024): e47321, https://www.ncbi.nlm.nih.gov/pmc/articles/PMC10809068; UK National Health Service, "Tackling Your Worries," Better Health, https://www.nhs.uk/every-mind-matters/mental-wellbeing-tips/self-help-cbt-techniques/tackling-your-worries/.

76   *the actress and activist Sophia Bush*: Deepika Chopra, "Sophia Bush on Being an Activist, Actress, and Avid Learner," September 2020, in *Looking Up with Dr. Deepika Chopra*, produced by Dear Media, podcast, MP3 audio, 50:38, https://open.spotify.com/episode/1LcNM5v2nm1tbGxQwPINjl?si=5cb388f0d3014e0b.

77   *a valuable but finite resource*: Adam Waytz, "The Limits of Empathy," *Harvard Business Review*, January–February 2016, https://hbr.org/2016/01/the-limits-of

-empathy; Jason Marsh, "The Limits of Empathy," Greater Good, Fall/Winter 2005–06, https://greatergood.berkeley.edu/issue_uploads/Limits_of_Empathy.pdf.

77 *how to talk to children*: Aisha Harris, "The History of Mister Rogers' Powerful Message," *Slate*, April 16, 2013, https://slate.com/culture/2013/04/look-for-the-helpers-mister-rogers-quote-a-brief-history.html.

78 *Studies show that simply observing*: SSM Health, "The Science Behind Kindness and How It's Good for Your Health," SSM Health, November 8, 2022, https://www.ssmhealth.com/newsroom/blogs/ssm-health-matters/november-2022/the-science-behind-kindness.

78 *the act of doing so not only boosts*: American Psychological Association, "When Doing Good Boosts Health, Well-Being," September 3, 2020, https://www.apa.org/news/press/releases/2020/09/doing-good-boosts-health; University of Texas at Austin, "Doing Good for Other People Is Contagious," Futurity, May 20, 2020, https://www.futurity.org/doing-good-prosocial-behavior-2369992/.

78 *graphic designer and digital creator*: Deepika Chopra, "Art, Politics + Virtual Protesting 101: How to Be Heard with Manassaline Coleman," August 2020, in *Looking Up with Dr. Deepika Chopra*, produced by Dear Media, podcast, MP3 audio, 43:22, https://open.spotify.com/episode/4zNYxb9QZAF6AQ5C1UGnRN?si=a8ab1dca3c134574.

78 *When he was in high school*: Deepika Chopra, "On Creating a Vibe of Love, Communiating without words, and Coming Out with Vince Coconato from Bob's Dance Shop," October 2021, in *Looking Up with Dr. Deepika Chopra*, produced by Dear Media, podcast, MP3 audio, 1:01:31, https://open.spotify.com/episode/3ZPk9CVEUzxNxwUBuZnUn6?si=49b3913ad3cb4e03.

78 *creates a feedback loop*: Tamara Bhandari, "This Is What Happens in Your Brain When You Take a Risk," World Economic Forum, July 29, 2016, https://www.weforum.org/agenda/2016/07/this-is-what-happens-in-your-brain-when-you-take-a-risk/.

Chapter 4: "Therapy Fixes Everything!"

88 *Our brain creates these beliefs*: Ralph Lewis, "What Actually Is a Belief? And Why Is It So Hard to Change?" Psychology Today, October 7, 2018, https://www.psychologytoday.com/us/blog/finding-purpose/201810/what-actually-is-belief-and-why-is-it-so-hard-change.

88 *known as the negativity bias*: Amrisha Vaish, Tobias Grossman, and Amanda Woodward, "Not All Emotions Are Created Equal: The Negativity Bias in Social-Emotional Development," *Psychology Bulletin* 134, no 3 (2008): 383–403, https://doi.org/10.1037/0033-2909.134.3.383.

89 *"[Our brain is like] Velcro"*: Deepika Chopra, "Neurodharma and the Negativity Bias: Blending Modern Science and Ancient Wisdom with Rick Hanson, PhD," July 2020, in *Looking Up with Dr. Deepika Chopra*, produced by Dear Media, podcast, MP3 audio, 48:58, https://open.spotify.com/episode/14MkEAkDpptCXXDFnalRuw?si=dcd2be4bc1c5441c.

90 *relationship between our thoughts, emotions, and behaviors*: Thomas A. Field, Eric T. Beeson, and Laura K. Jones, "The New ABCs: A Practitioner's Guide to Neuroscience-Informed Cognitive-Behavior Therapy," *Journal of Mental Health Counseling* 37, no. 3 (2015): 206–20, https://doi.org/10.17744/1040-2861-37.3.206.

92 *a list of common cognitive distortions*: Peter Grinspoon, "How to Recognize and Tame Your Cognitive Distortions," Harvard Health Publishing, May 4, 2022, https://www.health.harvard.edu/blog/how-to-recognize-and-tame-your-

cognitive-distortions-202205042738; Melissa Madeson, "Cognitive Distortions: 15 Examples & Worksheets (& PDF)," Positive Psychology.com, February 25, 2025, https://positivepsychology.com/cognitive-distortions/.

95 *to question the accuracy of your perception*: UK National Health Service, "Reframing Unhelpful Thoughts," Better Health, https://www.nhs.uk/every-mind-matters/mental-wellbeing-tips/self-help-cbt-techniques/reframing-unhelpful-thoughts/.

96 *the "twelve-second scheme"*: Olive Marie Morales, "12-Second Tactic: How to Train Your Brain To Be More Positive," *The Science Times*, January 30, 2021, https://www.sciencetimes.com/articles/29393/20210130/12-second-tactic-train-brain-more-positive.htm.

98 *"We have to see the good facts"*: Chopra, "Neurodharma and the Negativity Bias: Blending Modern Science and Ancient Wisdom with Rick Hanson, PhD."

100 *Research shows that simply having*: Andrew K. MacLeod, Emma Coates, and Jacquie Hetherton, "Increasing Well-Being Through Teaching Goal-Setting and Planning Skills: Results of a Brief Intervention," *Journal of Happiness Studies* 9, no. 2 (2008): 185–96, https://doi.org/10.1007/s10902-007-9057-2.

102 *Common traumatic events*: Psychology Today, "Trauma," https://www.psychologytoday.com/us/basics/trauma.

102 *Signs that someone is experiencing trauma*: National Institute of Mental Health, "Coping with Traumatic Events," https://www.nimh.nih.gov/health/topics/coping-with-traumatic-events.

102 *Through this different storage system*: Cleveland Clinic, "EMDR Therapy," https://my.clevelandclinic.org/health/treatments/22641-emdr-therapy; Danielle Gainer et al., "A Flash of Hope: Eye Movement Desensitization and Reprocessing (EMDR) Therapy," *Innovations in Clinical Neuroscience* 17, no. 7–9 (2020): 12–20, PMID: 33520399; Francine Shapiro, "The Role of Eye Movement Desensitization and Reprocessing (EMDR) Therapy in Medicine: Addressing the Psychological and Physical Symptoms Stemming from Adverse Life Experiences," *The Permanente Journal* 18, no. 1 (2014): 71–77, https://doi.org/10.7812/TPP/13-098.

Chapter 5: "You Can Have It All!"

107 *Of course this is human nature*: Dan Bates, "The 2 Faces of Social Comparison," Psychology Today, September 22, 2024, https://www.psychologytoday.com/us/blog/mental-health-nerd/202409/the-2-faces-of-social-comparison.

109 *Nearly half of American workers*: Matt Gonzales, "Here's How Bad Burnout Has Become at Work," SHRM, April 30, 2024, https://www.shrm.org/topics-tools/news/inclusion-diversity/burnout-shrm-research-2024; Anxiety & Depression Association of America, "Anxiety Disorders—Facts & Statistics," https://adaa.org/understanding-anxiety/facts-statistics.

109 *Parents, meanwhile, have become so stressed*: Vivek H. Murthy, *Parents Under Pressure: The U.S. Surgeon General's Advisory on the Mental Health & Well-Being of Parents* (Office of the U.S. Surgeon General, 2024), https://www.hhs.gov/sites/default/files/parents-under-pressure.pdf.

109 *Among the general population*: Jin Kyun Lee, "The Effects of Social Comparison Orientation on Psychological Well-Being in Social Networking Sites: Serial Mediation of Perceived Social Support and Self-Esteem," *Current Psychology* 41 (2022): 6247–59, https://doi.org/10.1007/s12144-020-01114-3.

112 *people who feel a keen sense*: Patrick L. Hill and Nicholas A. Turiano, "Purpose in Life as a Predictor of Mortality Across Adulthood," *Psychological Science* 25,

no. 7 (2014): 1482–86, https://doi.org/10.1177/0956797614531799; Aliya Alimujiang et al., "Association Between Life Purpose and Mortality Among US Adults Older Than 50 Years," *JAMA Network Open* 2, no. 5 (2019), https://jamanetwork.com/journals/jamanetworkopen/fullarticle/2734064.

112 *Purpose helps prevent stress*: Dariusz Krok, "Can Meaning Buffer Work Pressure? An Exploratory Study on Styles of Meaning in Life and Burnout in Firefighters," *Archives of Psychiatry and Psychotherapy* 18, no. 1 (2016): 31–42, https://doi.org/10.12740/APP/62154.

112 *The word originated in Okinawa*: Jeffrey Gaines, "The Philosophy of Ikigai: 3 Examples About Finding Purpose," PositivePsychology.com, May 13, 2025, https://positivepsychology.com/ikigai/.

112 *Several scientific studies have found that those who practice ikigai*: Yasuhiro Kotera et al., "Health Benefits of Ikigai: A Review of Literature," in Y. Kotera and D. Fido, eds., *Ikigai: Towards a Psychological Understanding of a Life Worth Living*, Concurrent Disorders Society Publishing, 2021, https://repository.derby.ac.uk/download/70627e36c5df9f61c017bf75372365219a6bd820b2f4b401519ebc685b94febd/192974/Health%20benefits%20of%20ikigai_%20A%20review%20of%20literature.pdf; Sakurako S. Okuzono et al., "Ikigai and Subsequent Health and Wellbeing Among Japanese Older Adults: Longitudinal Outcome-Wide Analysis," *The Lancet Regional Health Western Pacific* 21 (2022): 100391, https://doi.org/10.1016/j.lanwpc.2022.100391.

113 *designed to provide communal financial support*: Aislinn Kotifani, "Moai—This Tradition Is Why Okinawan People Live Longer, Better," Blue Zones, https://www.bluezones.com/2018/08/moai-this-tradition-is-why-okinawan-people-live-longer-better/.

120 *In fact, one survey found that*: Yukari Mitsuhashi, "Ikigai: A Japanese Concept to Improve Work and Life," BBC.com, August 7, 2017, https://www.bbc.com/worklife/article/20170807-ikigai-a-japanese-concept-to-improve-work-and-life.

120 *You'll be in good company*: Lane Gillespie, "Survey: 39% Have a Side Hustle, and 44% Believe They'll Always Need One," Bankrate, May 24, 2023, https://www.bankrate.com/personal-finance/side-hustle-survey/; Vistaprint, "STUDY: Millions of Americans Have a 'Side Hustle' to Boost Their Incomes and Pursue Their Passions," August 1, 2019, https://www.vistaprint.com/news/side-hustle-study-us.

Chapter 6: "Just Ask the Universe!"

127 *go ahead if you want to*: Tom Allingham, "14 Things More Likely Than Winning the Lottery," Save the Student!, April 10, 2024, https://www.savethestudent.org/save-money/things-more-likely-than-winning-lottery.html.

132 *World-class athletes*: Jessica Rovello, "5 Ways Katie Ledecky, Michael Phelps, and Other Olympians Visualize Success," Inc., August 23, 2016, https://www.inc.com/jessica-rovello/five-steps-to-visualize-success-like-an-olympian.html.

135 *Scientists believe mirror neurons are involved*: Sourya Acharya and Samarth Shukla, "Mirror Neurons: Enigma of the Metaphysical Modular Brain," *Journal of Natural Science, Biology, and Medicine* 3, no. 2 (2012): 118–24, https://www.ncbi.nlm.nih.gov/pmc/articles/PMC3510904/.

Chapter 7: "Believe in Yourself"

150 *Affirmation practices have been shown*: Catherine Moore, "Positive Daily Affirmations: Is There Science Behind It?" PositivePsychology.com, March 4, 2019,

https://positivepsychology.com/daily-affirmations/; Geoffrey L. Cohen and David K. Sherman, "The Psychology of Change: Self-Affirmation and Social Psychological Intervention," *Annual Review of Psychology* 65 (2014): 333–71, https://doi.org/10.1146/annurev-psych-010213-115137.

150 *In the early 1900s*: Émile Coué, *Self Mastery Through Conscious Autosuggestion* (New York: American Library Service, 1922, via Project Gutenberg).

152 *Importantly, psychologists who study self-affirmation*: Cohen and Sherman, "The Psychology of Change"; David K. Sherman et al., "Affirmed Yet Unaware: Exploring the Role of Awareness in the Process of Self-Affirmation," *Journal of Personality and Social Psychology* 97, no. 5 (2009): 745–67, https://doi.org/10.1037/a0015451.

152 *studies show that when presented*: Sherman et al., "Affirmed Yet Unaware."

152 *researchers asked participants to repeat*: BBC News, "Self-Help 'Makes You Feel Worse,'" July 3, 2009, http://news.bbc.co.uk/2/hi/8132857.stm.

153 *in one study African American*: Ada Ocampo, "Reducing the Racial Achievement Gap: A Social-Psychological Intervention," Stanford SFUSD Brief, summarized from Geoffrey L. Cohen et al., "Reducing the Racial Achievement Gap: A Social-Psychological Intervention," *Science* 313, no. 5791 (2006): 1307–310, https://doi.org/10.1126/science.1128317.

153 *participants were asked to rank*: Christopher N. Cascio et al., "Self-Affirmation Activates Brain Systems Associated with Self-Related Processing and Reward and Is Reinforced by Future Orientation," *Social Cognitive and Affective Neuroscience* 11, no. 4 (2016): 621–29, https://doi.org/10.1093/scan/nsv136.

153 *The impact of affirmations on physical health*: Cohen and Sherman, "The Psychology of Change."

154 *Couples who affirm one another*: Cohen and Sherman, "The Psychology of Change."

157 *when given the opportunity*: Sander L. Koole et al., "The Cessation of Rumination Through Self-Affirmation," *Journal of Personality and Social Psychology* 77, no. 1 (1999): 111–25, https://doi.org/10.1037/0022-3514.77.1.111.

159 *Timing is key*: Cohen and Sherman, "The Psychology of Change."

160 *Studies show, however, that when trying*: Nickola C. Overall, Jeffry A. Simpson, and Helena Struthers, "Buffering Attachment-Related Avoidance: Softening Emotional and Behavioral Defenses During Conflict Discussions," *Journal of Personality and Social Psychology* 104, no. 5 (2013): 854–71, https://doi.org/10.1037/a0031798.

161 *marriage counselor John Gottman*: The Gottman Institute, "What Is the Sound Relationship House?" November 30, 2020, https://www.gottman.com/blog/what-is-the-sound-relationship-house/.

162 *research shows that when we affirm*: Cohen and Sherman, "The Psychology of Change."

163 *the language you speak*: Lera Boroditsky, "How Language Shapes Thought," *Scientific American*, February 1, 2011, https://www.scientificamerican.com/article/how-language-shapes-thought/.

163 *the words we use can literally induce pain*: Maria Richter et al., "Do Words Hurt? Brain Activation During the Processing of Pain-Related Words," *Pain* 148, no. 2 (2010): 198–205, https://doi.org/10.1016/j.pain.2009.08.009.

163 *subjects who were exposed*: Alexander Ritter et al., "How Words Impact on Pain," *Brain and Behavior* 9, no. 9 (2019): e01377, https://doi.org/10.1002/brb3.1377.

163 *the language that doctors, caregivers*: Michael Stewart and Stephen Loftus, "Sticks and Stones: The Impact of Language in Musculoskeletal Rehabilitation," *Journal of Orthopaedic & Sports Physical Therapy* 48, no. 7 (2018): 519–22, https://doi.org/10.2519/jospt.2018.0610.

164 *people who struggle with mental illness*: Nora D. Volkow, Joshua A. Gordon, and George F. Koob, "Choosing Appropriate Language to Reduce the Stigma Around Mental Illness and Substance Use Disorders," *Neuropsychopharmacology* 46 (2021): 2230–32, https://doi.org/10.1038/s41386-021-01069-4.

Chapter 8: "Trust Your Gut"

173 *Thanks in large part to the work of*: Daniel Kahneman, *Thinking, Fast and Slow* (New York: Farrar, Straus & Giroux, 2011), 13.

174 *intuition is unique*: Naresh Khatri and H. Alvin Ng, "The Role of Intuition in Strategic Decision Making," *Human Relations* 53, no. 1 (2000): 57–86, https://doi.org/10.1177/0018726700531004; Galang Lufityanto, Chris Donkin, and Joel Pearson, "Measuring Intuition: Nonconscious Emotional Information Boosts Decision Accuracy and Confidence," *Psychological Science* 27, no. 5 (2016): 622–34, https://doi.org/10.1177/0956797616629403.

174 *While we are all born with*: Daniel Kahneman and Gary Klein, "Conditions for Intuitive Expertise: A Failure to Disagree," *American Psychologist* 64, no. 6 (2009): 515–26, https://doi.org/10.1037/a0016755; Kamila Malewska, "Intuition in Decision Making—Theoretical and Empirical Aspects," *International Journal of Business and Economic Development* 3, no. 3 (2015): 97–105.

174 *research shows that as we age*: Emma Seppälä, "The Science of Intuition—and How to Tune Into Your Own," *Time*, April 23, 2024, https://time.com/6837634/how-to-be-more-intuitive/.

175 *when people use intuition*: Lufityanto, Donkin, and Pearson, "Measuring Intuition"; Dijksterhuis, Ap, Maarten W. Bos, Loran F. Nordgren, and Rick B. van Baaren, "On Making the Right Choice: The Deliberation-Without-Attention Effect," Science, 311 (February 17, 2006).

175 *researchers found that intuitive decision-making*: Khatri and Ng, "The Role of Intuition in Strategic Decision Making."

176 *Another study from the business world*: Malewska, "Intuition in Decision Making—Theoretical and Empirical Aspects."

176 *For example, chess grandmasters*: Summarized in Kahneman and Klein, "Conditions for Intuitive Expertise"; for the full study, see William G. Chase and Herbert A. Simon, "The Mind's Eye in Chess," in William G. Chase, ed., *Visual Information Processing* (New York: Academic Press, 1973), 215–81.

176 *Likewise, fire ground commanders*: Summarized in Kahneman and Klein, "Conditions for Intuitive Expertise"; for the full study, see Gary A. Klein, Roberta Calderwood, and Anne Clinton-Cirocco, "Rapid Decision Making on the Fire Ground: The Original Study Plus a Postscript," *Journal of Cognitive Engineering and Decision Making* 4, no. 3 (2010): 186–209, https://doi.org/10.1518/155534310X12844000801203.

180 *intuition is strongest*: Erik Dane and Michael G. Pratt, "Exploring Intuition and Its Role in Managerial Decision Making," *Academy of Management Review* 32, no. 1 (2007): 33–54, https://doi.org/10.5465/AMR.2007.23463682.

180 *participants who were induced*: Carina Remmers and Thea Zander, "Why You Don't See the Forest for the Trees When You Are Anxious: Anxiety Impairs

Intuitive Decision Making," *Clinical Psychological Science* 6, no. 1 (2017): 48–62, DOI:10.1177/2167702617728705.

Chapter 9: "We Never Fight!"

188 *multiple high-quality relationships*: Zara Abrams, "The Science of Why Friendships Keep Us Healthy," *Monitor on Psychology* 54, no. 4 (2023), https://www.apa.org/monitor/2023/06/cover-story-science-friendship; Viviana Amati et al., "Social Relations and Life Satisfaction: The Role of Friends," *Genus* 74, no. 1 (2018): 7, https://doi.org/10.1186/s41118-018-0032-z, citing Karmel W. Choi et al., "An Exposure-Wide and Mendelian Randomization Approach to Identifying Modifiable Factors for the Prevention of Depression," *American Journal of Psychiatry* 177, no. 10 (2020): 944–54, https://doi.org/10.1176/appi.ajp.2020.19111158, and Rosemary Blieszner, Aaron M. Ogletree, and Rebecca G. Adams, "Friendship in Later Life: A Research Agenda," *Innovation in Aging* 3, no. 1 (2019): igz005, DOI:10.1093/geroni/igz005; Madeline Holcombe, "Why Most Men Don't Have Enough Close Friends," CNN.com, updated November 17, 2023, https://www.cnn.com/2022/11/29/health/men-friendships-wellness/index.html; Paula R. Pietromonaco and Nancy L. Collins, "Interpersonal Mechanisms Linking Close Relationships to Health," *American Psychologist*, 72, no. 6 (2017): 531–42, https://doi.org/10.1037/amp0000129; Kirsten Weir, "Life-Saving Relationships," *Monitor on Psychology* 49, no. 3 (2018): 46, https://www.apa.org/monitor/2018/03/life-saving-relationships.

188 *A landmark study out of Harvard University*: Liz Mineo, "Good Genes Are Nice, but Joy Is Better," *Harvard Gazette,* April 11, 2017.

189 *Another study found that close relationships*: Julianne Holt-Lunstad, Timothy B. Smith, and J. Bradley Layton, "Social Relationships and Mortality Risk: A Meta-Analytic Review," *PLoS Medicine* 7, no. 7 (2010), https://doi.org/10.1371/journal.pmed.1000316.

189 *only 39 percent of Americans*: Vivek H. Murthy, *Our Epidemic of Loneliness and Isolation: The U.S. Surgeon General's Advisory on the Healing Effects of Social Connection and Community,* Office of the U.S. Surgeon General, 2023.

191 *when optimists engage*: Kimberly K. Assad, M. Brent Donnellan, and Rand D. Conger, "Optimism: An Enduring Resource for Romantic Relationships," *Journal of Personality and Social Psychology* 93, no. 2 (2007): 285–97, https://doi.org/10.1037/0022-3514.93.2.285.

191 *both optimists and their partners*: Charles S. Carver, Lisa A. Kus, and Michael F. Scheier, "Effects of Good Versus Bad Mood and Optimistic Versus Pessimistic Outlook on Social Acceptance Versus Rejection," *Journal of Social and Clinical Psychology* 13, no. 2 (1994): 138–51, https://doi.org/10.1521/jscp.1994.13.2.138.

194 *Another strategy is to use* we *statements*: Bay Area CBT Center, "How Conflict Can Help Strengthen Your Relationship," August 9, 2023, https://bayareacbtcenter.com/how-conflict-can-help-strengthen-your-relationship-5-strategies-to-enhance-connection/.

198 *it takes ninety hours*: Holcombe, "Why Most Men Don't Have Enough Close Friends."

198 *People who hang out with friends*: Amati et al., "Social Relations and Life Satisfaction: The Role of Friends."

198 *Face-to-face interaction helps facilitate*: Kira M. Newman, "Why Your Friends Are More Important Than You Think," *Greater Good Magazine,* July 7, 2020, https:

//greatergood.berkeley.edu/article/item/why_your_friends_are_more_important_than_you_think.

198 *This helps explain why face-to-face communication*: Rick Hellman, "Just One Quality Conversation with a Friend Boosts Daily Well-Being, Study Shows," KU News, February 1, 2023, https://news.ku.edu/news/article/2023/02/01/just-one-quality-conversation-friend-boosts-daily-well-being-0.

199 *Researchers classified seven types*: Hellman, "Just One Quality Conversation with a Friend Boosts Daily Well-Being."

199 *While we usually think of our chats*: Abrams, "The Science of Why Friendships Keep Us Healthy," citing Gillian M. Sandstrom and Elizabeth W. Dunn, "Social Interactions and Well-Being: The Surprising Power of Weak Ties," *Personality and Social Psychology Bulletin* 40, no. 7 (2014): 910–22, https://doi.org/10.1177/0146167214529799.

200 *In a world where we spend*: Murthy, *Our Epidemic of Loneliness and Isolation*.

200 *research shows that while it's important*: Shelly L. Gable and Harry T. Reis, "Good News! Capitalizing on Positive Events in an Interpersonal Context," in Mark P. Zanna, ed., *Advances in Experimental Social Psychology* 42 (2010): 195–257, https://doi.org/10.1016/S0065-2601(10)42004-3, citing Michael Argyle and Monika Henderson, "The Rules of Friendship," *Journal of Social and Personal Relationships* 1, no. 2 (1984): 211–37, https://doi.org/10.1177/0265407584012005, and Christopher A. Langston, "Capitalizing On and Coping with Daily-Life Events: Expressive Responses to Positive Events," *Journal of Personality and Social Psychology* 67, no. 6 (1994): 1112–25, https://doi.org/10.1037/0022-3514.67.6.1112.

200 *People who disclose good news*: Gable and Reis, "Good News! Capitalizing on Positive Events in an Interpersonal Context."

201 *When people respond actively*: Nathaniel M. Lambert et al., "A Boost of Positive Affect: The Perks of Sharing Positive Experiences," *Journal of Social and Personal Relationships* 30, no. 1 (2012): 24–43, https://doi.org/10.1177/0265407512449400.

201 *according to some studies*: Shelly L. Gable et al., "Safely Testing the Alarm: Close Others' Responses to Personal Positive Events," *Journal of Personality and Social Psychology* 103, no. 6 (2012): 963–81, https://doi.org/10.1037/a0029488.

203 *multiple studies have found that simply talking*: Diane E. Dreher, "Why Talking About Our Problems Makes Us Feel Better," Psychology Today, June 11, 2019, https://www.psychologytoday.com/intl/blog/your-personal-renaissance/201906/why-talking-about-our-problems-makes-us-feel-better, citing J. W. Pennebaker, "Writing About Emotional Experiences as a Therapeutic Process," *Psychological Science* 8, no. 3 (1997): 162–66, https://doi.org/10.1111/j.1467-9280.1997.tb00403.x.

203 *Meanwhile, the mere presence*: Pietromonaco and Collins, "Interpersonal Mechanisms Linking Close Relationships to Health."

203 *providing a type of support*: Gable et al., "Safely Testing the Alarm"; Pietromonaco and Collins, "Interpersonal Mechanisms Linking Close Relationships to Health."

204 *Helping others is a well-known antidote*: Diksshita Jadhav and Kelly-Ann Allen, "Being 'There' for Others: What's in It for You?" Psychology Today, November 20, 2024, https://www.psychologytoday.com/us/blog/sense-of-belonging/202411/being-there-for-others-whats-in-it-for-you.

204 *By the end of the study*: Jeff Grabmeier, "Feeling Depressed? Performing Acts of Kindness May Help," Ohio State News, January 10, 2023, https://news.osu.edu/feeling-depressed-performing-acts-of-kindness-may-help/.

204 *By contrast, invisible support*: Maryhope Howland and Jeffrey A. Simpson, "Getting in Under the Radar: A Dyadic View of Invisible Support," *Psychological Science* 21, no. 12 (2010): 1878–85, https://doi.org/10.1177/0956797610388817.

205 *In a widely cited study*: James H. Fowler and Nicholas A. Christakis, "Dynamic Spread of Happiness in a Large Social Network: Longitudinal Analysis over 20 Years in the Framingham Heart Study," *BMJ* 337 (2008): a2338, https://doi.org/10.1136/bmj.a2338; Lorenzo Coviello et al., "Detecting Emotional Contagion in Massive Social Networks," *PLoS One* 9, no. 3 (2014): e90315, https://doi.org/10.1371/journal.pone.0090315.

205 *Studies show that disclosing*: Jenna L. Clark, Sara B. Algoe, and Melanie C. Green, "Social Network Sites and Well-Being: The Role of Social Connection," *Current Directions in Psychological Science* 27, no. 1 (2018): 32–37, https://doi.org/10.1177/0963721417730833.

205 *People who hang out with people who exercise*: Pietromonaco and Collins, "Interpersonal Mechanisms Linking Close Relationships to Health."

208 *that both negative relationships* and *ambivalent ones*: Newman, "Why Your Friends Are More Important Than You Think."

208 *In addition, if you have regular*: Pietromonaco and Collins, "Interpersonal Mechanisms Linking Close Relationships to Health."

Chapter 10: Optimism Is an Inside Job

213 *Greek philosopher Socrates*: Chris Taylor, "You've Been Getting Self-Care All Wrong. It's a Political Act and Always Has Been," Mashable, September 25, 2019, https://mashable.com/article/self-care-history; Aisha Harris, "A History of Self-Care," Slate, April 5, 2017, https://www.slate.com/articles/arts/culturebox/2017/04/the_history_of_self_care.html

214 *surveys show that 62 percent*: Adam Hardy, "American Workers Are Letting a Third of Their Vacation Time Go to Waste: Report," *Money*, July 24, 2024, https://money.com/workers-unused-vacation-time-pto-survey/.

214 *despite the fact that 44 percent*: Matt Gonzales, "Here's How Bad Burnout Has Become at Work," SHRM, April 30, 2024, https://www.shrm.org/topics-tools/news/inclusion-diversity/burnout-shrm-research-2024.

214 *for most people living*: Max Roser, "Proof That Life Is Getting Better for Humanity, in 5 Charts," *Vox*, December 23, 2016, https://www.vox.com/the-big-idea/2016/12/23/14062168/history-global-conditions-charts-life-span-poverty.

215 *With all these things to worry*: Wynne Parry, "The Power of Deep Rest," University of California, July 11, 2024, https://www.universityofcalifornia.edu/news/power-deep-rest.

215 *after studying how certain individuals*: Ferris Jabr, "Why Your Brain Needs More Downtime," *Scientific American*, October 15, 2013, https://www.scientificamerican.com/article/mental-downtime/.

215 *Other research has shown that most people*: Tomas Chamorro-Premuzic and Sunny Lee, "The Science of Resting (Well)," FastCompany, October 14, 2022, https://www.fastcompany.com/90795521/science-of-resting-well; Drake Baer, "Why You Need to Unplug Every 90 Minutes," FastCompany, June 19, 2013, https://www.fastcompany.com/3013188/why-you-need-to-unplug-every-90-minutes.

216 *Numerous studies show that*: Maureen Salamon, "Gratitude Enhances Health, Brings Happiness—and May Even Lengthen Lives," Harvard Health Publishing,

September 11, 2024, https://www.health.harvard.edu/blog/gratitude-enhances-health-brings-happiness-and-may-even-lengthen-lives-202409113071; UCLA Health, "Health Benefits of Gratitude," March 22, 2023, https://www.uclahealth.org/news/article/health-benefits-gratitude.

216 *Making gratitude a habit*: Prathik Kini et al., "The Effects of Gratitude Expression on Neural Activity," *Neuroimage* 128 (2016), 1–10, https://doi.org/10.1016/j.neuroimage.2015.12.040.

217 *Mindfulness has been shown to improve*: National Institutes of Health, "Mindfulness for Your Health: The Benefits of Living Moment by Moment," NIH News in Health, June 2021, https://newsinhealth.nih.gov/2021/06/mindfulness-your-health.

217 *the act of savoring positive feelings*: Claire Zulkey, "Breaking Down the Science of Savoring Summer Joy," Loyola Today, August 1, 2024, https://news.luc.edu/stories/research/breaking-down-the-science-of-savoring-summer-joy/.

219 *According to psychologist and author Dr. Rick Hanson*: Deepika Chopra, "Neurodharma and the Negativity Bias: Blending Modern Science and Ancient Wisdom with Rick Hanson, PhD," July 2020, in *Looking Up with Dr. Deepika Chopra*, produced by Dear Media, podcast, MP3 audio, 48:58, https://open.spotify.com/episode/14MkEAkDpptCXXDFnalRuw?si=dcd2be4bc1c5441c; Olive Marie Morales, "12-Second Tactic: How to Train Your Brain To Be More Positive," *The Science Times*, January 30, 2021 https://www.sciencetimes.com/articles/29393/20210130/12-second-tactic-train-brain-more-positive.htm.

220 *when asked to draw*: Robin C. Moore, *Childhood's Domain: Play and Place in Childhood Development* (London: Croom Helm Ltd, 1986), as cited in Nancy M. Wells and Gary W. Evans, "Nearby Nature: A Buffer of Life Stress Among Rural Children," *Environment and Behavior* 35, no. 3 (2003): 311–30, https://doi.org/10.1177/0013916503035003001.

220 *when asked to recall*: Rachel Sebba, "The Landscapes of Childhood: The Reflection of Childhood's Environment in Adult Memories and in Children's Attitudes," *Environment and Behavior* 23, no. 4 (1991): 395–422, https://doi.org/10.1177/0013916591234001, as cited in Wells and Evans, "Nearby Nature: A Buffer of Life Stress Among Rural Children."

221 *Many studies also show that spending time*: Sara Youngblood Gregory, "The Mental Health Benefits of Nature: Spending Time Outdoors to Refresh Your Mind," Mayo Clinic Press, March 4, 2024, https://mcpress.mayoclinic.org/mental-health/the-mental-health-benefits-of-nature-spending-time-outdoors-to-refresh-your-mind/.

221 *Children who live in close proximity*: Wells and Evans, "Nearby Nature: A Buffer of Life Stress Among Rural Children."

221 *with some reports indicating*: Amy Huxtable, "Prescribing Nature Can Improve Happiness and Reduce Anxiety, New Research Shows," University of Sheffield, September 4, 2024, https://www.sheffield.ac.uk/news/prescribing-nature-can-improve-happiness-and-reduce-anxiety-new-research-shows.

221 *If you find it hard to work nature*: Gregory, "The Mental Health Benefits of Nature: Spending Time Outdoors to Refresh Your Mind."

222 *Scientists have a name*: "Biophilia," Psychology Today, https://www.psychologytoday.com/us/basics/biophilia.

222 *experience something truly awe-inspiring*: Paul Wright, "The Neuroscience and Health Benefits of Experiencing Awe and Wonder," Nuvance Health, August 9, 2024,

https://www.nuvancehealth.org/health-tips-and-news/the-neuroscience-and-health-benefits-of-awe-and-wonder.

222 *Astronauts, for example*: Kyle MacNeill, "Can a Sense of Awe Inspire a New Worldview?" Atmos, February 3, 2025, https://atmos.earth/overview-effect-can-a-sense-of-awe-inspire-a-new-worldview/.

222 *our nervous system calms*: MacNeill, "Can a Sense of Awe Inspire a New Worldview?"; Hope Reese, "How a Bit of Awe Can Improve Your Health," *New York Times*, January 3, 2023, https://www.nytimes.com/2023/01/03/well/live/awe-wonder-dacher-keltner.html.

222 *researchers divided participants into two groups*: Virginia E. Sturm et al., "Big Smile, Small Self: Awe Walks Promote Prosocial Positive Emotions in Older Adults," *Emotion* 22, no. 5 (2022): 1044–58, doi:10.1037/emo0000876.

224 *In one wide-ranging meta-analytic study*: University of Sydney, "Dancing May Be Better Than Other Exercise for Improving Mental Health," February 12, 2024, https://www.sydney.edu.au/news-opinion/news/2024/02/12/dancing-may-be-better-than-other-exercise-for-improving-mental-h.html; Alycia Fong Yan et al., "The Effectiveness of Dance Interventions on Psychological and Cognitive Health Outcomes Compares with Other Forms of Physical Activity: A Systematic Review with Meta-Analysis," *Sports Medicine* 54, no. 5 (2024): 1179–205, https://doi.org/10.1007/s40279-023-01990-2; Alycia Fong Yan et al., "The Effectiveness of Dance Interventions on Physical Health Outcomes Compared to Other Forms of Physical Activity: A Systematic Review and Meta-Analysis," *Sports Medicine* 48, no. 1 (2018): 933–51, DOI:10.1007/s40279-017-0853-5.

224 *Another study out of UCLA*: Courtney Perkes, "'Free Moving' Dance Has Healing Benefits for Mental Health," UCLA Health, July 22, 2021, https://www.uclahealth.org/news/article/free-moving-dance-has-healing-benefits-for-people-with-mental-health-concerns.

226 *while the ideal length*: Jabr, "Why Your Brain Needs More Downtime."

226 *researchers who study the effect of nature*: Gregory, "The Mental Health Benefits of Nature: Spending Time Outdoors to Refresh Your Mind."

226 *spending time near water*: David Gallardo-Pujol, Jordi Renom Pinsach, and Laura Viñals Vilà, "How the Sea Is Good for Your Mind and Body," *Greater Good Magazine*, December 4, 2024, https://greatergood.berkeley.edu/article/item/how_the_sea_is_good_for_your_mind_and_body; Sarah Jacoby, "Just Being Near Water Can Help Boost Mental Health—Even Virtually," Today.com, August 29, 2022, today.com/health/mind-body/near-water-boost-mental-health-rcna45254.

227 *human beings need physical contact*: Jonathan Jones, "Why Physical Touch Matters for Your Well-Being," *Greater Good Magazine*, November 16, 2018, https://greatergood.berkeley.edu/article/item/why_physical_touch_matters_for_your_well_being.

229 *one of the studies I cited*: Gregory, "The Mental Health Benefits of Nature: Spending Time Outdoors to Refresh Your Mind."

230 *Every culture that has ever existed*: Nicholas M. Hobson et al., "The Psychology of Rituals: An Integrative Review and Process-Based Framework," *Personality and Social Psychology Review* 22, no. 3 (2018): 260–84, https://doi.org/10.1177/1088868317734944.

230 *several studies have found*: Karan Johnson, "The Surprising Power of Daily Rituals," BBC, September 14, 2021, https://www.bbc.com/future/article/20210914-how-rituals-help-us-to-deal-with-uncertainty-and-stress.

231 *participants who had experienced a major loss*: Michael I. Norton and Francesca Gino, "Rituals Alleviate Grieving for Loved Ones, Lovers, and Lotteries," *Journal of Experimental Psychology: General* 143, no. 1 (2014): 266–72, https://doi.org/10.1037/a0031772.

Chapter 11: The 33-Day Optimism Challenge

234 *The idea that it takes only three weeks*: Jocelyn Solis-Moreira, "How Long Does It Really Take to Form a Habit?" *Scientific American,* January 24, 2024, https://www.scientificamerican.com/article/how-long-does-it-really-take-to-form-a-habit/.

235 *it took participants anywhere from eighteen*: Solis-Moreira, "How Long Does It Really Take to Form a Habit?"

Index

acting example, 136
activism, 75–76, 239
adapting, 22–24, 47
addiction examples, 137–38, 207–8
adrenaline, 67
Adult I Spy (exercise), 68, 241
adversity, as struggle, 11–16
affirmations, 146–67
   connecting with others through, 160–62
   language used for, 162–65, 166–67, 203–4, 244
   process of, 150–54
   self-affirmation theory, 151–52
   self-image and, 146–50
   self talk and, 21, 96
   Seven-out-of-Ten Rule for, 154–62, 245
anagram experiment, 27
anxiety. *see* mental health
As Good As It Gets (film), 81
asking for help, 204–5
athletes as examples, 41–43, 135
autosuggestion, 150–51
The Aviator (film), 81
awe, 221–23, 248

balance, as impossible ideal, 10, 104–11. *see also* purpose
belief formation, 87–91. *see also* thinking and thought patterns
bias, confirmation, 43–46, 132–34, 149
bias, negativity, 88–89
bias, optimism, 23–24
blind optimism, real optimism vs., 27
Bob's Dance Shop, 79
boredom, 171–72, 181–82, 249

boundaries
   defined, 121, 207
   for mental health, 121–22
   in relationships with others, 206–9
   sacrifice and, 111
brain and mindset, 33–52. *see also* emotion; mental health; thinking and thought patterns
   adaptivity and, 22–24
   bias and, 23–24, 43–46, 88–89, 132–34, 149
   brain as future-oriented, 38–40
   brain's capacity for optimism, 36–37
   brain's response to fantasy and reality, 40–43
   changing thoughts, exercises for, 51–52
   default mode network (DMN), 222
   emotional wiring of brain, 46–47, 60
   memory cues and, 63–64
   mindfulness for, 218
   mirror neurons of, 134–35
   motivation for change, 36
   neural pathways of, 91
   neurons and "twelve-second scheme," 96–97
   neuroplasticity and, 49–50
   neuroscience discipline, 37
   optimism as choice, 33–36
   prefrontal cortex, 22
   seven truths, 36–50, 149
   shifting thoughts and, 7–8, 15–16
   sympathetic nervous system, 220
   thought suppression difficulty and, 47–49
breathing exercises, 67–68, 139–40, 240
broaden-and-build theory of emotions, 70–71
Bush, Sophia, 76

Index

cancer examples, 11–16, 26, 53–56
capitalization, 200
celebration, with others, 200–202
centering, of body/mind, 139–40
cephalic phase insulin response, 38
changing of thoughts. *see* thinking and thought patterns
children, 162, 197, 220–21
choice, optimism as, 33–36
Chopra, Deepika
  background of, xi–xviii, 6–8
  as Optimism Doctor, xiii, 2, 9
  podcast of, 42, 47, 76, 89
circadian rhythm. *see* sleep
Coconato, Vince "Coco," 79
cognitive behavioral therapy (CBT), 8, 87, 90, 91, 102, 204
cognitive distortions, recognizing, 92–95
communication. *see also* relationships with others
  digital vs. face-to-face, 198–200
  language of optimism, 162–67, 203–4, 244
  listening and, 203
  safe words for, 195–97
  trigger recognition in, 194–95
comparison to others, 108, 110
confidence. *see* affirmations
confirmation bias, 43–46, 132–34, 149
conflict. *see* relationships with others
control, 58, 94, 230
core beliefs, 159–60. *see also* values
cortisol, 67
Coué, Émile, 150–51
Create Your Perfect Self-Care Ritual (exercise), 232–33
curiosity, intuition and, 186
curiosity exercise, 17–18

Dana (case study), 53–57, 60, 65–66
dancing, 223–25
decision-making, 172–77. *see also* intuition
default mode network (DMN), 39–40, 222
defensive pessimism, 22. *see also* threat, perception of
Descartes, René, 150
digital communication
  distraction, 171–73, 200, 249
  face-to-face communication vs., 198–200
directions example, 184–85
Direct Your Own Mental Movie (game), 52
discomfort, embracing, 79–80
Discover Your Strengths (exercise), 99
divorce experiment, 23–24
dogs/electric shock experiment, 20–21
dopamine, 222

elephant example, 47–48
emotion, 53–80. *see also* mental health
  acknowledging feelings for resilience, 65–67
  broaden-and-build theory of emotions, 70–71
  channeling anxiety into activism, 75–76
  contradictory emotions, 68
  drawing strength from past, 71–72
  embracing discomfort, 79–80
  emotional wiring of brain, 46–47, 60 (*see also* brain)
  engaging with, 76–77, 241–42
  exercises for dealing with, 68–69, 71, 74–75
  inspiration sought for, 77–78
  mindset of, 46–47
  modeling behavior and, 205–6
  positivity vs. optimism, 56–62
  purposeful action and, 78–79
  regulation vs. dysregulation of, 58
  resilience and, 64–65, 71–72
  role of, 62–64
  scheduling worry time, 73–75
  seeking perspective and, 69–71
  showing respect in spite of, 193–94
  strategies for, 67–68
  toxic positivity and, 53–56, 202
engagement, 75–79
exercises. *see also* habits and routines
  Adult I Spy, 68, 241
  breathing exercises, 67–68, 139–40, 240
  for changing thoughts, 51–52
  Create Your Perfect Self-Care Ritual, 232–33
  daily affirmation practice, 159
  Discover Your Strengths, 99

How Optimistic Are You? (quiz),
  29–32
for joy, 97–98
limiting/scheduling worry time,
  73–75
smile challenge, 71
3×3 Breath, 67–68
visualization for beginners, 138–43
visualization to imagine your best
  possible self, 144–45
Wake Up and Dance, 223–25
walk-through scenario, 141–42
expectations, 127–28. *see also*
  visualization
exposure therapy, 81–84, 91–92,
  108
eye movement desensitization and
  reprocessing (EMDR), 102

familiar settings, power of, 135–36
A Family Affair (Netflix), xvi–xvii
family systems therapy, 102–3
fantasy vs. reality, brain and, 40–43
fear, 59–60, 63, 89–90
feedback, 21, 80, 95, 160–61
feelings, acknowledging, 65–67. *see
  also* emotion
feelings, thoughts vs., 59
fight, flight, or freeze response, 67,
  68–69
Find Your Reset Song (Mental DJ
  Game), 51, 241
Focused (3×3 Breath exercise), 67–68,
  240
4-7-8 Breathing (exercise), 183, 240
free-energy principle, 39–40
Full Body Scan (exercise), 183–84
future
  brain as future-oriented, 38–40
  as none of our business, xvi–xvii,
    xviii

Gandhi, M., 205
Garan, Ron, 222
goals, setting, 41–43, 100, 237. *see also*
  visualization
good news, sharing, 199–202, 244
Gottman, John, 161
grace, giving, 194
gratitude, 216–17, 229, 237, 238
Greene, Don, 42
groove, 38
gut feelings, 177. *see also* intuition

habits and routines
  affirmation as, 159
  changing (*see* brain and mindset)
  forming, 234–36 (*see also* 33-Day
    Optimism Challenge)
  gratitude as habit, 216–17, 229, 237,
    238
  intuition as, 181–86
  journaling as, 159, 216, 229, 238
  mindfulness for, 219–20
  morning routine, 212
  ritualizing, 228–32
Hanson, Rick, 89, 96–97, 98, 219
happiness, interacting with others and,
  199–202, 205, 244
Harvard University, 188–89
"having it all," 107, 110
health and well-being.
  see self-care
help, asking for, 204–5
Hicks, Esther and Jerry,
  125–26
Hill, Napoleon, 151
hockey metaphor, 11–16
Home Alone (film), 26
hormones, 67, 222
How Optimistic Are You? (quiz),
  29–32

I
ikigai, 112–20, 158
illusory truth effect, 235
inner voice. *see* intuition
inspiration, seeking, 77–78
intention, 126, 138–39
interpersonal relationships. *see*
  relationships with others
intuition, 168–86
  for decision-making, 172–77
  example of, 168–71
  as habit, 181–86
  meditation exercises for,
    183–84
  noticing, 170–73, 177–80
  self-awareness, 40, 119, 181
  System 1 and System 2 thinking,
    173–74

Jake (case study), 129–35, 138, 141,
  156, 159
journaling, 159, 216, 229, 238
joy, relishing, 97–98, 218–19,
  248–49

Kable, Joseph, 39
Kahneman, Daniel, 173–74
kindness, acts of, 204, 222–23, 245–46

labeling of emotions, 66, 94
labeling of rituals, 230–31
language of optimism, 162–67, 203–4, 244
Law of Attraction, defined, 123
The Law of Attraction (Hicks and Hicks), 125–26
learned helplessness, 20–21
learning, 20–21, 64–65
listening, 203
loneliness, 189
longevity, 5–6, 112
Looking Up (podcast), 89
Lorde, Audre, 213
lottery example, 127

Maltz, Maxwell, 234–35
manifestation, 123–26. *see also* visualization
massage example, 227–28
McGonigal, Kelly, 46
meaning. *see* purpose
meditation, 182–84, 217–20
memory cues, 63–64
Mental DJ Game (or Find Your Reset Song), 51, 241
mental health, 81–103. *see also* purpose
  asking for help from depressed people, 204–5
  belief formation and, 87–91
  boundaries needed for, 121–22
  changing thoughts for, 91–97
  cultivating optimism for, 25, 62, 97–100, 234
  facing adversity for, 4–5
  OCD example, 81–84
  power of thought and, 84–87
  seeking therapy for, 164
  self-worth work for, 86–87
  trauma and intervention for, 101–3
Merton, Robert K., 127
micro-moments of self-care, 225–28, 250
mindfulness, 217–20

mindset. *see* brain and mindset; emotion; thinking and thought patterns
The Miracle of Mindfulness (Nhat Hanh), 217
mission, purpose and, 113–20
Mister Rogers (Fred Rogers), 77, 78
modeling of behavior, 205–6
Monica (case study), 81–84, 87, 91, 103
mood, monitoring, 179
morning routine, 212
motivation, 22–24, 36
Murthy, Vivek, 189
muscle metaphor, 25
music, Find Your Reset Song (Mental DJ Game), 51, 241
Music, Meditate Through (exercise), 184
music listening example, 38

napping, 225
nature, 220–21, 222–23, 226, 229, 248, 249
needs. *see* self-care
negativity bias, 88–89
Netflix, xvi–xvii
neuroplasticity, 49–50
neuroscience discipline, 37
Nhat Hanh, Thich, 217
Nick (case study), 11–16, 25
nurturing of relationships, 202–5

obsessive-compulsive disorder (OCD) example, 81–84. *see also* mental health; therapy
optimism, 11–32. *see also* affirmations; brain and mindset; emotion; intuition; mental health; purpose; relationships with others; self-care; thinking and thought patterns; visualization
  as adaptive, 22–24
  cultivating, 25, 62, 97–100, 234
  defined, 16–18
  How Optimistic Are You? (quiz), 29–32
  language of, 162–67, 203–4, 244
  learning to be optimistic, 20–21
  mindset for (*see* brain and mindset)
  overcoming adversity and, 1–10
  positivity vs., 16, 56–62
  as realism, 26–27

real optimism, defined, 5, 126, 228
  for resilience, 27–28
  as spectrum, 18–19
  strengthening ability for, 25
  struggle and, 11–16
  uncertainty and, xi–xviii
  worldview of optimists vs. pessimists, 21
overview effect, 222
oxytocin, 222

passion, purpose and, 113–20
pausing, 179–80
Peale, Norman Vincent, 151
perception, questioning, 95
performance, enhancing, 41–43
perspective, seeking, 69–71
pessimism
  defensive pessimism, 22
  as permanent, pervasive, and personal (3 Ps), 21, 59, 92, 193
  perspective-shifting for affirmations, 162–65, 166–67
  relationships with pessimists, 191
  worldview of, 21
phone calls, 199, 246
physical exercise, 223–25, 247–48
positivity
  Law of Attraction (manifestation), 123–26
  optimism vs., 16, 56–62
  positive emotions, 46
  positive intention-setting, 138–39
  positive thoughts vs. positive feelings, 59
  positivity bias (Pollyanna principle), 23
  as toxic, 53–56, 202
post-traumatic stress disorder (PTSD), 101–3
The Power of Positive Thinking (Peale), 151
prioritizing
  ikigai and, 112–20, 158
  of purpose over productivity, 111–12
  relationships and true connection, 198–200
  seasons of life, recognizing, 110
Priya (case study), 146–50, 152, 155–57, 159–60
problem solving, 191
productivity, cycle of, 231

PsychoCybernetics (Maltz), 235
purpose, 104–22
  balance as impossible ideal, 10, 104–11
  boundaries and, 111, 121–22
  engaging in purposeful action, 78–79
  ikigai practice for, 112–20, 158
  prioritizing, over productivity, 111–12

realism, 26–27, 40–43
real optimism. *see also* optimism
  blind optimism vs., 27
  defined, 5, 126, 228
reason, intuition vs., 172–77
reflecting, 180, 238
reframing of conflict, 192–93
relationships with others, 187–209
  affirmation practices for, 154, 246
  boundaries in, 206–9
  celebrating wins and, 200–202
  conflict in, 187–91
  deepening quality of, overview, 197–98
  modeling behavior you expect from others, 205–6
  nurturing, 202–5
  phone calls and, 199, 246
  prioritizing true connection in, 198–200
  promoting optimism in, 192–97
  sharing affirmations in, 160–62
  toxic relationships, 208–9
resilience
  acknowledging, 65–67, 243
  drawing strength from past for, 71–72
  emotional resilience, 64–65 (*see also* emotion)
  optimism for, 27–28
  worst-case scenarios and preparation, 137–38
respect, 193–94
risks, importance of, 184–86, 247
Rogers, Fred (Mister Rogers), 77, 78

safe words, 195–97
scripting conversations, precaution about, 142
self-affirmation theory, 151–52

self-awareness, 40, 119, 181. *see also* intuition
self-care, 210–33
   Create Your Perfect Self-Care Ritual (exercise), 232–33
   importance of, 210–13
   micro-moments of, 225–28, 250
   routines as rituals for, 228–32
   simplicity of, 215–25
   for survival, 213–15
self-fulfilling prophecy, 127–28
self-gratitude, 217
self-image example (case study), 146–50, 152, 155–57, 159–60. *see also* affirmations
Self Mastery Through Conscious Autosuggestion (Coué), 150–51
self-talk. *see* affirmations
self-worth work, 86–87. *see also* affirmations
Seligman, Martin, 20–21, 28, 59
senses, engaging, 3, 219, 240–41
sensory-based visualization, 134–35, 140–41
Seven-out-of-Ten Rule, 154–62, 245
shower examples, 141, 182
side hustles, 120
sleep
   circadian rhythm and, 231
   importance of, 34
   napping, 225
small self, 221–22
smile challenge (exercise), 71
social connection and support
   community connection and, 239–40
   emotional needs and, 61, 66–67
   importance of, 188–91 (*see also* relationships with others)
   moai (Okinawan tradition), 113
   for physical health, 203
social media, 108
Socrates, 213
specificity, of affirmations, 157–58
"stealing time," 225–28
strengths, acknowledging, 98, 99, 245. *see also* affirmations
stress, as natural response, 46–47, 213–15. *see also* self-care
struggle, adversity and, 11–16
substance abuse examples, 137–38, 207–8
suppression of emotions, 60–61

suppression of thoughts, 47–49
swimmer experiment, 28
sympathetic nervous system, 220
System 1 and System 2 thinking, 173–74

ta-da list, 217, 238–39
therapy
   cognitive behavioral therapy (CBT), 8, 87, 90, 91, 102, 204
   exposure therapy, 81–84, 91–92, 108
   eye movement desensitization and reprocessing (EMDR), 102
   family systems therapy, 102–3
   seeking, 164
   talk therapy model, 39–40
   for trauma, 101–3
Think and Grow Rich (Hill), 151
thinking and thought patterns. *see also* brain and mindset; mental health; therapy
   belief formation and, 87–91
   changing thoughts/beliefs, 7–8, 15–16, 91–97, 128, 134–35 (*see also* visualization)
   cognitive reappraisal for, 204
   core beliefs, revisiting, 159–60
   creating space for, 181–82 (*see also* intuition)
   for making small changes, 119
   positive thoughts vs. positive feelings, 59
   power of thoughts, 84–87
   thought suppression, 47–49
   unwanted thoughts, 47–49
33-Day Optimism Challenge
   Days 1 through 33, 237–51
   developing habits with, 234–36
threat, perception of, 8, 22, 36–37, 243
3×3 Breath (exercise), 67–68
3 Ps of pessimism (permanent, pervasive, and personal), 21, 59, 92, 193
toxic positivity, 53–56, 202
toxic relationships, 208–9
trauma, intervention sought for, 101–3
triggers, recognizing, 194–95
"twelve-second scheme," 96–97

uncertainty, optimism and, xi–xviii
Under the Influence Game, 52
University of California Los Angeles (UCLA), 224
University of California San Francisco (UCSF), 214
unwanted thoughts, 47–49
The Upside of Stress (McGonigal), 47

vacation time, 214, 226
values, 153–54, 158, 247
visualization, 123–45
  for beginners, 138–43
  curiosity and, 17–18
  effectiveness of, 132–38
  as evidence-based manifestation, 128–31
  expectations and, 127–28
  to imagine your best possible self, 144–45
  manifestation vs., 123–26
  for performance enhancement, 41–43
  practicing, 17–18, 250–51
  walk-through scenario exercise, 141–42
vocation, purpose and, 113–20

Wake Up and Dance (exercise), 223–25
walk-through scenario (exercise), 141–42
water, time near, 226
well-being. *see* self-care
wins, celebrating, 200–202
Wood, Joanne, 152
working parent examples, 104–6, 109
worry time, limiting/scheduling, 73–75, 242–43
worst-case scenarios, preparing for, 137–38, 142–43
writing
  emotional processing and, 66
  journaling, 159, 216, 229, 238
  written agreements, 192

About the Author

Dr. Deepika Chopra is not your average shrink—she's *The Optimism Doctor*®. A professional psychologist and founder of Things Are Looking Up®, she blends science and soul to help people build resilience and joy. Creator of the hit science-based card deck by the same name, her insights appear frequently in *Forbes* and on NBC's *Today Show*. Dr Chopra holds a doctorate in clinical health psychology and completed a dual postdoctoral fellowship at the Cedars-Sinai Medical Center and the Simms/Mann-UCLA Center for Integrative Oncology. A regular media expert, and keynote and panel speaker, she's led workshops for Google, Amazon, and Amex, and spoken at events like the Aspen Ideas Festival. She lives in Los Angeles with her husband, three kids, a collection of '90s grunge records, and an unmatched talent for finding the perfect Arnold Palmer wherever she goes. *The Power of Real Optimism* is her first book.